WORK AND SOCIAL CHANGE IN ASIA

Essays in Honour of Jan Breman

WORK AND SOCIAL CHANGE IN ASIA

Essays in Honour of Jan Breman

Edited by
ARVIND N. DAS
MARCEL VAN DER LINDEN

MANOHAR
2003

This work is published under the auspices of the Indian Association of Labour Historians, New Delhi. It was prepared with financial support of the Changing Labour Relations in Asia (CLARA) research programme of the International Institute of Social History, Amsterdam, and the International Institute for Asian Studies, Leiden, the Netherlands.

First published 2003

ISBN 81-7304-485-6

Published by

Ajay Kumar Jain for
Manohar Publishers & Distributors
4753/23 Ansari Road, Daryaganj
New Delhi 110 002

Typeset at

Digigrafics
New Delhi 110 049

Printed at

Lordson Publishers Pvt. Ltd.
Delhi 110 007

Contents

1

Introduction

Marcel van der Linden

In memory of Arvind N. Das (1948–2000)

This anthology was first planned in early 1999, when Arvind Das and I realized that Jan Breman would have to retire in only two and a half years. We quickly agreed that Jan deserved a Festschrift, which should reflect the great geographical range of his considerable body of work. We were also in agreement in deciding that the book should focus largely on labour in Asia, since that subject had always been at the centre of Jan's scholarly and political interests. As is usual with projects of this kind, we drew up a list of colleagues and students of Jan who would be appropriate contributors and tried to make arrangements with them about the content and form of their articles and about deadlines. We assumed that we would be able to present the finished book to Jan in June 2001 at his farewell lecture at the University of Amsterdam.

During my visits to India and Arvind's (more frequent) visits to the Netherlands, we discussed the project's progress. Arvind was always enthusiastic and a source of good ideas, as he was with many other projects as well. His last visit to the Netherlands took place in the Summer of 2000 at the invitation of the Prince Claus Foundation. Just before he began his homeward journey, Arvind collapsed at Amsterdam Airport. He was brought speedily to the nearby Free University Hospital, where he died after being in a coma that lasted several days. His death was a shock to his numerous Dutch friends (including his close friend Jan Breman). It

* My thanks to Otto van den Muijzenberg for his generous help.

naturally evoked even more reactions in India. Arvind had been a leading progressive intellectual, who had exerted considerable influence through his books and lectures and above all through his review *Biblio*.

Arvind's death seemed to put a premature end to our plans for a Breman Festschrift. But I soon realized that Arvind would definitely have not wanted the project to grind to a halt. My friend Sabyasachi Bhattacharya, the eminent social and economic historian, declared unhesitatingly that he would be willing to work with me to bring the project to a successful conclusion. Without his energetic efforts, the present book would not have seen the light of day. Unfortunately we were no longer able to keep to the original timetable, so that the collection is being published many months too late.

Jan Breman was born in an Amsterdam working-class family on 24 July 1936. In the book *Down and Out: Labouring Under Global Capitalism*, that he co-authored with Ravi Agarwal and Arvind Das, Jan remarks that as a child he 'knew what poverty and oppression meant'.[1] Jan's father was a mailman; his mother came from a family of barge masters. While his intellectual prowess made it possible for him to escape from the poverty of his youth, Jan felt connected to his childhood social milieu throughout his life. It would not be wrong to say that Jan was driven, in his scholarship as in his politics, by rejection of a society that condemns people to material want and denies them fulfilment.

Jan's interest in the 'Third World' began quite early. As a boy he was sometimes brought by his father to the Royal Tropical Institute (originally called the Colonial Institute and later the Indies Institute), but a stone's throw distance from their home.

> High passageways, heavy doors, everything was meant to give a visitor the feeling that we Dutch were carrying out a great work over there. The institute was drenched in the colonial order and the 'white man's burden'. Imitation tea plantations, images of patients with leprosy before and after treatment in the colonies—all this was very familiar to me. The Central Book Depository had something exalted about it too. I didn't have the slightest mistrust of all this colonial storytelling.[2]

[1] Jan Breman, 'Prologue', in Ravi Agarwal, Jan Breman and Arvind N. Das, *Down and Out: Labouring Under Global Capitalism* (Oxford, 2000), p. 2.

[2] Remco Meijer, 'Jan Breman', in idem, *Oostindisch doof: Het Nederlandse debat over de dekolonisatie van Indonesië* (Amsterdam, 1995), pp. 143–51, here p. 144.

At the University of Amsterdam, Jan studied social geography from 1956 to 1962 (he would rather have studied history, but that was not possible with the high school diploma he had). Jan approached his studies 'with the attitude: Dutch society has made a fantastic leap forward; how did this happen and how will it happen in the ex-colonial societies?'[3] During his years at university Jan came under the influence of the Professor of 'non-Western' sociology Wim Wertheim (1907–98), an internationally renowned scholar who was trying to break with Orientalism by systematically taking Asians' own interests and perceptions seriously. Jan remembers his earliest collaboration with Wertheim as follows:

> Wertheim did his teaching from the Department for the Modern History and Sociology of South and South-East Asia that he had founded, which was housed in a wing of what was first called the Colonial Institute and is now the Royal Tropical Institute. Its premises consisted of two stately rooms, one of which he reserved for his own use while the other was filled by his accompanying foot soldiers: a part-time secretary, an associate and a couple of student assistants. I entered the last category in 1959 with a stipend of 600 guilders.[4]

Wertheim, who had worked as an attorney and professor in the Dutch East Indies, was initially interested primarily in Indonesia. Stimulated by his mentor, Breman wrote his Master's thesis on Javanese demography.[5] But in the late 1950s, when deteriorating relations between the Dutch and Indonesian governments reduced the Dutch social scientists' chances of doing fieldwork in Indonesia to almost zero, Wertheim looked for another region for ongoing research.[6] He had previously visited South Asia during a trip in 1956. Influenced by Indian sociologist Ishvarlal Pragji Desai, Wertheim began to look towards Gujarat.[7] Together with a fellow professor, the anthropologist André Köbben (who had the ex-

[3] Ibid.

[4] Jan Breman, 'W.F. Wertheim: De sociologie van het niet aan de Universiteit van Amsterdam', in J. Goudsblom, P. de Rooy and J. Wieten (eds), *In de Zevende: de eerste lichting hoogleraren aan de Politiek-Sociale Faculteit in Amsterdam* (Amsterdam, 1998), p. 171.

[5] Published as 'Java: bevolkingsgroei en demografische structuur', *Tijdschrift van het Koninklijk Aardrijkskundig Genootschap*, second series, 80 (1963), pp. 252–308.

[6] See also Sediono Tjondronegoro's article in this collection.

[7] I.P. Desai's published works include *The Patterns of Migration and Occupation in a South Gujarat Village* (Poona, 1964).

perience of fieldwork in Ivory Coast in 1953–4), Wertheim was able to secure a substantial grant from the Foundation for Pure Scientific Research for doing research in this Indian state. After his associates Cora Vreede-de Stuers and J.J.A. van Straten had made a preliminary visit, three Ph.D. students left for Gujarat. The first two were Jan Breman and his friend Chris Baks, who were based in south Gujarat from September 1962 to January 1964.[8] A year later, Klaas W. van der Veen and Enno Hommes followed. The young researchers, who chose a wide range of research topics, published their dissertations in 1969–70.[9] Wertheim observed that in a sense the four studies formed 'a whole, since in broad outline they concern the same area—south Gujarat—and, despite or perhaps because of the diversity of the topics selected, more or less complement each other'.[10] It is striking, however, that even in this early period Breman can be singled out for treating class contradictions most centrally.

The 'group of four' ushered in a long-lasting Dutch research tradition: since that time research projects have succeeded each other regularly in south Gujarat. A 'second wave' took shape in the early 1970s, when the now experienced researchers like Breman returned to Gujarat (1971–2) with new Ph.D. students like Hein

[8] The third student, Igle Ronner, was based in central Gujarat. Ronner published several articles about his work in Gujarat but received his Ph.D. for a study on internal migration in Sri Lanka. See his book *Interne migratie in Ceylon als bevolkingspolitiek* (Meppel, 1967).

[9] Klaas W. van der Veen was the first to receive his doctorate, with the thesis 'Huwelijk en hiërarchie bij de Anavil Brahman van Zuid Gujarat: sociale verandering en ideologische continuïteit in de Indiase kastensamenleving' (1969). Van der Veen's book *I Give Thee My Daughter: A Study of Marriage and Hierarchy among the Anavil Brahmans of South Gujarat* (Assen, 1972) is based on this thesis. The second dissertation was: Chris Baks, 'Afschaffing van pacht: een onderzoek naar de sociale gevolgen van pacht in twee dorpen van Zuid-Gujerat, India [The Abolition of Tenancy: An Enquiry into the Social Consequences of Tenancy in Two Villages in South Gujarat, India]' (1969). The next was Enno W. Hommes, 'Over de evaluatie van plattelandsplanning in India' [On the Evaluation of Rural Planning in India] (1970). Jan Breman received his Ph.D. with highest honours for 'Meester en knecht: een onderzoek naar de veranderingen in betrekkingen tussen landheren en landarbeiders in Zuid-Gujarat, India [Master and Servant: An Enquiry into Changing Relationships between Landowners and Rural Labourers in South Gujarat, India]' (1970).

[10] 'Ten Geleide', in van der Veen, *Huwelijk en hiërarchie*.

Streefkerk in their wake.[11] Breman's students such as Mario Rutten followed later.[12]

In the meantime Jan Breman himself had become fully integrated into the academic life. In 1962, he accepted a teaching position at the Erasmus University in Rotterdam under Professor Jacques van Doorn. Together with Enno Hommes and Philippines specialist Otto van den Muijzenberg (the latter was also one of Wertheim's students) Breman regularly edited 'non-Western' issues of the journal *De Sociologische Gids* from 1967 on. He was also active in the 'non-Western' section of the sociological association.

Jan's international scholarly breakthrough came in 1974, when University of California Press published an English version of his dissertation.[13] It was even less common at that time than it is today for Dutch social scientists to have their work accepted by prestigious international publishing houses. The publication of Jan's *Patronage and Exploitation* thus marked a milestone. In 1976, Jan was appointed Reader at the Erasmus University in Rotterdam. In accepting this position he gave a 'public lecture' on the informal sector that (in English translation) has become one of his most cited publications.[14] When a governmental decision promoted all Readers in one fell swoop, Jan Breman also officially became a Professor.

Together with Van Doorn, Jan established a Comparative Asian Studies Programme (CASP) in Rotterdam, which was inaugurated on 22–3 May 1980 with a conference.[15] After a few years, however,

[11] Hein Streefkerk, *Lichte industrie in een kleine Indiase stad: ondernemers en arbeiders in Zuid-Gujarat sinds 1900* (Amsterdam, 1978). English version: *Industrial Transition in Rural India: Artisans, Traders and Tribals in South Gujarat*, trans. Larry Hirschfeld and Ann Stoler (London, 1985).

[12] Mario Rutten, *Farms and Factories: Social Profile of Large Farmers and Rural Industrialists in West India* (New Delhi, 1995).

[13] Jan Breman, *Patronage and Exploitation: Changing Agrarian Relations in South Gujarat* (Berkeley, 1974).

[14] Jan Breman, *Een dualistisch arbeidsbestel: een kritische beschouwing van het begrip 'de informele sector'* (Rotterdam, 1976). Published in English as 'A Dualistic Labour System? A Critique of the "Informal Sector" Concept', *Economic and Political Weekly*, 2 (1976), pp. 1870–6, 1905–8, 1939–43; republished in Breman's *Wage Hunters and Gatherers: Search for Work in the Urban and Rural Economy of South Gujarat* (New Delhi, 1994), pp. 3–45.

[15] See the proceedings in Otto van den Muijzenberg, Pieter Streefland and Willem Wolters (eds), *Focus on the Region in Asia* (Rotterdam, 1982).

this programme fell victim to budget cuts. Wertheim's successor, Otto van den Muijzenberg, and a few faculty members at the two universities in Amsterdam (the secular University of Amsterdam that Jan had attended and the Protestant Free University), therefore, brought Jan back to the Dutch capital. In 1987, he was appointed Professor of Comparative Sociology at the University of Amsterdam and Director of the new postgraduate Centre for Asian Studies Amsterdam (CASA). CASA soon earned an outstanding reputation and became an important meeting place for Asian and European scholars, in part because it recruited students not only from the Netherlands but also from Asia itself. Its continuity with the Asian research done in Amsterdam since the 1950s and 1960s was expressed in 1990 with the establishment of the annual 'Wertheim lectures'.[16]

Alongside his scholarly activities, Jan has always been politically active. He has been a member of the Dutch Labour Party (Partij van de Arbeid) for decades, although he believes that in recent years the party has acquiesced too much to neoliberal thinking. From time to time he has joined directly in party-political discussions. He has, however, most often intervened in the political debate when the so-called 'Third World' and so-called 'development aid' have been in question. He has always taken a forceful stand against those who postulate a false harmony between rich and poor countries. He wrote, for example, in 1967:

> The argument that our interests and those of developing countries are not in conflict is a stubborn one, but in the existing situation it is simply not true. Achieving a fairer division of labour and income will unavoidably require a more fundamental approach—including changes in the terms of trade and in our own economic structure.[17]

In later publications, Jan advocated 'indicative global planning', through which 'the desired level and composition of production, consumption, savings, investment and so on in the different countries would be indicated'.[18] This could be the beginning of an

[16] A close connection soon developed between CASA and the Postdoctoral Institute for Sociology (PdIS) established a few months earlier by Abram de Swaan and his associates. The Amsterdam School for Social Science Research arose out of this connection.

[17] J.C.B [Breman], 'Marginaal', *De Sociologische Gids*, 14 (1967), p. 349.

[18] Jan Breman and Jan Pronk, 'Internationaal ontwikkelingsbeleid, een poging tot nationale beleidsontwikkeling', in Cor Boef et al., *Mooi rood is niet lelijk* (Rotterdam, 1969), pp. 41–2.

international development policy 'that would be part of the overall global process of income provision, income distribution and income expenditure'.[19]

Jan has always viewed with suspicion efforts to raise living standards in the capitalist periphery through development aid. First of all, he sees most forms of aid as continuations of colonialism:

> [Development experts] travel from Peru to Bangladesh with exactly the same baggage in their suitcases. [They] are the colonial officials of today. They work according to scripts that were also used in colonial times. . . . Their expertise is not good enough, because it's expertise from the outside. There is never a relationship among equals; instead there's a paternalistic relationship between guardian and ward.[20]

Second, Jan opines that what rich countries give as development aid with one hand is take away many times over by them with the other hand (the global uneven accumulation of capital). As he wrote recently: 'The contradiction between rich and poor in the world is greater than ever before and is still increasing. Since international aid programmes started up almost half a century ago, the number of people living in poverty has continued to rise. . . .'[21]

Over the years, Jan has written many articles about development issues in both Dutch and Indian journals. The trend towards a greater instead of a smaller role for the market in the world economy has been a particular source of concern to him, because it further increases global social inequality. Some of his sharpest criticisms have been directed at neoliberalism, regardless of whether it has been propagated by the World Bank or by his fellow Labour Party members.[22]

[19] Ibid., p. 42.

[20] Ageeth Scherphuis, 'Jan Breman: "De ontwikkelingsdeskundigen zijn de moderne koloniale ambtenaren" ', in Kees Schaepman (ed.), *Zware shag en gironummers: twaalf Nederlanders over de Derde Wereld* (Amsterdam and The Hague, 1991), pp. 46–52, here p. 50.

[21] Jan Breman, 'Ontwikkeling en de kwaliteit van het bestuur', *Socialisme en Democratie*, 58 (2001), pp. 276–81, here p. 276.

[22] For example, Jan Breman, 'Labour Get Lost: A Late-Capitalist Manifesto', *Economic and Political Weekly*, 30 (1995), pp. 2294–2300; idem, 'Van ontwikkelingssamenwerking naar internationale armenzorg', *Socialisme en Democratie*, 56 (1999), pp. 375–87.

Jan's scholarly activities have always been carried out in the charged area where academies and the political arena overlap. On the one hand he has always strived for great scholarly precision, but on the other hand the questions he poses and the rhetorical presentation of his work are politically inspired. Jan is the prototype of the committed scholar, and in this sense an inspiration to many.

Memories

2

Academic Journeys between Amsterdam, Gujarat, and Cheribon

Sediono M.P. Tjondronegoro

Sitting down to start writing a verbal contribution to a Festschrift for a colleague at the end of his fruitful career always pushes one to dig up common experiences in the past—particularly if the two colleagues have built their respective careers in different countries on different continents far from where they began their studies together, and yet there has been a strong tie ever since that binds them together. This is how I have felt throughout my long friendship and good-fellowship with Jan Breman, perhaps eight years my junior.

My first acquaintance with Jan was in the east wing of the Royal Institute for the Tropics (Linnaeusstraat 2A) in Amsterdam, where the Department—then called the Seminarium—for the Modern History and Sociology of South and South-East Asia of the University of Amsterdam was housed. The institute, chaired by the late Professor Wim Wertheim, had been a centre for those students interested in non-Western sociology. Though the institution had a regional focus, it also dealt with a much wider geographical area, since its coverage also included South Asia. Students who were interested in Africa and Latin America, similarly excluded from the notion 'Western', may have taken the course as well to broaden their comparative perspectives. The inclusiveness of the term 'non-Western sociology' undoubtedly attracted many students, so soon after the devastating Second World War and the subsequent reconstruction and development of so many countries and newborn states, which were later referred to as countries of the Third World, a term that I think Georges

Balandier had invented in the early 1950s (*Tiers Monde*).

If my memory serves me correct, Jan began his university studies in Amsterdam in 1956, where, more specifically, he was enrolled at the United Faculties for Mathematics, Physics, Letters and Philosophy (Verenigde Faculteiten voor Wiskunde en Natuurkunde, Letteren en Wijsbegeerte) and where, during his postgraduate studies, he became a regular visitor to the above-mentioned Seminarium. The regional focus on South-East Asia was broadened in practice to South Asia, and in particular, India. The longest period that Professor Wertheim stayed and worked in Asia, in his younger years and at the start of his foreign career, happened to be in Indonesia, beginning in 1931. Although his interest extended beyond the geographical boundaries of South-East Asia to include India and China, most of the students who took the courses were interested in South-East Asia.

Perhaps rather unfortunately for him at that time, Jan focused on Indonesia as he prepared to do his research in that part of the globe. Due to worsening diplomatic relations between Indonesia and the Netherlands, whose roots lay in the conflict about sovereignty over West New Guinea (later called Irian Jaya by the Indonesians), the regional focus of his study had to be shifted to South Asia. The outcome of the Round Table Conference (RTC) between the Netherlands and Indonesia at Scheveningen in the second half of 1949 included a postponement of the transfer of sovereignty over West New Guinea to Indonesia until a later and undecided date. As the difference of opinion dragged on in the 1950s, the Indonesian government broke diplomatic relations with the Netherlands in 1958 by abrogating the 1949 RTC agreements and nationalized all Dutch companies, including trading houses as well as plantations. The conflict worsened to the brink of a military confrontation in the early 1960s. It required the mediation of no less a personage than the late US Senator Robert Kennedy to reach a peaceful resolution. Meanwhile, many Dutch citizens with their domicile in Indonesia, and also many members of the Eurasian community, preferred in this period to repatriate to the Netherlands. These political tensions gave rise to serious concern as to whether fieldwork in Indonesia was advisable and feasible for Dutch students and scholars.

Practically all the students who took Professor Wertheim's courses were discouraged from doing fieldwork in Indonesia and had to shift their interest to other South-East Asian countries. Jan

Breman and a good friend of his, Chris Baks, decided to redirect their interest to India instead. Their major interest in the fate of the poor in the bottom layers of society, however, remained unchanged. Jan's personal interest in Indonesia had begun to take form earlier in a demographic study of Java's population during the Raffles administration.[1] Raffles wanted to determine the population of Java, and for this purpose a census was held, which included registration of rural landholdings. Raffles needed this information for purposes of taxation, apparently in accordance with his practice in India, where he was posted by the British government before administering Java. Jan drew on the rich archival material that he found at the Rijksarchief in The Hague. I found this approach rather typical of students in sociography; but through the use of such descriptive information Jan was able to arrive at a total population figure of five million. Raffles has become well known for the cadastral registration on Java that he accomplished during his administration. If he had had more time, he might have carried out such a registration on other islands of the Indonesian archipelago too. Five years' rule, however, was not enough time to achieve that! My guess would be that he could have carried it out in the southern part of Sumatra, since the British had built a stronghold in Bengkulu overlooking the Indian Ocean.

Whatever the case, archival statistics led Jan to conclude that there were close to five million people inhabiting the island of Java during Raffles' administration.[2] This finding was challenged a few years later, however, by a junior colleague at the same Faculty, namely Bram Peper. On the basis of additional archival sources and a reinterpretation of Raffles' population census, Peper arrived at a higher figure than Breman.[3] These divergent results may have arisen from the fact that, as Breman himself admitted in his study, Raffles' figures were based on counting households (*cacahs*) and then multiplying the total by an estimated average number of

[1] Editors' note: Sir Thomas Stanford Raffles was the British Lieutenant-Governor of Java and its dependencies during 1811–16.

[2] Jan Breman, 'Java: bevolkingsgroei en demografische structuur', *Tijdschrift van het Koninklijk Aardrijkskundig Genootschap*, Tweede Reeks, 80 (1963), pp. 252–308.

[3] Bram Peper, *Grootte en groei van Java's inheemse bevolking in de negentiende eeuw* (Amsterdam, 1967).

household members. If this average multiplier was inaccurate, the total outcome would also necessarily show a clear deviation. According to Bram Peper, this might have happened. Thus the point is that anyone who could come closer to the exact average could also present a more realistic and accurate total. The interesting thing for me as a foreign student was that Breman and Peper had both had the late Professor Wertheim as their academic advisor. It showed that hypotheses can differ openly in a collegial atmosphere, which reflects the predominance of academic objectivity over personal findings and sentiments. This has become an academic and intellectual norm in my learning process ever since. Perhaps in Indonesian academic life—where traditions are shorter—one would not easily find an academic advisor accepting two such divergent findings. Academically speaking, there is clearly—now I can say this with more conviction—no controversial point here, since any hypothesis can be corrected by a subsequent finding based on scrutiny of more data and uncovering of new sources of information.

Apart from the above discussion, however, I want to point out that Jan's interest has always been in the lower strata and socio-economically more disadvantaged groups in Asian society. In those years this also meant that his interest was in rural rather than in urban communities, since both India and Indonesia were predominantly agrarian countries. Millions of poor people were indeed to be found in rural villages in Asia, though in India poor people were also struggling to survive in urban centres. Personally I know too little about the teeming millions populating the cities of South Asia. The poor's 'dependency relationship' with more well-to-do farmers also attracted Jan's intellectual interest and attention.

At times I felt that Jan's empathy for the disadvantaged layers of society was reflected in his appearance, particularly the way he used to dress when he was in the field to do interviews. Perhaps he sought as a white man not to appear so strikingly different from those he worked among? Whatever his considerations or the psychological factors at work, he was absolutely correct in not dressing too showily when meeting respondents and interviewees. Dressing showily would have led to a greater distance between the interviewer and the interviewees, which would in turn have lessened his chances of establishing a rapport. His modest appearance must have made it easier for him in any event to develop a rapport with the lower class people, who are often and understandably suspicious of strangers whom they perceive as upper class.

Also typical of the way Jan dresses and equips himself is the woven linen or cotton bag that he used to put his notebook in. I have never known him to carry a tape recorder or even a small camera. I assume that the cotton bag was originally a product of Indian village handicraft. He has usually slung this single-strap bag over his shoulder, so that he resembles an innocent tourist more than a researcher. He takes only brief notes, even if he conducts long interviews that he later writes up at length, requiring long hours of work. Apart from the notes Jan takes about what has been said, his descriptions of the spirit or atmosphere in which the interview took place are also important. Frankly speaking, I do not have any clear knowledge of Jan's mastery of local languages, so that I cannot tell whether he can communicate better directly in India or in Indonesia. What I do know, however, is that he takes care while in Indonesia to be accompanied by a native speaker who can translate and interpret people's answers.

In India, Jan decided to choose the state of Gujarat as his research site; in Indonesia, he has visited and revisited certain districts (*kabupatens*) in west Java. His first visit to Gujarat was in the year 1961–2, and if I recall correctly his visit to Indonesia occurred in late 1971 and early 1972, when he toured rural Java with a senior staff member of Bogor Agricultural University. By revisiting his research areas frequently, Jan has certainly gained an intensive and detailed knowledge of the communities and areas he studied. One of his fellow research workers who accompanied him to a village in the district of Cheribon told me that even after a couple of years Jan could still remember the alleys in that particular village, which his Indonesian fellow researchers could not even recall.

As Jan himself reported in his research findings, his recurrent visits enabled him to gain a better picture of the progress or regress of communities in his research areas, in India as well as Indonesia. Indeed, the situation of the poor has improved in the course of time in both countries—not only the food situation but also housing. Death rates among the young have declined and educational opportunities, have increased. Among the more intangible indicators of poverty, the poor's consciousness of enjoying greater freedom—an awakening from their position of dependency on the richer classes or their patrons—is also a measure of declining poverty. It enables them to voice their claims to better education, health care, etc., more forcefully and loudly. Such non-materialistic indicators are important in understanding the emergence of a growing demand for better amenities. Public claims will inevitably grow more forceful, in other words, since more of the formerly most disadvantaged people will make more demands and make them more forcefully.

Examining and analysing the bottom of the social structure, Jan could inevitably observe quite detailed phenomena, which he tried to place in a more theoretical framework. Defining the observed phenomena brought him to question such sociological jargon as dualism, formal or informal sectors, waves of population mobility between rural and urban centres, and so on. Jan's observation that the boundaries between the informal and formal sectors are rather vague is correct. Some of the indicators used to assign workers to one of these two sectors, such as level of education, employment registration, regular income, and so forth, can change within a relatively short time span. Such rapid changes in workers' status make it hard to assign them to a social category, so that statistics used to measure these sectors may not be very reliable. In terms of characteristics, however, there is greater permanency and continuity.

The recent monetary and economic crisis in Indonesia has clearly shown that mass layoffs have almost overnight caused unemployment in the formal sector, and simultaneously swelled the informal sector. I observed this same instability in developing countries after the crisis of the 1980s in Thailand. Thousands of workers from the formal sector were laid off in Indonesia and had no better choice than entering the urban informal sector by opening food stalls, newspaper stands, and other small business enterprises with petty capitalistic features. A return to their villages of origin in rural areas to find employment was no longer possible because there was no more land for them to cultivate. The distinction between formal and informal sectors is not applicable in fact to Indonesia's rural areas, since there is generally only an informal sector.

As has been experienced by almost all researchers everywhere, the first area that one has researched intensively remains a nostalgic location to return to in subsequent years. This has also been the case with Jan Breman, who began his research in Gujarat and revisited the area most recently in February 2000. I am not certain about how many times he has been there—presumably more than a dozen times over almost thirty years. Despite all that, he has not forgotten his sincere interest in and perhaps first love for Indonesia. Though his visits to Indonesia have been less frequent, he must have revisited west Java and Yogya every four or five years over the past three decades.

The target populations he has studied in these two countries, India and Indonesia, have been largely parallel. However, he has never, to my knowledge, attempted to do a comparative study, focusing on certain subjects and comparing the phenomena in the two countries. Rather he began with a theoretical conception and enriched it by using cases in the two countries to illustrate his conclusions. This has made the subject-matter more complex; it has made his work a many-splendoured thing. A comparative study between India and Indonesia's rural villages would in my opinion have been interesting, because Indian society is more profoundly stratified due to its caste system than are Indonesia's village communities. Consequently, vertical and perhaps even horizontal social mobility may follow different patterns. I have heard that even horizontal mobility in India is not that easy; certain professions within one stratum are also closed. A few studies have been undertaken in Bali where a similar—but not equally rigid—stratification exists.

Jan has had a rather traditional approach as far as methodology is concerned, combining literature study, archival research, and fieldwork. Every combination of two out of these three has been possible for him. In a few publications, he has limited himself to archival research into particular writings about the nineteenth century. In most cases, however I feel that he has preferred a combination of literature and fieldwork. Two of Jan's studies—the one already mentioned about the population census in Raffles' time and his study of coolies and planters on the east coast of Sumatra—were based purely on archival material. The latter publication, which was translated later into Indonesian, unleashed a wave of reactions in his own country.[4] Even though the publication on Sumatra received extensive coverage in the press—not all of it positive—it was definitely well received in Indonesia since it revealed the inhuman side of colonialism.

[4] Jan Breman, *Koelies, planters en koloniale politiek: het arbeidsregime op de grootlandbouwondernemingen aan Sumatra's Oostkust in het begin van de twintigste eeuw* (Dordrecht, 1987).

One of Jan's limitations is that he does not have an active command of the Indonesian language. This would have made it possible for him to gain a much deeper insight into his subjects. Yet his sharp observations and great empathy for many of the people he has observed and interviewed has made up for this limitation. Work by research assistants, each of them doing his or her own research in the same area on a related topic, has also proven to be most helpful to Jan's deeper insights. As I have already mentioned, long interviews and detailed note taking and discussion with assistants have added greater clarity to his reporting.

There are several noteworthy initiatives that Jan has taken and for which he deserves credit. Though he began his career at the University of Amsterdam, he introduced a programme in non-Western sociology at Erasmus University in Rotterdam, which was then chaired by Professor J.A.A. van Doorn. The department had a general sociological orientation, although Professor van Doorn was, like Jan, also interested in Indonesia; van Doorn had spent some time there almost immediately after the proclamation of the Republic of Indonesia. Evidently, van Doorn and Jan were on opposite sides of the great divide over Indonesian independence. Coincidentally, van Doorn and Jan had the same regional interest, namely west Java. While van Doorn had studied subjects in the district of Sukabumi, Jan was more attracted to the district of Cheribon, where agricultural workers were involved in sugar factories before the war and land and labour issues predominated.

Here again, we see Jan's interest and concern for the disadvantaged. Jan thus became one of the founders of the Comparative Asian Studies Program (CASP) at Erasmus University, a research centre within the Sub-Faculty for Social and Cultural Sciences. CASP has had a strong orientation towards sociology and historical research in South as well South-East Asia since its inception. This ran almost parallel with the former Seminarium in Amsterdam, where Jan began his studies. I understand that in reaction against the Leidsche School, which had a stronger inclination towards ethnography and anthropology, CASP has had a bias towards the kind of Modern Indonesian Studies that were first introduced by the Modern Indonesia Program at Cornell University in Ithaca, New York.

One of Jan's studies published by CASP brought together all the factors mentioned above, under the title 'Agrarian Crises and Land

Reforms in East Cheribon' (1981).[5] As the author explained in the publication's subtitle, it examines an example of late colonial development. The colonial administration often referred to the cane sugar industry as one of the fundamental and flourishing industries upon which the colonial economic system was based (the sea upon which the cork of the Netherlands Indies floated) from the second half of the nineteenth century up until the 1930s. Then the world crisis set in and also struck the sugar industry in the Netherlands Indies. A wave of unemployment was one of the results, due to the decline in sugar exports to Europe.

During his tenure at Erasmus University, Jan was also affiliated with the Institute of Social Studies in The Hague, a government-sponsored educational institution that offers opportunities for comparative study to students from developing countries, leading to a Master's degree at the beginning and later to doctorates as well. The restructuring of the Dutch university system (two-phase structure) that began in the early 1980s brought a change in the arrangements, clustering and relocating the so-called *vakgroepen* (clusters of disciplines), as a consequence of which *vakgroepen* were centred and housed at certain universities. I understand that, due to this restructuring, Jan decided to move to the University of Amsterdam, where a graduate school was established under the name Center for Asian Studies Amsterdam (CASA), of which he was director until 1999. The Centre also provides scholarships to Dutch students as well as students from developing countries in Asia, Africa, and Latin America. The two-phase structure had provoked student protests early on, since the duration of studies was shortened, very much like the American system.

The most recent field research that Jan conducted in west Java, Indonesia, was in the same area where he had been much earlier, namely the district of Cheribon. Jan visited villages in that district twice in 1999 to evaluate the implementation of a project backed by the World Bank, namely the establishment of a social safety net (in Indonesian, abbreviated as Jaringan Pengaman Sosial: JPS). This programme was set-up after the mid-August 1997 economic and financial crisis to help the poor, whose numbers have grown since the crisis to approximately 40 million people. A few sources

[5] Jan Breman, *Agrarische crises en hervormingen in Oost-Chirebon: Een voorbeeld van post-koloniaal ontwikkelingsbeleid op het platteland van West-Java* (Rotterdam, 1981).

estimated the number to be as high as 80 million. As the bureaucracy was no longer trusted to supply the poor's most basic needs, many non-governmental organizations (NGOs) were enlisted so as to bypass bureaucratic channels. Jan's report tells us, however, that things have not changed drastically at the grass-roots level. In fact it still remains a problem to identify the poor who are suffering the most from the economic and monetary crisis, and it is even more difficult to target them as aid beneficiaries. Tentative findings have been presented at a national-level seminar in Jakarta, where not only researchers and government officers but also representatives of several NGOs were present. All in all the discussions reached conclusions that were not as positive as the social safety net implementers had hoped.[6] Jan's findings have underlined the weaknesses of the programme's functioning. A final publication is forthcoming, but the problem of poverty will still be there.[7] I wish Jan a productive life even after retirement!

[6] Jan Breman, 'Politics of Poverty and a Leaking Safety Net', *Economic and Political Weekly*, 34 (1999), pp. 1177–8.

[7] Jan Breman and G. Wiradi, *Good Times and Bad Times in Rural Java* (Leiden, 2002).

Gujarat

3

The Inevitable Decline of the Small Farmer's Social Position, Eastern Surat District, India

Chris Baks

> *Un chercheur est parfois à la limite entre l'imaginaire et la réalité; espérons qu'il nous avise à bon escient et ne nous raconte n'importe quoi.*
>
> D'APRÈS YVES COPPENS

The focus in this essay is on a specific group of cultivators, the Adivasi small farmers in Valod Taluka, the administrative unit on the border of the forest belt or jungle to the east of the central plain in the Surat District of Gujarat state. It is the area adjacent to Bardoli Vibagh in which Breman did part of his early and subsequent fieldwork.[1] In India small farmers enjoy special attention in national and state planning, while the Adivasis (i.e. original inhabitants) or Scheduled Tribes have preferential rights under the 6th Schedule of the Indian Constitution. Small farmers are a broad category in Indian development programmes, into which a majority of rural poor families is classified. In the last 25 years, special attention has been paid to this category in these programmes in order to improve the living conditions of the

* The author wishes to thank Anton Ploeg, Yves Quéro, and Joke Schrijvers, who were so kind as to comment on the text, as well as Peter Drucker who thoroughly checked the English text.

[1] Jan Breman, *Of Peasants, Migrants and Paupers: Rural Labour Circulation and Capitalist Production in West India* (Delhi, 1985). Small farmers are examined on pp. 52–60, pp. 159–87 and in the context of special themes like migration. In this study Breman analyses the transformation of

families in the process of rural transformation. Referring to Valod Taluka, one can assume that the wide range of public support has contributed favourably to small farmers' economic situation. It cannot be denied that some have benefited, but many of the small farmers have not taken advantage of the development programmes. Evidence for this statement is provided in the following pages.

The data provided in this essay are derived from fieldwork carried out in Valod Taluka between 1962 and 1986 and from written sources. Some past events have been singled out to help readers understand the small farmers' present position as situated in the classic framework of space and time. The selected issues are: colonial land revenue system, incorporation in the market, industrialization, and population increase, with the underlying assumption that legal, economic, and demographic factors have added to the disintegration of Adivasi communities in the area of research. The subject is dealt with here in only a few pages, so this article cannot be compared with the extensive studies Breman has dedicated to the changing social position of the agricultural labourer in western India. In spite of this, this article may serve some useful purpose. The essay is divided into six sections: an introduction on current Gujarat in general and south Gujarat in particular; a brief overview of the region's history with special reference to the Adivasis; British colonial interference in land rights; Indian and state government planning; the Adivasi small farmer and development programmes; and a critical note.

Industrial and Agricultural Development

At the end of the twentieth century, Gujarat and its southern neighbour Maharashtra are India's leading industrial states. Together they outdistance West Bengal, while Punjab and Haryana lag behind in economic growth.[2] Gujarat's industrial activities are not a recent

south Gujarat's agrarian society and its consequences. Attention is paid to the role of big farmers and the position of agricultural labourers, but small farmers figure in Breman's account as well.

[2] Bengal was in the lead in industrialization on the subcontinent for decennia on end in pre- and post-Independence India. Since 1991, West Bengal has attracted only 3 per cent of India's direct and on-the-ground private investment as against 19 per cent for Gujarat and 16.5 per cent for Maharashtra. In 1995, West Bengal lost four-and-a-half times more man-days than Gujarat (Sumit

development, for it has an artisanal history going back several centuries. The region was well known for its high quality cotton, which was locally spun and woven as well, and for its dye-works. In the past, industry was established in small pockets in central Gujarat and in some coastal ports like the town of Surat in south Gujarat. The Industrial Revolution reached western India in the second half of the nineteenth century, when central Gujarat's cotton industry received a new impetus. Notable industrial development, however, dates from the 1960s, when it increased in both variety and extent. It is concentrated in a long belt running along the coast of south Gujarat towards the north. This belt in turn is connected with the economic activities of the Mumbai (Bombay) region.

Today, a near-uninterrupted stretch of industrial estates with their factories and suppliers have created an important labour market. Following this track through south Gujarat, the estates are mainly situated on the Mumbai–Ahmedabad national highway and railway line.[3] Surat and the surrounding area are a strong growth-pole. Heavy industries like chemical and fertilizer plants, oil refineries, and metal industries alternate with textile and service companies. Information technology and high technology are still to be developed. More and more establishments are being set-up in the rural areas to the east of the Mumbai–Ahmedabad track. These factories are primarily processing locally grown agricultural products. By now they have eclipsed the traditional small-scale industries.

In the last 40 years, a number of cultivators have employed scientific methods and adopted better technological equipment, using better transport, storage, and processing. They have adjusted their farms to a capitalist mode of production and followed a pattern of monocropping, primarily non-food cash crops that need abundant irrigation at fixed times, chemicals, fertilizers, new seed varieties, and also a developed trade system and easily available

---

Mitra, 'Speedbreakers Ahead: Potential Investors Remain Wary of the State's Reputation', *India Today*, 1 February 1999, p. 45). In constant 1980–1 prices Gujarat's annual growth rate in 1992–7 (industry, agriculture, commerce, and services) was 12.1 per cent, while Maharashtra's was 9.6 per cent (Jairam Ramesh, 'Punjab's Paradoxes', *India Today*, 19 April 1999, p. 40).

[3] In a vivid description, Streefkerk paints in glowing terms his revisiting of this belt focused on the industrial estate of Vapi. Hein Streefkerk, 'Thirty Years Later', *Newsletter International Institute for Asian Studies*, 20 (November 1999), p. 17.

credit facilities. This high-yield farming with high cost technology has profoundly changed rural institutions and rearranged social positions at an intra- and inter-caste level.

Valod Taluka has missed the opportunity to be part of this remarkable industrialization. As Breman has convincingly shown in various studies, this type of development has brought many problems to the people at the bottom of the agrarian ladder. Capital investment and new technology have made deep inroads in the agrarian sector, further widening existing social disparities. In Valod Taluka, agricultural modernization has benefited a limited number of cultivators who owned about 4 to 5 per cent of the holdings in 1985, most of whose owners were Adivasis with at least 8 hectares of land. They are large cultivators, but compared with the farmers mentioned before, the big sugar cane and banana farmers in Bardoli Vibagh, they have a modest income and certainly a less than exuberant lifestyle. The middle-sized holdings, about 27 per cent, mostly belonging to Adivasis with 2 to 8 hectares of land, show a great variety in income and progress. Sugar cane, a profitable crop, is decisive for the cultivators' economic position and their ability to be members of the sugar cane cooperative societies. None of the landowners having less than 2 hectares had land under sugar cane cultivation in 1985. According to the official classification this is the category of small farmers, with roughly 50 per cent of the holdings, with the 18 per cent who are landless at the bottom of the scale. In the two last categories Adivasis far outnumber non-Adivasis.[4]

In Valod Taluka, the cultivators have scarcely profited from public financing, in this case irrigation works. On the other hand, the taluka's population has taken advantage of rural electrification and road construction, which have facilitated the movement of goods and labour. Financing has also come from private capital—wealthy Gujarati entrepreneurs in India and abroad—whose

[4] The figures are derived from research data of a Valod-based non-governmental organization (NGO) and collected under the supervision of Praful Trivedi. The NGO investigated the socio-economic development of Adivasi cultivators and labourers by means of a random survey. Data were principally used for institutional purposes. Since the data cover a fairly long period of investigation, from 1963 to 1985, they give researchers a coherent idea of the cultivators' situation in the taluka. They show a steady decline in the size of holdings, fragmentation, and an increase of poverty. Valod Tramodyog, *Surveys*, series from 1963–85.

transactions have furthered economic activities across the continuum of urban and rural sectors. The Adivasis of Valod Taluka are absent from this network, and apart from a few exceptions, for the great majority of Adivasis prosperity is a vain hope. Due to a variety of reasons they are still engaged in a traditional form of agriculture, in spite of being part of a capitalist economy. Characteristics of a special type of land tenure, such as fragmentation, tiny parcels coupled with a lack of proper equipment, inadequate instruction, and shortage of capital, have remained unaltered. In the eyes of government officials, these Adivasis have remained backward cultivators.

Population growth deserves particular attention. Public information, journals, films, and other forms of publicity acquaint people with the seriousness of the rise in population. But family planning is making only slow progress and population growth will continue for some time to come.[5] Demographers expect that Gujarat's overall fertility rate will slow down to 2.1 by about 2015. Even then, population growth will not stop, because of the age distribution; about a third of the state's population is below the age of 15 years. At the beginning of the twenty-first century, Gujarat has about 45 million inhabitants, more than 3 million of them in Surat District alone. Population growth has been noticeable from the 1950s onwards, because of a declining mortality rate and a steady increase in life expectancy. In the past few decades an influx of immigrants into Surat District has added to the population increase, owing to the high demand for labour in the urban and industrial sectors. Population pressure is especially high in the western urbanized and industrialized zone and in the central plain with its dense tillage. The eastern part, including Valod Taluka, is less populated, but the population pressure is high there as well.[6] The soil is of poor fertility compared to land in the central plain,

[5] Readers of an article on population policy in a regional journal are not spared some drama and a built-in bias. The 'man-land ratio in Surat District is disproportionate. As a family of five had 2 acres of land twenty years ago, today the family has swelled to ten, whereas the holding is the same. This increase is disastrous for our economic development, and will ultimate result in the district's demise'. *Gujarat Mitr,* October 1985; translation from Gujarati by Jyotish Solanki.

[6] In 1985 the population of Valod Taluka numbered 66,508 on a surface of 528 sq km, a density of 126 per sq. km. In the Central Plain density is over 250 sq km. These data are from a survey by the Valod-based NGO (see n. 4).

its infrastructure is underdeveloped, and there are few employment opportunities outside agriculture. Consequently, an increase in the population aggravates the situation and puts more pressure on local resources.

Some Historic Events

In past centuries, south Gujarat was not a remote corner of the Indian subcontinent. It borders the Arabian Sea and has a long commercial history. Before the Portuguese set foot in Gujarat, Banias from the region had a special quarter in Jatur (Ormuz). They and the Arabian merchants carried on long-distance trade in the triangle between Gujarat, the Persian Gulf, the Red Sea, and East Africa.[7] Later on in this triangle Gujarati textiles were traded by Dutch and English merchants. In south Gujarat, two principal caravan routes linked Surat to Agra, the Mughal centre, far into the nineteenth century. One of them, the so-called eastern route, followed the Tapti river, on which the port of Surat was situated. At regular distances *sarais*, local markets to which Adivasis took agricultural and forest produce, provided the travelling merchant with food and security.[8] The necessaries were provided by local peasants and craftsmen and by Adivasis. The peasants belonged to Hindu castes and lived in fortified villages in which some artisans and petty traders were active as well. Apparently the eastern route

[7] Sanjay Subrahmanyam, *L'Empire portuguais d'Asie, 1500–1700: histoire politique et économique* (Paris, 1999), pp. 23–8; Apart from this study, the following chapters were consulted in *The Oxford History of India*: Book IV, Ch. 4; Book V, Ch. 2; Book VII, Ch. 6; Book VIII, Ch. 6. The coastal regions of western India were traditional sites of interaction between the subcontinent of Asia, the Middle East and the East African coast. On the subcontinent there were transregional networks of trade, administration, and religion, held together by military force. Drawing an analogy to what Blussé writes about the South China Sea, the Indian Ocean could be portrayed '[. . .] as a whole within Braudel's triple analytical framework of space, time and history', Leonard Blussé, 'Chinese Century: The Eighteenth Century in the Chinese Sea Region', *Archipel*, III/58 (1999), pp. 107–29, p. 109. Subrahmaniam's study has points in common, though on a vastly wider scale: see Ch. 1, 'Les debuts de l'Asie moderne', pp. 21–45.

[8] On a map entitled 'Magni Mogolis Imperium' by Joh. and Corn. Blaeu (Amsterdam, 1664), a replica of an early Portuguese map copied by William Baffin in 1618, the *sarais* on the caravan routes are reproduced as tiny dots like cogwheels in a paper print.

was preferable to the northern one because it passed for the most part through Mughal territory, which meant greater safety.[9] The Hindu castes already mentioned had close relationships with caste members on the coast. Together they made up a highly structured society in which trading castes attended to the storage and transport of rural produce grown by the peasant castes and of the handmade piece goods fabricated by artisans.

The northern part of Valod Taluka lies within 20 km of the eastern caravan route. There were contacts between some Adivasi groups and the outside world of the *sarais*. There were Adivasis who lived in permanent settlements, but most of them pursued a way of life alternating between slash-and-burn agriculture, hunting, and gathering. The south Gujarat Adivasis were part of the Great Tribal Belt of Bhil-speaking peoples. Two of these tribal groups, Chodhras and Gamits, are still in the majority in Valod Taluka today. Chodhras are organized into hierarchical endogamous units, each of which is divided into exogamous groups and headed by a council of elders that settles differences, chiefly family quarrels. The Gamits do not have a similar organization in other respects, but they do have the institution of the council of elders. Both tribal groups follow patrilineal descent and virilocality. These characteristics of their social system have simplified the process of their integration into the Hindu caste system, as tribal castes in the system's lower ranks.[10]

The Adivasis and Hindus of Valod Taluka, as elsewhere, have differing views on the original ownership of the land. Informants in oral history may give a similar account of events, but their interpretation varies.[11] The Adivasi explanation says that they lived in the region before the Hindus arrived. The land and forests were theirs, they say, before they got involved in the Hindu economy and were cheated out of their property by the Hindus'

[9] J.Ph. Vogel (ed.), *Journaal van J.J. Ketelaar's Hofreis naar den Groot Mogol te Lahore, 1711–1713* (The Hague, 1937), pp. 34-5.

[10] A detailed study by Ghanshyam Shah gives a good view of the Chodhra world. This study covers a wider area than one taluka of Surat District. Ghanshyam Shah, *Socio-Economic Conditions of Chodhras: A Restudy* (Surat, 1977).

[11] P.E. Josselin de Jong, 'The Participant's View of Their Culture', in idem (ed.), *Structural Anthropology in the Netherlands* (The Hague, 1977), pp. 231–52. This is an interesting approach, but it pays little attention to power relations, as mentioned at the end of section 2 of this article.

devious tricks. Their claim to the land is based on descent, an argument which is denied by the Hindus, mainly Banias, Desais, and Parsis. The Hindus say that the land and forest were unowned when they arrived, and that their ancestors rightfully occupied and cultivated the soil. The Hindu version was endorsed by the British and entered in the land registers. In any event, Hindu families had lived in the small towns and villages since time immemorial.

The Adivasis traditionally perceive land as a spiritual bond between humans and their ancestors, thus raising land from a material to an ideational level. People or families are seen not as landowners but as occupants on behalf of the ancestors, with user rights vested in a family. In early Adivasi society, land was pivotal in the organization of the social system: it shaped the conditions for economic and social security. Through land, families were related by marriage; the bride-takers received the usufruct of a part of the territory of the bride-givers and the other way around, thus reciprocally linking family groups. Land was an imaginative way through which families maintained contacts, for example by borrowing food or exchanging labour. Alliancies were a precondition for survival in a harsh environment vulnerable to famine and droughts, with meagre resources and a limited carrying capacity of the soil. A society like the Adivasis' was in a permanent state of disequilibrium, and land was a collective defence mechanism for withstanding calamities. Splitting up the land into smaller units would have been too great a risk.

A reconstruction of the past can easily give rise to fallacies, particularly if those in power use a fictitious past for their own ends in the field of administration.[12] The Adivasis' and Hindus' two views interpret events in a different time scale, given that the Adivasis have the precolonial period in mind and the Hindus refer to a later, very British period. The Desais were tax-collectors on behalf of indigenous rulers, most recently the Marathas, and their presence in the eastern part of Surat District was negligible before 1850. But under British rule they acquired forest contracts and, after some time, land from the Adivasis, who ran up debts.[13]

[12] Eric J. Hobsbawm and Terence O. Ranger, *The Invention of Tradition* (Cambridge, 1983), Introductory part, pp. 4ff.

[13] Klaas W. van der Veen, *I Give Thee My Daughter: A Study of Marriage and Hierarchy among the Anavil Brahmins of South Gujarat* (Assen, 1972). The historic part of this study deals with the position of the Desais or Anavil Brahmins, for a long time the dominant caste in south Gujarat.

Banias had a different instrument of power: they lent money among the Adivasis who bought on credit. Parsis acquired liquor contracts and wielded power by selling alcohol and lending the police a helping hand hunting down illegal distilleries. In these ways land was obtained from debtors and given as security.

The Adivasi position resembles the history of other tribal people and peasant groups that endured similar alienation by foreign rulers of their traditional rights to land. In a recent article, Durand reviews the historiography of tax collection in the Netherlands East Indies. In his conclusion he argues that around 1940 the agricultural situation was disquieting as a consequence of colonial rulers' inability to resolve the conflict between Western interests and indigenous land rights.[14] In the less developed islands of eastern Indonesia, land tenure legislation had little impact on indigenous land rights, but conditions changed after Independence, as can be gathered from a study by Visser.[15] More data are provided by Ploeg on colonial land policy in Papua, formerly Irian Jaya.[16]

The Adivasis make a reasonable case in claiming their historic rights. Besides, alienation of land is traceable in the land registers kept since British colonial times, which are proof that the Adivasis were the original holders and losers of the land. Starting from De Josselin de Jong's concept,[17] we can say that the Adivasis are in the right but the powerholders determine the course of events, meaning that the Adivasis' rights will not be acknowledged by the legal system. As a consequence, the Adivasis' view has been overruled, much the same as what has happened and continues to happen to tribal people in Indonesia.

[14] Frédéric Durand, 'La question foncière aux Indes Néerlandaises: enjeux économiques et luttes politiques', *Archipel*, III/58 (1999), pp. 73–88. Durand takes advantage of an elaborate survey by Tjondronegoro and Wiradi in which various authors discuss the problem in specific regions and in different periods. The colonial tax policy became oppressive with the rise of population in Java, and tax policy was detrimental both to the small peasant and to customary law, thanks to the effects of indebtedness and loss of land.

[15] Léontine Visser, *My Rice Field is My Child: Social and Territorial Aspects of Swidden Cultivation in Saha, Eastern Indonesia* (Dordrecht, 1989). This study is not devoted to indigenous law but indirectly gives some important information.

[16] Anton Ploeg, 'Colonial Land Law in Dutch New Guinea', *The Journal of Pacific History*, 34, 2 (1999), pp. 191–204.

[17] Josselin de Jong, 'The Participant's View of Their Culture'.

Colonial Interference

In colonial times present-day Gujarat was divided into a number of princely states under British tutelage, so-called indirect rule, and British Gujarat under direct rule, of which Valod Taluka was a part. British involvement developed gradually, by means of the establishment of an administration to raise taxes and maintain order. As regards the agrarian sector, the colonial government took the line that the state was the ultimate landowner, which empowered the government to raise taxes. 'All land is liable to pay assessment', in the words of Elphinstone, the former governor of Bombay and writer of Indian history.[18] For this reason, tribals who were occupants of ancestral lands prior to these measures now became proprietors under British colonial law. To collect taxes, a reorganization of land tenure was necessary, as was a new revenue system. Known as *ryotwari* (a *ryot* is a peasant), the new system was introduced in Valod after 1870. A bureaucratic apparatus with appointed and salaried public servants was established, having jurisdiction down to the local level. By 1900 each village in Valod Taluka had a book-keeping system with entries on the holder's name—occasionally a woman—the size of holding, type of soil, the amount of tax paid or as yet unpaid, and changes such as sale of land or mortgage. An official accountant was in charge of keeping this record of rights up to date. After several decades the document acquired the status of a record of titles, a proof of ownership, and was recognized as such after Independence.

There were two categories of tax that the Adivasis had to deal with: tax was directly collected from the cultivator and levied on produce, and, since forests were declared Crown Land, forest produce was liable to tax. The tax had to be paid to the village accountant and the forest contractor. They represented the administration and, together with another official, the police-patel, colonial law and order. Under *ryotwari* the Adivasis of Valod Taluka became the acknowledged holders of former ancestral land, enjoyed free tenure, and could freely dispose of their yield, provided that they paid their legal assessments on time. However, in gradual stages the Adivasis were deprived of free entry to the jungle or forest. The District Court, meanwhile, kept a watchful eye on the state of affairs.

[18] The phrase is cited in R.U. Parikh, *Land Policy* (Ahmedabad, 1960), p. 2.

The British rationale was that this would stimulate agricultural production, which was not possible under the Mughal administration. Under the Mughal tax system, intermediaries purchased the right to collect taxes, and ruined the rural people with their exorbitant demands. It was expected that the British colonial policy would free the cultivators, henceforth provided with secure tenurial rights, from extortionate taxes. *Ryotwari* guaranteed a balanced level of revenue under British supervision and left the cultivators with sufficient means to take part in the broader market. However, in this approach the colonial government omitted to establish a sound credit organization; credit facilities were left to the long-standing custom of moneylending. Nor did it take the local power structure into consideration. Members of the higher castes seized the opportunity to staff the lower and middle echelons of the tax-collector's office and court, where they exerted their influence over land, taxpayers, and debtors. Their participation legitimized the *ryotwari* system and assured them of continued local dominance.

British interference provoked profound changes in Adivasi traditional law. Their society based on kinship ideology was relational, person-focused, and situational. *Ryotwari* imposed upon it an alien administration and connected it to money as a mediating standard. Revenue had to be paid in cash and the Adivasis were obliged to produce sufficient crops to earn money. In the former subsistence economy, a recurrent problem was how to build up a sufficiency of food. Barter and transmission prevailed among family groups; in other words, spreading of risks prevailed to maintain an equilibrium. This balance of reciprocity was upset by the revenue system. An additional problem was the splitting up of Adivasi family holdings into smaller units. From now on, *ryotwari* obliged several members of a family group to pay taxes for the allotted land. The obvious way to earn money was to give priority to cash crops. An increase in productivity per acre—the ultimate colonial objective—was not feasible, because old techniques were continued on poor soil and the crops, coarse grains and beans, were not in much demand. Later on, cotton was grown, but of inferior quality, and not much money was earned. Peasants became involved in the colonial market system but did not profit much from it. The cultivator depended on monsoon rains, which sometimes failed or were irregular. Hardly any surplus could be stocked beyond what was needed for daily life. As a result, a recurrent food problem and insufficient yields for the market were linked to a limited elasticity of the money supply.

It comes as no surprise to read in official publications that around 1900 the great majority of Adivasi cultivators was in debt.[19] The Hindus and Parsis supplied them with loans and bound them to the soil as sharecroppers. Eastern Surat District was an area of labour shortage; the Adivasis remained near or on their former land, and for both parties the arrangement met a temporary need. In the Adivasis' eyes, the land was only mortgaged and could be redeemed in instalments, but this rarely happened. With Köbben's article on slavery at hand the Adivasis can be classified into the category of debt-bondage.[20] Debt-bondage served the interests of the Hindus and Parsis, since it gave them legal control over Adivasi land and assured them a supply of labour. British presence resulted in more safety in the countryside and creditors availed themselves of the opportunity to settle near their debtors.

In Valod Taluka and in other Adivasi settlements, society changed in appearance and customs faded away, yet some were maintained: for example, marriage in direct exchange between families persisted but without the exchange of usufructuary rights to land, since the bride-wealth was the result of a moral transaction. In later years, some Adivasi families accepted money when a daughter was married off. This element of Sanskritization was fiercely disputed by Gandhi because the bride-givers often got into debt, as mentioned by Vreede-de Stuers.[21]

[19] The following government publications were consulted: *Gazetteer of the Bombay Presidency,* II, 1877; *Gazetteer of the Bombay Presidency,* IX, 1899; *Gazetteer of the Bombay Presidency,* IX, 1901; *Gazetteer of the Surat District,* n.d.

[20] André J.F. Köbben, 'Why slavery?', in Tom Brass and Marcel van der Linden (eds), *Free and Unfree Labour: The Debate Continues* (Berne, 1997), p. 88. Slavery did not exist among the Adivasis; there was no stratified society, though natural resources were scarce or closed to use the terms of Nieboer's theory. Tribal groups often moved, as recorded in literature, but this should be attributed to their economy and their belief that it was wrong to stay in the same location after the sudden death of a family member.

[21] There are numerous studies on the dowry problem. See van der Veen, *I Give Thee My Daughter*, a study of marriage customs and social change among the Anavil Brahmins, the former elite of south Gujarat. Vreede-de Stuers gives an outline on various castes in India with particular reference to women's position, Cora Vreede-de Stuers, *De Hindoese vrouw en moeder: traditie en nieuwe denkbeelden* (Amsterdam, 1962), pp. 26–33.

Planning and Development Programmes

The colonial land revenue system could be seen as an early attempt at land reform or planning. The colonial government's tax reform was meant to increase the efficiency of agricultural production by reorganizing the size and structure of the unit of production, and to free the cultivator from an oppressive tax burden. *Ryotwari* was presented as an unbiased approach based on scientific and quantitative criteria. The main criteria were the exact measurements of a holding and the type of soil, climate, and crops. The underlying philosophy was simple enough: put the cultivator in charge of a sufficient amount of land, guarantee his land legally, make him liable, and put him in contact with the market. Unfortunately, the cultivator suffered from over-assessment, as the share of government tax was fixed at 40 to 50 per cent of the estimated net value of the crop in this part of India. British officials, moreover, were often ignorant of the local situation and of Indian officials' self-seeking behaviour. Notwithstanding later improvements through legal reforms, for example Tenancy Acts, a Debt Relief Act and Small and Scattered Holdings Act, at the end of the colonial period the government could not prevent a majority of the Adivasis from living in poverty. There were Adivasi families in better circumstances, but only a few.

On the eve of Independence, the ideological struggle within the National Congress party, which formed the first and later national and state governments, hindered the policymakers and planners of the new India from choosing a distinct development strategy. The main ideas at work in the party were the views of the utilitarians; the Bombay Plan, the liberal blueprint for industrialization; M.N. Roy's concept of the collectivization of the agrarian system; and Gandhi's view of the Indian village economy.[22] Finally the Planning Commission, established after 1947, succeeded in combining these ideas in the Five Year Plans. These general Plans are formulated at the national level and worked out in detail at the state level. From the outset, emphasis was put on socio-economic change in a society based on social justice. Gujarat began with redistribution of the ownership of land, actually an amelioration of former colonial measures that had abolished middlemen. British reforms had not

[22] Enno W. Hommes, 'Over de evaluatie van plattelandsplanning in India' (Ph.D. thesis, University of Amsterdam, 1970), Ch. 3.

prevented the growth of a new category of middlemen. These were large landowners who blocked improvements through their indifference to agriculture and absenteeism. Therefore, the concept of personal cultivation was introduced as the major way to restructure agrarian society and stimulate productivity. Many protective measures have been promulgated: among other things, changes in the tax-collecting system and protective rules to prevent easy land transactions in a free market. Gujarat continued its land policy based on earlier British legislation, specifically on tenancy, indebtedness, and small holdings. Eventually, tenancy was abolished altogether, the ultimate step to personal cultivation.[23]

An endless number of Acts, regulations, and modifications have given shape to an impressive land reform, that is impressive from the point of view of policymakers, planners, and administrators. Two concepts—economic holding and ceiling—have guided reform and development measures since their introduction. An economic holding is an agro-economic concept, whereas a ceiling has a redistributive or social function. Both concepts have been revised at intervals in view of altered conditions, i.e. when technical progress enabled the cultivators to carry out agriculture more intensively. There is a close connection between the two concepts, since the ceiling and the economic holding are interwoven. After all, technological development and productivity affect the size of a holding. In Surat District in 1949, about 59 per cent of owner-cultivators had less than 5 acres of land, which was not an economically viable holding at that time.[24] Thirty-five years later, the situation had not changed in Valod Taluka. The very object of land reform policy is to make tillers the owners of the soil, but to ensure increasing productivity per unit other things, viz., availability of capital, irrigation, and modern equipment, are need too.

[23] Indian politicians were of the opinion that tenancy is objectionable in itself. In Gujarat the politicians wanted a thorough change of the tenurial system and decided to abolish it altogether. Two agricultural economists, M.S. Desai and R.S. Mehta, studied the early effects of the Act and were convinced that 'the agriculturists are today worse off than under the previous Tenancy Acts which aimed at giving them relative security of tenure and fair rent. The abolition of tenancy seems to take us back to the pre-land reform days'; M.S. Desai and R.S. Mehta, 'Abolition of Tenancy Cultivation', *Indian Journal of Agricultural Economics*, XVII, 1 (1962), pp. 127–34, here p. 133.

[24] M.B. Desai and C.H. Shah, 'Rural Economy of Reconstituted Gujarat', *Journal of the Gujarat Research Society*, XIV, 3 (1952), pp. 111–48.

A small farmer's success, as Desai said in the early 1960s, depends on his capability to secure enough nourishment for subsistence and to earn cash with the surplus.[25] Desai summed this point up in a short article: 'The productivity of [a] peasant farm can be considerably increased by investment on well-cultivated and well-fertilised crops in a system of mixed farming with well-cared for livestock, which will maintain and increase the soil fertility. Without this there are little chances of increasing the earnings of the peasant and raising his standard of living'.[26]

Apart from legislation, the Five Year Plans have initiated supplementary action to stimulate productivity in the agrarian sector. The Government of Gujarat has produced a series of village development programmes regarding community development, cooperatives, rural banks, and the political institution of *Panchayati Raj,* the elected government councils from the village up, to ensure a broad base within the rural polity. Legislation and development programmes have succeeded in replacing non-cultivating castes with cultivating castes, whose members belong to the top of the present agrarian hierarchy. They have written the success story of agricultural commercialization. At the bottom of the hierarchy, however, the outcome is different.

The Small Farmer and Development Programmes

Given their numbers, the small farmers, not only men but also women and their families, are a serious problem in Valod Taluka. They dominate the taluka's society, though at first sight they are almost invisible. The small farmers' dwellings are grouped in hamlets which are scattered in the interior off the main roads, and a traveller glancing casually at the scenery does not notice the huts, which for most of the year are hidden in the dusty fields and during the monsoon are difficult to reach through the mud. Still, the dwellings are somewhat better than the ramshackle huts of the Halpatis, the tribal caste of agricultural labourers thoroughly studied by Breman. Not until 1970 did small farmers get their own development programmes in line with the overall economic

[25] Personal communication.

[26] N.K. Desai, 'Concept of Economic Holding', *Khadi Gramodyog*, 2 (1956), pp. 1–8, here p. 8. A peasant farm is a small farmer's unit of production, about 5 acres of land or 2 hectares.

strategy, though on a modest scale. The first organization in Surat District, the Small Farmers Development Agency, supported pilot projects for potentially viable holdings, in fact a designation of the minimum size for an economically viable holding. Its size depends on various criteria but it is below 5 acres of land. Later on, the organization extended the programme to all small farmers. A special subcategory, marginal farmers with non-viable holdings, was subsequently added; these farmers received aid and advice on poultry farming and goat-raising supported by loans from cooperatives or commercial lending institutions. All programmes have now been subsumed under the Integrated Rural Development Programme. To complete the planning in the agrarian sector, landless families are also involved in public work projects, such as the upkeep of roads and maintenance of small irrigation canals.[27] In a recent study, Breman has once more described these men, women, and children, who often live in utter poverty by the roadside or along the canals.[28]

Development planning has evolved a complex organization as a means of action, an effort to rationalize collective activities, in which the small farmer has a delimited sphere. In Valod Taluka the small farmers are mostly Adivasis, at least 80 per cent of the category and half of the cultivators. As we said before, Adivasis have been distinguished as an administrative category since British times and have enjoyed preferential treatment as Scheduled Tribes in education and vocational training since Independence, and are helped to get government jobs. The Chodhras and Gamits of Valod Taluka are multiply scheduled and as such have an established legal position. Other organizations, which have developed a workable model of grass-roots organizing, are also devoted to the Adivasis' welfare. These Indian-style non-governmental organizations (NGOs) have already existed for many years in Valod Taluka. Before the word came into use, they were centres

[27] For a chronological survey of the establishment of the development programmes for small farmers in India, see Johannes E. Nielen, 'Rural Transformation and the Small Farm Sector: A Sociological Study in Two Districts of Andhra Pradesh, India' (Ph.D. thesis, Free University, Amsterdam, 1993), Ch. VII.

[28] Jan Breman, *Footloose Labour: Working in India's Informal Economy* (Cambridge, 1996).

for Adivasi uplift. The origin of the ashrams was a social movement of some educated Adivasis from the former state of Vadodara (Baroda). They introduced a social programme to teach Adivasis not to abuse alcohol and to observe sanitary regulations. It was Gandhi who established an ashram in Bardoli Vibagh soon after the movement began; Gandhi's ashram was followed by a second one founded by one of his followers in the Valod area. These were and still are educational centres, but they are also concerned with politics. Before Independence, social workers were already acting for Adivasi tenants and debtors in court.[29]

It is true that these NGOs *avant la lettre* organized resistance to the British, but the movement did not produce socio-economic change for the Adivasis. It was a political movement under Hindu leadership and with undeniable earmarks of patronage. To this day its leaders take great care to forestall Adivasi rebellions against their landlords and moneylenders. This point of view has also been the guiding principle of the ashrams established since 1950; the ashram leaders guide the Adivasis' emancipation so as to integrate them peacefully into Hindu society.

The early ashram movements may fit in with Wertheim's counter-point concept, but the concept is not applicable to the present ashrams' way of acting, because an emancipatory movement under Hindu supervision is in fact an obstacle to Adivasi empowerment.[30] It is well-known that the NGOs or ashrams arrange their work with local and regional politicians and administrators to such a degree that in the eyes of the Adivasi small farmers government organizations and ashrams are interchangeable. Incidentally, those in touch with these organizations become well aware of the problems with them. 'The successful Adivasi farmer gets attention from government', one hears, and, 'If we could have educated a son in the ashram, we would have attracted the staff's attention.' Yet the ashram leaderships cannot

[29] Desai, in his study of the Vedchi ashram in Valod, points out that Indian Independence had its origins in the Bardoli and Valod social movements. I.P. Desai, *The Vedchhi Movement*, Vol. I (Surat, 1969), pp. 56–63.

[30] W.F. Wertheim, 'Society as a Composite of Conflicting Value Systems', in idem, *East-West Parallels: Sociological Approaches to Modern Asia* (The Hague, 1964), pp. 22–37. Here the concept is understood in its broadest sense, as a protest to force social change.

be blamed for making deals with the Adivasis' adversaries so as to secure their interests. The ashrams often lack an adequate professional staff and suffer from weakly developed strategies.[31] Caste is the basic Indian reality, and underrating caste loyalty and the role of kin (the widespread 'kin-itis') would be a sign of ignorance and naivety. Influential local caste members are related to politicians and development officials, and so are ashram staff members. Planning and programmes are defined on a supra-local level and implemented down a sequence of organizations; lobbying can only be to one's advantage, since the state hoards scarce resources. A researcher making an assessment of government development organizations, and also of NGOs or ashrams, would discover consecutive personal nuclei in the administration. Contacts with regional and state political centres go through *Panchayati Raj,* which are excellent bases for strengthening horizontally organized institutions like cooperatives and credit organizations. In recent years a new power centre has appeared, better organized than the traditional one, a multi-caste-based composite of big farmers, industrialists, and service sector managers. The state's view regarding planning is defined by this new elite, since the federal state has been withdrawing into the background. A wider region, including parts of Gujarat and Maharashtra, is taking shape, in which the new elite is gaining influence over economics and politics. This has not escaped the ashram leaders' notice; they have redoubled their efforts to gain access to this new formation and politics.

These things entirely escape small farmers and their families. Ashram clients are mostly middle-sized and large farmers, who keep their distance from the poorer members of their tribe. The younger generation is moving away, and, with a few exceptions, leaving the tribal poor to fend for themselves. They are the new Adivasi elite on their way to a niche in Hindu society.

[31] A conscientious exposé of the working of a government programme and an NGO project in Andhra Pradesh is given by M.J. Put, 'Innocent Farmers? A Comparative Evaluation into a Government and a NGO Project Located in Semi-Arid Andhra Pradesh, India' (Ph.D. thesis, University of Amsterdam, Amsterdam, 1997). In Valod Taluka, one of the ashrams ventured to establish a sugar cane factory, but mismanagement and opposition from vested interests, i.e. board and farmer-members of other cooperative sugar cane factories in Bardoli Vibagh, contributed to its fiasco.

A Critical Note

One of the features of Indian government planning is the contrast between the number of cultivators in need of improving their production and the limited means available to reach this goal. This may have led the government to give priority to develop viable holdings, but it should be added that from the outset Indian planning was rooted in economic theories and economic growth as an all-embracing principle. This starting point in planning has marginalized a great number of farmers, including the small farmers of Valod Taluka, who could not meet the conditions of an economically viable holding. The Small Farmers Programme does not produce these conditions either, and is at best a type of poor relief. It is quite understandable that a number of problems have been passed on to the NGOs.

Another feature of government planning is a partiality for male farmers as the only skilled actors in agriculture, thus neglecting women's role in the production process. Schrijvers convincingly describes the ignorance of the lower social strata and officials' opposition and gender-insensitivity. All this has led to women not taking an active part in development programmes. Women have always worked in the fields and contributed to the family's income, and women's additional earnings are vital nowadays for the survival of the household.[32]

These lines also apply to Valod Taluka. For more than a century, the Adivasis have experienced the influence of the market and its ever increasing emphasis on capital and technology as a precondition to increasing productivity per unit of land. Desai and Shah indicate that from the 1930s onwards there has been a small group of Adivasis who have benefited, a small upper stratum in which women do not work in the fields.[33] They see themselves as

[32] In various studies Schrijvers explains in detail the obstacles small farmers' wives have to cope with to earn a living and bear the double burden of work in the household. Her fieldwork was in Sri Lanka but she often refers to Indian situations. Joke Schrijvers, "Questions of Gender in Development Planning: Women's Experiences in a New Settlement of the Mahaweli project in Sri Lanka', *Asia-Pacific Journal of Rural Development*, 3, 1 (1993), pp. 44-57.

[33] Desai delineates the stratification process of the Adivasis, the rise of 'a mobile and upward looking middle class' to which the ashram workers belong; Desai, *The Vedchhi Movement*, pp. 139ff. Shah explains the pursuit

different from poorer women, whose lack of money results in lack of food and education, and among whom illness is a calamity. Poor women have no choice but to work to survive together with their children and elderly family members, because their husbands are away in search of work or are casual labourers in low-paid agricultural or industrial jobs. Those engaged in such insecure and vulnerable labour are in fierce competition with each other. Among the poor families in Valod Taluka there are marginal farmers, landless people, and a great number of small farmers.

The prospects of the small farmer in Valod Taluka are uncertain, as is the future of other cultivators with small plots in India or the rest of the world. Ploeg stresses the problems of small farmers in a tribal area *par excellence*, in Papua New Guinea. He mentions the impact of market forces, population increase, and availability of arable land as important factors that undermine the Papua small farmers' future.[34] If we move on from New Guinea via Indonesia to India, then phenomena such as population density, scarce rural resources, insufficient economic and social infrastructure, illiteracy, and an uneven distribution of the economic surplus take on ever greater proportions. Most Adivasi small farmers in Valod Taluka live in a world of gradual degradation. Economic decline is followed by the breakdown of the endogamous family group, in most cases ending in an incomplete household consisting of women, children, and old people attached to their small holding, which they tenaciously hang on to. The incomplete household groups account for the fact that these people live on the very bottom of society in terms of poverty, malnutrition, and neglect by development agencies.

The poor small farmers and their families feel abandoned. After the land reform measures of the 1950s and 1960s the Adivasi

---

by the better-off strata of the Adivasis' integration into the Hindu social order, 'for their own advantage'. Shah, *Socio-Economic Conditions of the Chodhras*, p. 197.

[34] Anton Ploeg, 'Little landlessness, but . . .' , in George N. Appell (ed.), *Modernization and the Emergence of a Landless Peasantry: Essays on the Integration of Peripheries to Socioeconomic Centres* (Williamsburg, VA, 1985), pp. 371–99. Recently doubts have arisen concerning the Papua small farmers' willingness to continue agricultural activities, because working in the mines is more remunerative. In any event the Papuans have non-farm employment possibilities so that they can improve their lives.

cultivators made a new start, but price fluctuations, scant credit facilities, bad harvests, and illness of people and cattle have 'started the sequence of misery again'. As one poor Adivasi woman summed the situation up, 'Once we derived our pride from our *jati* (endogamous group); there was land for cultivation, there was our jungle, we had our tradition, but we lost the land, and so our pride.' Today, *jati* members live scattered and meet only occasionally. Conflicts are not kept under control by the elderly, and the disintegration of tribal organizations continues.

Alternative development strategies—efforts to reach the poor with the alternative approach of appropriate and intermediate technology—to relieve poverty have had meagre results.[35] Poverty alleviation measures have been taken long ago but there has always been an urban bias in the aid programmes, as in the case of the fair price ration shops or the Public Distribution System (PDS), and its newer branches, the Targeted PDS. Measures designed to provide cheap food to the poor are actually reaching a laughably small proportion of the rural poor. The government pours money into subsidies—on rice, wheat, and gas cylinders—but the bulk of the goods remain in the urban areas. These programmes are part of a charity policy but with insufficient means, and resemble the overall development programmes of the government, which are focused on proprietors of economically viable holdings, who, incidentally, also get income tax breaks.

The long process of detribalization has ended in impoverishment. and possibly in a process of depeasantization too. If so, in accordance with Brass' theorizing, the Adivasi casual labourer—in Valod Taluka, also a small farmer—will be a useful instrument in the restructuring of the labour process of the urban zone of Surat District and in the highly capitalized rural Bardoli Vibagh.[36] In this essay, there are no data to confirm or reject the thesis of depeasantization, but if it could be proved it would imply a further degradation of the Adivasi small farmer's position in society.

[35] Floris Paul Blankenberg, 'Implementation of Rural Technology Projects in India: An Exploratory Research' (Ph.D. thesis, University of Twente, Enschede, 1985). See Chs. 3, 4, and 5 on Gujarat and the use of windmills, solar cookers, and biogas projects.

[36] Tom Brass, 'Some Observations on Unfree Labour, Capitalist Restructuring and Deproletarianization', in Brass and van der Linden, *Free and Unfree Labour*, pp. 57–75.

Years ago an informant observed, 'The Adivasi jungle was our home but now we are exiles in our old jungle.' In a short article, Kloos suggests that the researcher who sets out for Sri Lanka read Woolf's book on the jungle in the dry zone.[37] The novel is about the tragic demise of a village and its inhabitants, swidden cultivators and forest gatherers. It is about the struggle of a man and his daughters against the evil world (that is, Sri Lanka), a struggle they lose—in the end the jungle swallows the village. In Valod Taluka, the jungle is the metaphor for the current economic world which destroys tribal communities and drives small cultivators and their families into poverty and a life of semi-permanent migration.

[37] Peter Kloos, 'The Jungle in the Village: Leonard Woolf on Sinhalese society', in idem (ed.), *True Fiction: Artistic and Scientific Representations of Reality* (Amsterdam, 1990), pp. 159–67.

South Asia

4

Working through Partition: Making a Living in the Bengal Borderlands

Willem van Schendel

In the Indian subcontinent, the word 'Partition' conjures up a particular landscape of knowledge and emotion. The break-up of colonial India has been presented from vantage points which privilege certain vistas of the postcolonial landscape. The high politics of the break-up itself, the violence and major population movements, and the long shadows which Partition cast over the relationship between India and Pakistan (and from 1971, Bangladesh) have been topics of much myth-making, intense polemics, and considerable serious historical research. As three rival nationalisms were being built on conflicting interpretations of Partition, most analysts and historians have been drawn towards the study of Partition as a macro-political event. Let us portray these scholars as the mountaineers of Partition studies.

A second trend in the literature has focused on Partition as a cultural and personal disaster, the fissure of two major regional cultures (Punjab and Bengal) which were divided between the successor states, and the personal suffering and traumatic memories of millions of uprooted refugees. Those who study these themes are the fishermen of Partition, casting their nets in its deep waters. It is these two groups of scholars who have determined how we see the mental landscape of Partition—a landscape dominated by the jagged peaks of Mount Recrimination reflected in the dark surface of Lake Nostalgia.

Other parts of that landscape, however, are still in the shadows. We must explore them if we are to make sense of how Partition shaped social life in South Asia in the second half of the twentieth century. What lies between the mountains and the lake? What was happening in the foothills, on the plains, the rivers, and their banks? How did ordinary people experience the macro-political event of state fragmentation? And how did their actions influence the shape of post-Partition societies?

We still know remarkably little about many aspects of Partition, particularly its socio-economic impact on different localities and individuals. The nationalist historiographies of Pakistan, India, and Bangladesh have elevated the moment of Partition (14–15 August 1947) to the status of an absolute caesura in the history of the subcontinent. Till now, few have challenged the resulting state-centred periodization. But in many regions, and in the lives of numerous individuals, the realities of Partition were slow to make their mark; in their constructions of history, 1947 does not always appear as the sharp break of historiographical convention. Gyanendra Pandey's remarks for India are equally applicable to Pakistan and Bangladesh:

> The historians' history of Partition has, in India, been a history of crisis for the Indian nation and the nationalist leadership. It has been a history of the machinations which lay behind this event, and the lessons to be drawn by the nation for the future. This is not a history of the lives and experiences of the people who lived through that time, of the way in which the events of the 1940s were constructed in their minds, of the identities or uncertainties that Partition created or reinforced. Even as a history of crisis for the Indian nation, therefore, this history is inadequate.[1]

This inadequacy is even more glaring in the case of the historians' social and economic history of Partition.[2] In order to construct

[1] Gyanendra Pandey, 'The Prose of Otherness', in David Arnold and David Hardiman (eds), *Subaltern Studies VIII: Essays in Honour of Ranajit Guha* (Delhi, 1994), p. 194.

[2] In the years following Partition, a few attempts were made to quantify the economic impact at aggregate levels (e.g. Vakil) and some studies have compared trends in East and West Bengal without focusing specifically on Partition (Boyce, Bose, Rogaly et al.). Studies such as Dasgupta's, comparing the long-term economic impact of Partition on a divided region, are very rare. C.N. Vakil, *Economic Consequences of Divided India: A Study of the Economy of India and Pakistan* (Bombay, 1950); James K. Boyce, *Agrarian Impasse in Bengal: Institutional Constraints to Technological Change* (Oxford, 1987); Sugata Bose, *Peasant Labour and Colonial Capital: Rural Bengal Since 1770*. The New Cambridge History of India, Vol. III/2 (Delhi,

adequate social and economic histories of Partition we need to reconsider the historical sources which have informed Partition studies so far. Students of Partition have been returning time and again to a few particularly rich sources: high-level state records (most famously the ones published in *The Transfer of Power*[3]) as well as the private papers, correspondence, and memoirs of prominent politicians and bureaucrats. The possibilities offered by other source material have been much less diligently pursued. With few exceptions, the many voices speaking from low-level and local records, newspapers, diaries, letters, and oral and written testimony by ordinary people have been underused.[4]

In this essay we consider how Partition affected working people's livelihood. India—much more than Bangladesh and Pakistan—has a lively tradition of labour history and labour studies.[5] Studies in this tradition often take 1947 as their cut-off point, but otherwise they hardly intersect with studies on Partition. Many years ago, Jan Breman argued that 'to understand the present situation of the

---

1993); Ben Rogaly, Barbara Harriss-White and Sugata Bose (eds), *Sonar Bangla? Agricultural Growth and Agrarian Change in West Bengal and Bangladesh* (Dhaka, 1999); Abhijit Dasgupta, *Growth with Equity: The New Technology and Agrarian Change in Bengal* (Delhi, 1998).

[3] Published in 12 volumes by Her Majesty's Stationery Office, London, between 1970 and 1983, and edited by Nicholas Mansergh, E.W.R. Lumby et al.

[4] Interesting recent examples of analyses on the basis of such material are Ritu Menon and Kamla Bhasin, *Borders & Boundaries: Women in India's Partition* (Delhi, 1998); Joya Chatterji, 'The Fashioning of a Frontier: The Radcliffe Line and Bengal's Border Landscape, 1947–52', *Modern Asian Studies*, 33 (1999), pp. 185-242; Dipesh Chakrabarty, 'Remembered Villages: Representation of Hindu-Bengali Memories in the Aftermath of the Partition', *Economic and Political Weekly* (10 August 1996), pp. 2143–51; Gautam Ghosh, ' "God is a Refugee": Nationalism, Morality and History in the 1947 Partition of India', *Social Analysis*, 42, 1 (1998), pp. 33–62; and Prafulla K. Chakrabarti, *The Marginal Men: The Refugees and the Left Political Syndrome in West Bengal* (2nd edn., Calcutta, 1999).

[5] For a recent overview, see Sabyasachi Bhattacharya, 'South Asian Labour History: Historiography—And Where Do We Go From Here?' Paper presented at the conference on Global Labour History in the Twenty-first Century, International Institute of Social History, Amsterdam, November 2000.

rural labourers it is essential to know their position in the past',[6] and his impressive research output since then has done much to historicize the study of labour relations in South Asia. It is in this spirit that we explore the effects of Partition on labour, a topic which has received scant attention by students of labour as well as by students of Partition.

This is an exploratory essay, and its scope is restricted in several ways. First of all, it deals only with the north-eastern part of South Asia where Partition created an international border separating East Bengal—which became East Pakistan, then Bangladesh—from West Bengal, Bihar, Assam, and other regions which joined the new state of India. Second, it concentrates on the new borderland and how labour relations changed there. Third, it is confined to the period of the late 1940s and 1950s. And finally, it is based largely on evidence contained in 'low-level' state records. Because these records are more readily accessible in Bangladesh than in India, this essay contains more information on how people worked through Partition on the Pakistan side of the borderland than on the Indian side.[7]

The aim of this essay is modest: to initiate the study of labour in the Partition borderland across the divide of 1947. It does so by briefly introducing several categories of workers whose situation changed, often dramatically, as a result of Partition. The archival evidence on these changes is rather limited as state officials were interested only in certain aspects of labour, and their capacity for monitoring these was quite restricted. A more comprehensive understanding of how people 'worked through Partition' requires the use of other sources, particularly oral ones.

Despite its limited scope, this essay underlines the need to rethink the categories of labour history in South Asia. In a recent

[6] Jan Breman, *Meester en Knecht: Een onderzoek naar de veranderingen in de betrekkingen tussen landheren en landarbeiders in Zuid-Gujarat, India* (Amsterdam, 1970), p. 2.

[7] In this paper, reference is made to three series of relatively 'low-level' state records in the National Archives of Bangladesh in Dhaka. These are B. Proceedings of the Home Department of the Government of (East) Bengal, records which were supposed to be destroyed after a number of years. In the following, records of the Confidential Records Branch start with *CR*, records of the Political Branch with *Plt.*, and records of the Police Branch with *Police*. I wish to thank the staff of the National Archives, in particular Dr Sharif Uddin Ahmed and Md Hashanuzzaman Hydary, for their help.

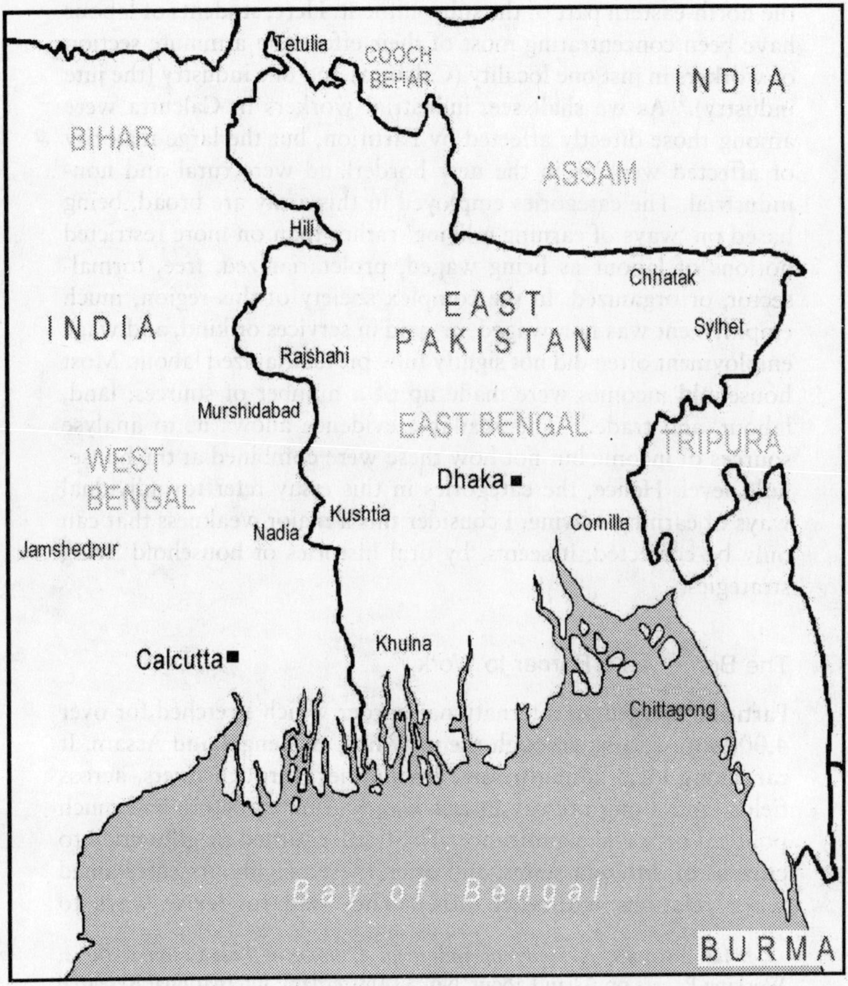
Tetulia
COOCH
BEHAR
INDIA
BIHAR
ASSAM
Hili
Chhatak
INDIA
EAST
PAKISTAN
Sylhet
Rajshahi
Murshidabad
EAST BENGAL
TRIPURA
WEST
BENGAL
Dhaka
Kushtia
Comilla
Nadia
Jamshedpur
Khulna
Calcutta
Chittagong
Bay of Bengal
BURMA

publication, Jan Breman has analysed and criticized the narrowing of the focus of Indian labour studies to the study of urban industrial labour.[8] This criticism is certainly relevant to the study of labour in the north-eastern part of the subcontinent. Here, students of labour have been concentrating most of their efforts on a minute section of workers in just one locality (Calcutta) and one industry (the jute industry).[9] As we shall see, industrial workers in Calcutta were among those directly affected by Partition, but the large majority of affected workers in the new borderland were rural and non-industrial. The categories employed in this essay are broad, being based on 'ways of earning a living' rather than on more restricted notions of labour as being waged, proletarianized, free, formal-sector, or organized. In the complex society of this region, much employment was non-waged, or paid in services or kind, and wage employment often did not signify fully proletarianized labour. Most household incomes were made up of a number of sources: land, labour, and trade.[10] The available evidence allows us to analyse sources of income but not how these were combined at the household level. Hence, the categories in this essay refer to individual ways of earning a living. I consider this a major weakness that can only be corrected, it seems, by oral histories of household living strategies.

The Border as a Barrier to Work

Partition created an international border which stretched for over 4,000 km, cutting through the provinces of Bengal and Assam. It ran along local administrative boundaries, through rivers, across fields, and along railway lines which had never before had much political or social significance. The border turned neighbours into citizens of different states, and often these neighbours entertained work relations with each other. They had to devise ways to

[8] Jan Breman, *A Study of Industrial Labour in Post-Colonial India*; Working Papers on Asian Labour, No. 3 (Amsterdam: International Research Programme Changing Labour Relations in Asia (CLARA), 1998). See also Jan Breman, *Footloose Labour: Working in India's Informal Economy* (Cambridge, 1996).

[9] See list of references in Bhattacharya, 'South Asian Labour History'.

[10] On the multiplicity of sources of income in rural Bengal, see Willem van Schendel, *Peasant Mobility: The Odds of Life in Rural Bangladesh* (Assen, 1981), pp. 302–3, 313–15, 320–2.

continue these relations, or create new ones. Many found that the border did not change life overnight but only gradually came up as a barrier to cross-border work. Eventually, many were confronted with the stark choice between giving up their job or moving across the border in order to keep it.

Wage Labour

The imposition of the border, and the population movements that took place as a result of it, had lasting effects on the labour market in the borderland. Both employers and labourers gradually had to adapt to new conditions which privileged labour ties on either side of the border and made cross-border labour ties less attractive. For example, a serious problem was how to take your wages home without being detected by the border police. The states of India and Pakistan, on bad terms with each other, prohibited the free flow of commodities across the border and returning wage labourers, whose wages were often largely in the form of food grains, were seen as smugglers. In 1951,

> Mangal Majhi [of Jakirpur village, West Dinajpur, India] worked as a day labourer in the house of Masoruddin Mondal of Bheram [the adjacent village in Dinajpur, Pakistan], who gave him one maund [36 kg] of paddy as his wages. He was arrested by a patrol constable of Rudrani Border Out Post within Pakistan territory while he was attempting to smuggle this paddy across the border. He was sent up in charge sheet and convicted.[11]

The situation was even more complicated if wages were paid in cash. Pakistan and India imposed various restrictions on the import and export of currency, and border police could use this to harass cross-border labourers.[12]

But even day labourers who merely went to look for employment

[11] Government of East Bengal, Home (Political) Department, Confidential Records Branch, CR 1B2-28/50 (B. Proceedings, November 1952) (hereafter: CR 1B2-28/50 (11-52)).

[12] On 12 March 1952, Salam Mia, a day labourer of Hussanpur village (Tippera (Comilla) District, Pakistan), had the Pakistan Customs Liaison Officer enter into his Complaint Book: 'I got Rs. 51/- at Agartala [in Tripura, India] as my wages for three month service. With the said amount I was coming to my home—Pakistan when I reached the India border, the Customs officer on duty seized the entire amount of Rs. 51/- and gave me a receipt for Rs. 50/- only' (CR 3I-68/52 (1-54)).

across the border could get into trouble. Jahura Bibi, a widow from Sylhet (Pakistan), sent her 20-year-old son Taibullah across the border to find her some employment. He did not return, so the next morning she went to the Indian side herself, only to find that he had been arrested. The police told her that her son 'would be released if she could produce witnesses to prove that her son [was] not a spy'.[13] Two days later, a similar case occurred, this time involving a labourer from a village in Tripura (India) who had gone over to Pakistan to find some work. Near the border the labourer, Hiralal Das, was caught by a Pakistan border guard who suspected him of being a spy. Hiralal assured him that he was just looking for some work. The guard then proceeded to beat him up, after which he interrogated him about the strength of the military in Tripura, the location of the Tripura treasury, and where the Tripura royal family kept their valuables. As Hiralal could not give him any answers, the guard and a colleague beat him with their rifle butts, kicked him with their boots, and threatened to kill him. Eventually he was set free and returned to India, after which he filed a complaint with the local police.[14] It is clear that cross-border day labour held special risks but nonetheless it must have also been very common.[15]

Working for the other State

A subset of border commuters, and one which is relatively well documented, were employees of the other state. During the colonial period many people had been employed by state institutions which were now in the other country. Despite this, their employment was not terminated even after Partition. For example, the district authorities of Rajshahi District (Pakistan) continued to employ boatmen from the adjacent District of Murshidabad (India). When these men got caught up in a border dispute between the two states in

[13] CR 1A1-6/51 (3-53).

[14] CR 1A2-3/51 (3-53).

[15] Another risk was being tricked into accepting a day-labour job across the border and then being arrested. This happened to Babar Ali, an Ansar (Pakistan volunteer) from Sylhet in 1952. Safu Mia from Tripura (India) asked him and two others to work in his field across the border in India. As they were working there, they were arrested by Indian police in connection with a recent theft. The plot had been hatched by Tamaruddin Addadar of Tripura who had asked Safu to engage Babar with whom he had 'previous enmity . . . for some family affairs' (CR 1A7-1/52 (4-53)).

1948, they 'were severely beaten, arrested, remanded [in] custody [by the Indian authorities] and subsequently released on a bail of Rs. 200/- each. Their relations are also being oppressed. Their fault is said to have . . . originated from the fact that they are serving under an enemy and hence are traitors.'[16]

Such state employees would commute daily across the border. But a much larger group of state employees, who worked for one state but lived in the other, served too far from their homes to commute daily.[17] They remitted their earnings and visited their homes during holidays. Many of them worked as policemen or in the armed forces. Their movements attracted little attention except when they got into trouble, usually because they were arrested while on home leave, on suspicion of espionage. This happened to Santi Ranjan Chakraborty of Comilla District (Pakistan) who was arrested in 1951. His father wrote to the East Pakistan authorities from his village home in Comilla:

> I have the honour to state, that my eldest son Sreeman Santi Ranjan Chakraborty is an employee of Indian Navy, Bombay, before the partition of Bengal. He was coming on leave in his own house. After staying home some days he went to his father-in-laws house. . . . There he had been arrested. . . . He left his pay book, identity card, leave ticket, in Calcutta on the way of his coming from Bombay. . . . He is the only person of earning [capacity] in our family. . . . We live on his earnings only.[18]

[16] CR 1W-1/49 (1-53). Another example from Murshidabad was Maulvi Zuadur Rahim of Kaitha village who worked as Head Assistant, Finance Department, Government of East Bengal (CR 1I-156/48 (11-50)). Arabinda Gupta from Cachar (Assam, India) worked as Agricultural Demonstrator in Sylhet (Pakistan) (CR 3I-324/52 (9-53)). Jatindra Nath Ganguly of Satkhira (Pakistan) was Khas Mahal Peon in 24-Parganas (India) (CR 1A3-8/49 (11-50)).

[17] Just before Partition, some categories of state personnel were given the option to take employment in either Pakistan or India. For details on these Optee Government Servants, or Optees, see Md. Mahbubar Rahman and Willem van Schendel, '"I Am *Not* A Refugee": Rethinking Partition Migration', paper presented at the Conference on Displaced People in South Asia, Chennai, 2–4 March 2001.

[18] Letter from Nolini Mohan Chakraborty (Kashimpur village, P.O. Nashirkot, District Tippera (Comilla)), 11/12/51 (CR 1A2-1/51 (3-54)). For other cases of employees in the Indian Army and Air Force, see CR 1A3-8/49 (11-50), CR 1A6-1/52 (3-54); and CR 1A2-1/51 (3-54). The governments of Pakistan and India regularly exchanged armed forces personnel captured in the other country (CR 1A6-1/52 (3-54)).

Policemen regularly got into trouble when on home leave. Nurun Nabi, a constable at Tetulia (Pakistan), went home to Murshidabad (India) in 1952 to give money to his mother. On his way back to Pakistan he was arrested near the border by a Bihar constable who robbed him and threatened to 'shoot me dead in retaliation of the death of one Bharati *havildar* [Indian sergeant] who was reported to have been shot dead by the Pakistani police at Patagara (Bharat)'.[19]

A complex case was presented by Haripada Biswas from Khulna District who worked for both governments at the same time. During the week he was a permanent employee of the Office of the Accountant General, West Bengal, in Calcutta (India), and every weekend he was in Khulna (Pakistan) where he held the office of President of the Barrackpur Union Board No. IV. He was an Indian citizen.[20]

Unlike other cross-border commuters—whose employment never ended completely (although it was disrupted at times of border tension or war) and would expand considerably in the closing decades of the twentieth century—cross-border state employees found it increasingly difficult to continue after 1952, when India and Pakistan introduced passport and visa controls.

Minding the Shop

The border also played havoc with the marketing system in the borderland which was based on rotating village markets. Village shops were relatively rare and goods reached customers through periodical markets which would assemble in substantial villages on two days each week. These days differed for individual villages in a region so there was always a market on in a nearby village. The border meant that for borderlanders, marketing became a cross-

[19] Nurun Nabi spent three months in an Indian jail and his case led to correspondence between the Ministry of External Affairs in Delhi and the High Commission for Pakistan in Delhi (CR 1A6-1/52 (3-54)). For similar cases, see CR 1A3-8/49 (11-50); CR 1A6-1/52 (3-54); and CR 1A2-1/51 (3-54)).

[20] This double function seems to have created no problem, unlike his 'actively agitating for the inclusion of the Khulna District in Bharat [India]'. The District Magistrate of Khulna externed him from the district for 'prejudicial activities' for six months in 1950 (CR 1I-12/50 (3-53), CR 1I-16/53 (1-55)).

border affair and exposed them to harassment by state personnel.[21] The small town of Hili was cut in half by the border, and the market on the Indian side was deprived from 'even fish and vegetables arriving by train to Hili Railway Station [which was in Pakistan]'.[22] Panchanan Poddar, who lived in the Indian half of the town, earned his living in the Pakistan part where he had a goldsmith's shop. In 1954 he was arrested in Pakistan on the ground of not having the correct papers to work there.[23]

Cross-border Landholding

Perhaps the most extensive impact of Partition on work in the borderland had to do with agricultural work. In a strip more than 4,000 km in length, almost all of it rural, numerous cultivators found that they had become separated from their most valuable source of income, land. There were basically two ways in which this happened. First, some landowners found that the border ran between their home and (some of) their fields. In Bengal, landownership tends to be fragmented, and it is quite common for even small peasants to own several small plots. Second, inhabitants of the borderland decided to migrate across the border, thereby becoming separated from (some of) their fields. In either case, cultivators faced enormous organizational problems. Working the land on the other side of the border continued to be a common

[21] For example, on 30 March 1948 the Secretary to the Premier of West Bengal sent a long list of cases to his counterpart in East Bengal. One of these concerned eight merchants from Gangarampur (West Dinajpur, India) who had gone to collect 'salt, mustard, dal, cocoanut, oil, mustard oil, spices, soap, ground-nut, oranges etc from Dinajpur town [Pakistan] as usual. But the carts were detained near Pulhat and subsequently taken to Kotwali P.S. (Dinajpur). They were told that under no circumstances should anything go to the Indian Dominion from Pakistan. Eventually they returned all the articles from whom they had made the purchase but they did not get back the money' (CR 1W-1/49 (1-53)).

[22] CR 1W-1/49 (1-53).

[23] The District Magistrate of Dinajpur [Pakistan] wrote to his colleague in West Dinajpur [India] in January 1955: 'I am sure you would agree that persons like Panchanan Poddar should not receive your support or sympathy. Evidently, many people on either side of the border near Hili have been carrying on activities which offend against the Laws of both the countries besides harming their economic and financial interests' (CR 1B2-13/55 (12-55); for a case of a shopkeeper who lived in Pakistan and owned a shop in India, see CR 1A7-1/52 (4-53).

practice but there were several problems: How to protect the standing crop? How to take bullocks and ploughs safely back and forth across the border? How to make sure that you could take your harvest home without being accused of smuggling? And how to fight off claims by refugees on the other side of the border that your land there should be confiscated as enemy property and given to them?

It is clear that landowners followed various strategies to cope with this unprecedented situation. If the fields were close to the borderline, they tended to do the cultivation work themselves, continuing much as in the past with family labour and occasional day labour. When fields were too far away for daily inspection, or where militant new settlers would not allow the owners from across the border to cultivate their own fields, it was often best to give land in share-cropping, try to exchange it for land on this side of the border, or sell it. In many cases these were not real options, as lands were simply occupied by newcomers who could not be made to leave. And where fields happened to be located in territory that was disputed between Pakistan and India (as was quite common along the undemarcated border[24]), cultivation became impossible for years on end, and such fields would have to be left lying fallow.

It is impossible to quantify the agricultural disruption caused by the imposition of the border. A large number of state records dealing with cross-border landholding and conflict suggests, however, that it was massive. Often local cultivators managed to involve border police in their conflict, creating an inter-state incident. The following example is typical. In February 1951 the District Magistrate of Kushtia (Pakistan) wired his colleague in Nadia (India) that 'Bharati [Indian] civilians backed by armed police have arrived at Bhatapara field to harvest paddy grown by Pakistani cultivators' and on the same day 'one Reazuddin of village Shoulmari P.S. Meherpur was reaping paddy on his land with six labourers [when] thirty Indian nationals backed by armed

[24] By 1953, about 3,500 km (or 81 per cent) of the border remained undemarcated, and by 1965, about 1,500 km (or 34 per cent). India and Pakistan quarrelled over the exact location of many sectors of the border, and even now parts of the border remain unsurveyed and undemarcated. The same is true for the entire border between Bangladesh and Burma (Myanmar).

police scared Reazuddin and his labourers away by your police firing six rounds and trespassed into Pakistan teritory and removed the paddy cut by Reazuddin'.[25]

Such cross-border landholding and cultivation was treated as an affair involving individual landholders' claims. But in one case it was treated as a collective affair. This was the case of the *ziratia* tenants. Certain parts of colonial Bengal and Assam had been ruled 'indirectly', through local princes. These territories were not involved in the Partition of British India (i.e. the directly ruled parts) but were supposed to accede to either Pakistan or India. Two such Princely States bordered East Pakistan—Tripura State in the east and Cooch Behar State in the north—and both acceded to India. A complication arose because the Maharajas of both these states had not only been rulers over their own territories but had also been considerable landowners (*zamindars*) in 'directly ruled' Bengal.[26] After accession, they were rulers over Indian territory but at the same time remained landlords in Pakistan. This situation persisted till 1952, when Pakistan abolished landlordism and the Maharajas' holdings in Pakistan were taken over by the State.

In the case of the Maharaja of Cooch Behar this was a straightforward case of dispossession, but the Tripura case was much more complicated. The Maharaja of Tripura was the landlord of an enormous estate covering over 1500 villages in the Pakistan borderland.[27] Inhabitants of these villages also had land across the

[25] CR 1B2-11/51 (3-53). The Kushtia–Nadia border was a hot spot for cross-border land conflicts at the time. For Pakistanis reaping crops on the Indian side, see, e.g. CR 1B2-22/50 (5-52), CR(2) 1B2-22/50 (5-52). Sometimes such conflicts were reported in newspapers. See *Hindusthan Standard*, 11 January 1949 (see Government of East Bengal, Home Department, Police Branch, P10C-28/49 (B. Proceedings, June 1949); hereafter: Police P10C-28/49 (6-49).

[26] The Maharaja of Cooch Behar was also *zamindar* of the Chaklajat Estates in the districts of Rangpur and Dinajpur. The Maharaja of Tripura was *zamindar* of the huge Chakla Roshnabad Estate in the districts of Tippera (Comilla) and Noakhali.

[27] J.G. Cumming, *Survey and Settlement of the Chakla Roshnabad Estate in the Districts of Tippera and Noakhali, 1892–99* (Calcutta, 1899), p. xvi. According to the Purbo Shimanto Pakistani Proja Union (Union of Tenants of the Eastern Borderland of Pakistan), it yielded more than Rs. 2 million annually (Government of East Bengal, Home (Political) Department, Political Branch, CR1B-5 (B. Proceedings, December 1949); hereafter: Plt.CR1B-5 (12-49).

border in Tripura State and in that capacity were known as *ziratia* tenants. There was also a customary right, from well before the colonial period, for them to gather wood and bamboo and graze their cattle in the hill forests of Tripura.

Partition caused this economy to unravel, and the border people did not take it lying down. Forming themselves into a number of organizations,[28] they started petitioning the authorities in Tripura and Pakistan, explaining that both their agricultural work and their gathering of forest produce were being seriously jeopardized.[29] They argued that 'these Ziratia subjects can not enter their lands within the state. Tripura police militaries and Kirit Bikram Bahinies [a voluntary militia] are reaping the paddies of lands of Pakistanies in border at places.'[30] When the Tripura authorities continued to harass them whenever they crossed over to Tripura, they launched a no-rent movement in the Maharaja's estate in Pakistan.[31] In a leaflet entitled *A Call for Preparation* they stated: 'we claim that the citizens of Pakistan bordering the Tripura State have full rights over the natural produce of Tripura State and no power on earth can deprive them of these rights',[32] and in another leaflet they made quite clear that 'The incidents . . . constrain the Hindu and Muslim people of the Roshnabad [Estate]

[28] Notably the Purbo Shimanto Pakistani Proja Union (Union of Tenants of the Eastern Borderland of Pakistan) and the Roshnabad Proja Samiti (Tenants Organization of the Roshnabad Estate) and its Committee of Action.

[29] For example, *Roshnabad Zomidarir Shimantobashir O Tripura Rajyer Projagono Pokkhe Shrishrimoti Mohamanya Matamoharani Shomipe Binite O Shokorun Prarthona* [A humble and woeful petition to Her Exalted Majesty the Queen Mother on behalf of the border people of the Roshnabad Estate and the subjects/tenants of Tripura State] 1949; Representation by Moulvi Sk. Wahidullah Chowdhary B.A., Secretary, Committee of Action, Roshnabad Proja Samiti, Feni (Plt.CR1B-5 (12-49), Plt.1I-77/48 (9-48)).

[30] CR 1B-3/48 (9-49).

[31] In a letter to the Secretary, Home (Inter-Dominion) Department (Tripura, India) of 30 November 1949, the District Magistrate at Comilla (Pakistan) wrote: 'The Ziratia tenants are seeing me daily in large numbers, complaining of the troubles given to them by petty officials and other unfriendly elements. When they set foot in Tripura territory, they are chased out or threatened, intimidated and belaboured.' In another letter to the Chief Commissioner, Tripura, the District Magistrate wrote that day: 'The Ziratias are tenants of Tripura and their welfare and happiness is as much the concern of Tripura as ours, nay, even more' (Plt.CR1B-5 (12-49)).

[32] Plt.CR1B-5 (12-49).

to adopt the following resolutions, and there is no communal motive behind them.'[33] The incidents did not stop, and *ziratia* tenants found it increasingly hazardous to work on the Indian side of the border.

In 1951, the Tripura government initiated a policy of requisitioning land of Muslim landowners (including *ziratias* from Pakistan) in order to rehabilitate Hindu refugees from East Pakistan.[34] *Ziratia* tenants found it increasingly dangerous to cross the border to work either on their fields or in the forests collecting bamboo, timber, and other forest products. The Pakistan authorities did not support them either. When Pakistan abolished landlord (*zamindari*) rights in the 1950s, the Maharaja of Tripura lost his huge income from the Chakla Roshnabad estate. By a stroke of the pen his tenants in Pakistan were freed from their landlord but they had to pay a high price: as landholders in Tripura they suffered a crushing defeat—they lost all their lands and income from the forests. Within a few years, they went from being regarded as the Maharaja's loyal subjects to being seen as Pakistani foreigners without any rights. The state of Pakistan diverted the income from the Chakla Roshnabad estate to its own coffers. It compensated the Maharaja lavishly but the *ziratias* were not compensated in any way. By the late 1950s, cross-border landholding in this part of the borderland, whether by superior tenure holders such as the Maharaja or by lowly *ziratias*, had come to an end.[35]

In all these cases—wage labour, marketing, and cross-border landholding and forest rights—the new international border acted as a barrier. It cut off individuals and households from sources of

[33] Plt.CR1B-5 (12-49).

[34] Published in the *Tripura Gazette* in the period March–June 1951. See also 'Tripura State', *Morning News* (Dhaka), 23 April 1951; letter to the editor, *Pakistan Observer*, 12 June 1951 (CR 3T4-1/51 (3-54)).

[35] In 1957, *ziratia* rights were linked to railway transit facilities for Indian food grains through East Pakistan to Tripura. In exchange for these facilities, *ziratias* were allowed to take up to 40 *maunds* (1,440 kg) of paddy per family from Tripura to East Pakistan. When this transit trade was blocked, however, these last remaining *ziratia* rights lapsed. See Shreedhar and John Kaniyalil, *Indo-Pak Relations: A Documentary Study* (New Delhi, 1993), pp. 137–40. See also 'Kumillay Purbo Pakistan o Tripura Rajjo shommelon: Shimanter golojog o bibhinno shomosshar mimangsha prochesta', *Azad*, 13 October 1949.

income on which they had depended and forced them to replace these with new ones. The border forced labour, produce, and land markets into a new territorial straitjacket, and borderlanders had to adapt their living strategies accordingly. Cross-border relations never disappeared completely but they were subject to new uncertainties and risks. For some borderlanders, however, the new barrier itself was a workplace.

The Border as a Workplace

Many people had been working on what was now the new Partition border. Some continued to do so and others found employment because of the border. The various ways in which these border workers negotiated the new dangers and opportunities was crucial in giving different sections of the borderland their particularly local characters.[36]

About 1,000 km of the border actually ran through water, and those who worked on the border rivers and marshes faced a dangerous but potentially lucrative situation. Local ferries suddenly became illegal or (rarely) blossomed into officially designated border crossings.[37] They turned into crucial nodes in new networks of cross-border commuting, migration, trade, and smuggling. Rivers had always been important avenues of traffic and trade, linking coastal Bengal with inland towns and villages. Regular steamer services had provided public transport, often over hundreds of kilometres, and goods had moved primarily over water. As a result of Partition, however, some of the most important river routes simply died, together with the river ports that had depended on them and the employment they had generated. Large border rivers became too dangerous for steamers (e.g. the Ganges (Padma)), and officials would reject local demands for re-

[36] See Andrew Walker, 'Borders, Frontier Communities and the State: Cross-River Boat Operators in Chiang Khong, Northern Thailand', *Canberra Anthropology*, 19, 2 (1996), pp. 1–28.

[37] If border ferries were allowed to continue, they were also taxed, sometimes by both states. It took till 1952 before such double taxation was removed in the case of the ferry between Balla (Sylhet) and Khowai (Tripura). This agreement was extended to all 16 'Inter-Dominion ferries' in 1955 (CR 3I-104/52 (7-54); CR 3C1-2/55 (11-55)).

establishing steamer stations out of fear of facilitating smuggling.[38] Trade in small boats on the smaller border rivers and fishing in border marshes, lakes, and rivers became risky because of disagreements over where the actual borderline was located. Not surprisingly, those who operated non-designated ferries and country boats on border rivers (often wage labourers employed by the boat owners) frequently found themselves to be the target of cross-border shootings. Their work was suspect because of its location: here the line between legal trade and smuggling, exploitation of domestic and foreign resources, and being a citizen or an alien was wafer thin. Nobody has ever bothered to record how many boatmen and fishermen lost their lives on the border rivers over the years but the records are full of border incidents in which they were involved.[39]

The land borders were usually easier to locate. Over a period of years, considerable stretches were demarcated and marked by boundary pillars but some areas remained undemarcated and even border guards were not exactly sure where the border was. Indian, Pakistani, and Burmese villagers who worked near the border had to be careful: straying cows often crossed the line and the responsible cowherd could get harassed, arrested, or killed by border guards. Woodcutters in deep forest might cross the border unawares and get attacked or, in more recent times, blown to pieces by an anti-personnel mine.[40] Cultivators with land in areas claimed by both Pakistan and India could work their fields only at

[38] On the death of the steamer service on the Ganges, see Willem van Schendel, 'Easy Come Easy Go: Smugglers on the Ganges', *Journal of Contemporary Asia*, 23, 2 (1993), pp. 189–213. On the refusal to allow a steamer station at the border town of Zakiganj in Sylhet in 1951, see Plt. 32C-1/51(3-53).

[39] On boatmen being arrested, shot at, or killed by border guards, see, e.g. Police EBP10C-23 (9-48); CR 1B2-11/50 (3-51); Police P10C-12/49 (10-49); CR 1B2-1/51 (2-54); CR 1B1-4/53 (6-54); CR 1B2-46/51 (7-54); CR 1B5-1/52 (8-54); CR 1B2-9/54 (2-55); CR 1B2-40/53 (12-55); on fishermen, CR 1B2-6/49 (7-52) and CR 3I-20/53 (11-54); on *char* inhabitants, CR 1W1-1/51 (5-53), CR 1B1-4/53 (6-54). Others whose work took them to the border rivers were also at risk, e.g. collectors of stones in the Pyain river on the Assam/Sylhet border (see CR 1A1-6/51 (3-53)).

[40] CR 1I-16/48 (Part) (11-50), CR 1I-120/48 (1-51). 'Mine explosions along Myanmar border: 57 Bangladeshi woodcutters killed in 18 months', *The Daily Star*, 4 June 1998.

great risk or under the protection of border guards.[41] And finally, the work of border guards itself was fraught with danger: shoot-outs between border guards were an important tool for India and Pakistan to give expression to their territorial disagreements.

Manning the Border

One of the first consequences of Partition was a sudden need to police the new border. To this end, the states created new sets of border personnel. Immediately after Partition, the situation was chaotic. First, voluntary militias were formed, often with state support, in which refugees were usually prominent.[42] There were many different outfits, some of them shortlived, and it was a major task for the state to impose some semblance of a monopoly of violence in the borderland. Spontaneous vigilante parties and party-based groups (like the Indian Congress Volunteers and the Muslim League National Guards) had to be streamlined into state-based militias. On the Indian side of the border, the paramilitary volunteers were usually known as Home Guards, although there were several other names.[43] On the East Pakistan side, volunteers were assembled in the new Ansar organization.[44] Discussions about this force were initiated in October 1947. 'At first the names "Home Guard" and "National Guard" were tentatively used, but the name "Ansar" was adopted as expressing within itself, with historical and religious significance, the whole ideal of voluntary service to the community and to the nation.'[45] Although 'membership of the organization would be entirely honorary and voluntary, and open to all Pakistanis between 18 and 48 years of age', many Ansars in the border areas were soon embodied in the police in order to man border outposts and prevent the smuggling

[41] For example, CR 1B2-33/52 (3-54).

[42] CR 1I-120/48 (1-51); cf. CR 1B3-1/49 (3-51).

[43] For example, the Assam Home Guards, the Bihar Home Guards, Tripura Rakshmi Bahini (Tripura Protection Corps), Jatiya Rakshmi Bahini (National Protection Corps), Banga Rakshmi Bahini (Bengal Protection Corps), West Bengal National Volunteer Force. The last three may be alternate names for the Bangiya Jatiya Rakshi Dal (Bengal National Protection Brigade), formed in March 1948 (Chatterji, 'The Fashioning of a Frontier', pp. 237–9).

[44] Police 13C-1 (10-48).

[45] James Buchanan, 'First Annual Report on the Ansars' (1948); in Police P10A-76/49 (11-49).

of jute to India.[46] In this way they became waged servants of the state.[47] On the Indian side, volunteers were similarly used by the state in guarding the border.[48]

The state offered other important employment opportunities at the border, especially in the Customs and Excise Departments which grew rapidly. Customs officials were active at a number of designated border crossings and at railway stations in the borderland.[49] They soon acquired a reputation for bullying, harassment, extortion, and theft;[50] in order to control them Pakistan and India decided to employ 'customs liaison officers' who were stationed on

[46] The number of border outposts grew rapidly. For example, in 1949 Pakistan increased the number of border outposts on the North Bengal border from 85 to 162. The outpost had been manned by a Border Militia which was now withdrawn as it was deemed unreliable (i.e. involved in smuggling). In their place came Ansars who had been embodied in the Border Police (CR 1C-2/50 (11-50)). See Chatterji, 'The Fashioning of a Frontier', pp. 236–7.

[47] Police P10A-76/9 (11-49), Appendix C.

[48] Although it is not clear from the evidence at hand whether this included paying a wage. In the early 1950s, according to the Provincial Commandant of the West Bengal National Volunteer Force (WBNVF), 'a good number of volunteers' joined the Indian border outposts. On 19 December 1953 five of them were arrested by Pakistani border police in Khulna District for crossing the border without any papers. During their 'usual night patrol' in the Basirhat area (in India) the unarmed volunteers had encountered smugglers who had put up a fight and forced them to flee to the Pakistan side (CR 1A2-2/53 (10-54)).

[49] There was continual pressure from local authorities to increase the number of 'land customs stations' in order to legalize cross-border trade, which was going on anyway, and to allow the state to tax it. But since the establishment of such official customs stations required that both India and Pakistan agree, the opening up of a local customs station could easily become a pawn in complex diplomatic games between the two governments. (Plt.32C-1/51(3-53)); CR 3C2-5/50 (3-53); CR 11C1-9/52 (1-54); and CR 3I-239/51 (8-54)). At times positions in the customs department were created in an attempt to block cross-border trade, as when East Bengal tried to stop jute smuggling to West Bengal in 1949 (CR 1C-2/50 (11-50). By 1954 there were less than three dozen check posts on 'a border of 1700 miles' (CR 8M-1/54 (1-55)).

[50] See letters of victims of highhandedness, e.g. CR 2R3-9/50 (3-53); CR 10C-9/50 (5-53); and CR 1W1-1/51 (5-53).The topic also came up regularly in high-level meetings between the governments of East Bengal and West Bengal (e.g. CR 3C2-5/50 (3-53)).

each other's territory and who could be approached by people with a complaint against customs officials.[51]

All this employment was new and it was much sought after by members of hitherto independent militias in the borderland as well by immigrants. These jobs were popular because they provided an entry into the state bureaucracy and therefore promised a steady income, career prospects, and prestige; public recruiting drives attracted many more hopeful young men than could possibly be given a job.

Borderland Industries

Little is known about the effects of the border on industries which were located in the new borderland. Some industries found themselves actually straddling the new border. For example, from precolonial days lime burning had been an important cottage industry on the border of two administrative units in Assam, namely Sylhet and the Khasi and Jaintia Hills. In 1943 a cement factory had been started here. When Assam was partitioned, Sylhet fell to Pakistan and the Khasi and Jaintia Hills became part of India. The factory was in Chhatak in Sylhet, some 10 km from the new border, but its raw material was in India. Even though there was no official border crossing along this entire stretch of border, this sole cement factory in East Pakistan survived. In 1953, an official reported: 'the transport of lime stone from the Kasi and Jiantia Hills [*sic*] in Assam takes place by the rope-way of the Assam Bengal Cement Factory and coal from the Boshera colliery in India is transported by river route to the factory'.[52] But supplies were insufficient, and the factory could produce only half its capacity until limestone quarries in Pakistan came into production and the kilns and boilers were converted from coal to gas firing in 1960. Employment at the factory, in the quarries and in the colliery was adversely affected, but not eliminated, by the imposition of the border.

[51] The Delhi Pact of 1950 stated: 'There shall be no harassment by the Customs authorities. At each Customs post agreed upon by the Governments concerned, liaison officers shall be posted to ensure this in practice.' (CR 1C-1/50 (11-50)). For examples of complaints against harassment, see CR 1B3-2/50 (7-52); CR 26A-1/50 (12-52); CR 3I-68/52 (1-54); and CR 11C1-4/53 (2-54). On liaison officers, see also CR 1A7-1/52 (4-53).

[52] CR 11C1-9/52 (1-54). See also *East Pakistan District Gazetteers: Sylhet* (Dacca, 1970), pp. 15-17, 190, 193–4, 370.

As a workplace, the border was a mixed blessing. We have seen that its creation forced many workers to look for alternative ways of earning a living whereas it provided new jobs to others. Those who worked on or near the border were exposed to unprecedented danger because violence could easily erupt in the tense atmosphere between two nation-building projects at loggerheads.

The Border as a Resource

Before Partition, there had been considerable trade flows criss-crossing what would become the borderland. After August 1947, the new states had to devise policies to cope with the fact that such trade had suddenly turned into international flows. However, neither India nor Pakistan could develop a straightforward trade policy; they were pulled in different directions.[53] On the one hand, the two states sought to disentangle the economy of the partitioned regions in order to integrate their portion of the region into their own national economy. But at the same time, they were keen to profit from any cross-border trade which they saw as supporting their own national cause because it provided strategic or scarce goods, or because it could be taxed.

As a result, a high level of uncertainty surrounded border trade, and borderlanders were continually picking up clues as to the newest obstructions and opportunities. Trade which was encouraged yesterday might be criminalized today, only to be tolerated unofficially tomorrow.[54] In other words, the creation of the border set-up a new, haphazard dynamics that nobody in the borderland could control. Right after the establishment of the border, the flow of certain goods was interrupted or hampered, other goods

[53] Little is known about Burma's trade policy *vis-à-vis* East Bengal. In the early years after Independence, the government in Rangoon had little say over the regions bordering on East Bengal and only gradually established control. Initially there were problems as the currencies of Burma and Pakistan were not convertible (see 'Rangoon o Pak-Borma shimante mudrar jor chorakarbar . . .', *Azad*, 29 May 1949). Trade relations were much less restricted by political considerations in this section of the borderland.

[54] For example, in December 1950 the export of vegetables and fish through a ferry crossing on the Sylhet–Tripura border was suddenly disrupted, apparently merely as a result of a new contingent of Pakistan armed forces being posted there. See CR 5T-1/50 (2-53), also for similar cases.

continued to flow freely, and yet others began to flow in response to new opportunities opening up. Borderlanders soon learned that this pattern of flow and blockage would be subject to sudden and unpredictable change.

The best documented case of disruption is the movement of jute fibre from the fields of East Bengal to the jute mills around Calcutta. The case of jute shows the coercion and resistance which was involved in such disruption, particularly in the borderland. The new border separated the jute industry from its raw material, and it made perfect economic sense to continue the trade which had existed for about a century. But it did not make political sense. The Pakistan government was keen to develop a jute industry of its own and forbade the export of jute. Since it could not offer the prices that jute fetched across the border, the jute trade was driven underground. Selling jute to Calcutta suddenly became an anti-national act.

For this reason, the Pakistan state had to give special attention to the borderland. New border outposts were established on the border between West Bengal and East Bengal to curb the smuggling of jute to India. In 1949, the Pakistan Jute Board concluded that earlier measures to curb smuggling to India had not had the desired effect, that 'smuggling is still going on on a fairly large scale', and that 'the smugglers were being actively helped by certain elements in the Police, Ansars and Customs Staff'.[55] For this reason the government organized a Jute Purchase Drive in the borderland. The task of the thirty purchase teams were formed it was to 'comb through each section [of the borderland] and buy as much jute as possible'. It was clear that they expected resistance. The mood among jute growers in the borderland was described as one of growing discontent because they were forced to hold on to large stocks of jute 'strangulated in villages', and therefore faced financial crisis.[56] For this reason, the purchase teams were accompanied by armed Ansars.

In many other cases, cross-border traders also defied the state. Many parts of East Bengal produced paddy which was sold to deficit areas that were now across the border in India. The East Bengal authorities were keen to stop this and special police officers

[55] CR 1C-2/50 (11-50); CR 1B2-35/51 (1-55).

[56] CR 1C-2/50 (11-50).

were given the task of preventing paddy leaving the country. This was not an easy task, as events after the first major post-Partition harvest in December 1947 showed. One officer wrote to his superior for support. Describing himself as a 'helpless but undaunted servant of Islam and Pakistan', he explained that, after he had been stationed on the border at Rajshahi, 'I became aware of a large area in Murshidabad district opposite my camp faced with an acute crisis and the smugglers on our side disastrously active. I set to work at once and was successful in stopping this huge drainage of food grains from Eastern Pakistan.' He was then threatened by smugglers, armed Indian border guards, and a landlord, but persisted 'as a selfless Guard of my National Home'.[57] Some of his colleagues, however, failed to stop a breakthrough.

On 11 January 1948, no less than 500 boats laden with paddy were taken through Chanchkoir, on the river Atrai in Rajshahi, on their way to India. The police ordered them to stop but as there were only a few policemen, they proved no match for the many armed men accompanying the boats. The next day the police learned that paddy boats were assembling up-river again. This time the Cordoning Officer detailed his men for duty. That afternoon a fleet of boats accompanied by at least 60 armed men on the river banks came rushing towards Chanchkoir. The boatmen and their protectors shouted '*Allahu Akbar!*' (God is Great!) and refused to listen to the officer telling them to stop and show their permits. On the contrary, they attacked and wounded the officer with a pointed bamboo. He fled to a police boat. The crowd pursued him by jumping into the water and caught up with him in mid-river. Then the officer ordered his men to open fire, jumped into the river himself, and swam across with the crowd in hot pursuit. The police party fired in all directions for 20 minutes, using 102 rounds of ammunition, while the men surrounded them and pelted them with bricks. Then the paddy boats queezed past the police party, collected about 20 injured and 4 dead bodies, and disappeared towards the border.[58]

[57] Letter from Syed Ghulam Nabi Ahmadi, Patrol Officer, Ghughumari Ghat and Panka Ghat, to the Regional Controller of Procurement, through the Regional Cordoning Officer, Region I, Rajshahi, 25 February 1948 (CR 1W-1/49 (1-53)).

[58] 'Report of the executive enquiry on the firing resorted to by the Armed Police Party posted at Chanchkoir on 12.1.48' (Police P5R-10/48 (10-48)).

Similarly, in April 1950, two border guards in the northern district of Rangpur were on patrol when they came across 'a large number of Hindu migrants with about a thousand heads of cattle and other restricted articles proceeding towards Cooch Behar [India] by a village path'. When told by the senior guard to proceed to India through the prescribed customs route, they did not pay heed to his instruction but 'adopted a defiant attitude and tried to assault him'.[59]

It is difficult to say how often such confrontations occurred. It was not only thwarted pre-Partition trade that was at issue. Soon new commodities also found their way across the border, and a lively two-way network of unauthorized trade, or smuggling, developed. It provided many borderlanders with an income as traders, coolies, ferrymen, and day-labourers of various descriptions.[60] In this way, the border developed into an important resource for workers in the borderland.

The Border as a Refuge

Partition resulted in the movement of large numbers of people, some of them as labour migrants but others as refugees. The border acted as a refuge for those who were driven from their place of work by discrimination, or fear of violence. Among the many groups affected were 'minority' workers—Hindus in industries in East Bengal (Pakistan) and Muslims in industries in West Bengal (India). Our information is largely restricted to Muslims working in factories in West Bengal. The late 1940s and early 1950s were a period in which categories of citizenship and religious affiliation were seen as closely intertwined. Till 1952, when citizenship became more formalized with the introduction of passports and visa between India and Pakistan, it was not always clear who was a citizen of which country. Did one's place of domicile make one a citizen of the state that controlled that territory? Was one's religion a sign of citizenship—being Muslim

[59] The confrontation ended in arrest, and confiscation (and subsequent auctioning) of cows. A petition, accusing the police of demanding a huge bribe, was later filed by Rupkanta Barman and five others of a village in P.S. Dimla (Pakistan), suggesting that these were local Rajbongshi cattle traders rather than emigrants (CR 1A3-5/50 (3-54)).

[60] See van Schendel, 'Easy Come Easy Go'.

signifying Pakistani citizenship and being non-Muslim (especially Hindu) signifying Indian citizenship?

In both countries, communal intimidation was used to promote citizenship-by-religious-community, and communal violence, or the threat of such violence, became an important instrument for driving out Muslims from India and Hindus from Pakistan. When communal violence occurred in industrial settings in West Bengal, local Muslim workers might feel forced to leave for East Bengal and so become Pakistanis.[61] This happened to Mehbub, now a citizen of Bangladesh, who remembered his family's flight from Calcutta during the riots in 1950:

My name is Mehbub. I am from Kankinara, Calcutta, 24-Parganas. I was born there. My father had migrated to Kankinara from Bihar, from Arrah District. He was a foreman (*shordar*) in a jute mill—a very important man. His name was Haji Abdur Razzak. He was a Line Shordar at the Bhatpara Jute Mill, and later at the Gouripur Jute Mill and then the Haora Jute Mill. . . . We had a lot of property there—we still do but it is all illegally occupied now: our house, a cinema hall and land. . . . We left all that because of a huge riot that broke out in 1950. We had to leave our neighbourhood and gathered in one place. There we were besieged from all sides. The government took a decision and Sarojini Naidu told us: 'You go to Pakistan.' Then they loaded us onto trains like pilgrims. There were separate carriages for us in the trains at Sealdah Station. We could not take any possessions with us. Only the clothes we were wearing. From there we went to Ishurdi [in East Pakistan] and then to Rajshahi. [Over here,] Father began a copper and brass business. . . . He returned to India in 1958 but he did not get back our old house. Instead he rented a house in Noyabazar (Kankinara) and took a job in a jute mill again. He is dead now but my nephews still live there, in India. They are doing well.[62]

[61] For example, in March 1949 an anti-Muslim riot occurred in Kankinara, a mill town near Calcutta where, according to Dr B.C. Roy, the Premier of West Bengal, in his statement in the West Bengal Assembly, 'the majority of the residents are Muslims and up-country Hindus working in the mills. Periodically they fall out and disturbances ensue'. During the Holi festival a Hindu sprinkled coloured water 'on a Muslim belonging to the Kankinara Jute Mills and residing in the coolie lines of those mills'. This set-off a riot resulting in several casualties and the temporary closure of the mills (CR 5R-2/49 (3-50)).

[62] Mehbub, interviewed by Md. Mahbubar Rahman, Rajshahi (Bangladesh), February 1999. For more on migrants and refugees in the borderland in the 1940s and 1950s, see Rahman and van Schendel, '"I Am *Not* A Refugee"'.

This case reveals Mehbub's family's multiple identities in terms of both class and citizenship: Mehbub's father, a foreman in a factory, was also the owner of an enterprise. After 1947, he became an Indian citizen but changed his citizenship to Pakistani after fleeing to Pakistan in 1950, only to return to India eight years later where he died as an Indian citizen.

But some Muslims working in Indian industries were officially considered as Pakistani citizens on the basis of their religion as well as their place of origin. This was the case with several thousands of Muslims from East Bengal who were working as permanent labourers in the industrial belt of Jamshedpur (India).[63] Before 1947, many of them had been active members of the Muslim League and had supported the campaign for Pakistan. According to the High Commissioner for Pakistan in India, who took up their case in 1949 because he considered them Pakistan nationals, they had 'declared their allegiance to the Dominion of India' after the division of the two countries but were being 'victimised by the local authorities for their past activities'. The Indian authorities replied that only a small number of 'Pakistani Muslims' had been detained or externed for 'indulging in subversive activities which could not be ignored'.[64]

In early 1950, widespread rioting in both India and Pakistan, in which Mehbub's family got caught up, forced large numbers of Muslims to flee to East Bengal and large numbers of Hindus to flee to India, especially to West Bengal, Assam, and Tripura. Among the Muslim refugees were some 30,000 industrial labourers from West Bengal. It is not clear how many of these refugees were 'Pakistani' in the sense of being labour migrants from East Bengal, and how many were 'Indians', being Muslims from West Bengal, Bihar, or other parts of India.[65] According to an agreement reached

[63] Almost 3,300 East Bengali Muslims were reported to work in ten large steel and other factories in Jamshedpur and Asansol (Bihar, India) in March 1949, remitting more than Rs. 4,00,000 to their families back home each month (CR 1'O'-3/49 (3-54)).

[64] Ibid.

[65] Although the vast majority of Muslim labourers in West Bengal industries felt that their lives were in danger if they stayed in their jobs, a select group of Muslims working in strategic industries (electricity works, arms factories) were given state protection in special Muslim protected quarters. Abdus Satter, 'An Eye-Witness Report on Greater Calcutta Mill Areas; Latest Situation As On 15-7-50' (CR 3I-154/52 (3-53)).

between Pakistan and India, the governments of West Bengal, Assam, and East Bengal would persuade employers of industrial labour to reinstate returning refugees to their old jobs.[66] The Government of West Bengal was unwilling to implement this agreement, and the result was that hardly any Muslim refugees could return to their old jobs. The industrial labour force in West Bengal was renewed with locally recruited, largely Hindu, labourers.[67] This lack of reinstatement remained a bone of contention between East and West Bengal for years.[68]

Whenever political tensions between India and Pakistan intensified, as happened frequently, workers in the Calcutta region who

[66] This agreement, known as the Delhi Pact or the Nehru–Liaquat Pact (in India)/Liaquat–Nehru Pact (in Pakistan), was signed on 8 April 1950; the statement about industrial labourers was included in the annexure of 15 August 1950 (CR 1C-1/50 (11-50)).

[67] The government of West Bengal pleaded inability to persuade employers to take back the refugee Muslim labourers despite 'doing their best and using whatever influence they had with the mill authorities'. They pointed to the fact that 'under standing orders in force in Jute Mills, a workman was liable to be dismissed for absence without leave for more than 10 days' and that the employers, faced with a serious labour shortage after the riots, had to employ new hands. Also, 'the sudden defection of these workers seriously hampered national production. The vacancies caused by their continued absence had to be filled in by new recruits to prevent further loss to production'. If refugee labourers would now approach their former employers for re-instatement, this was 'likely to disturb the peace in the mill area as the Sirdars who are now in control of the mill area (and are said to be overwhelmingly Hindus), might create trouble'. 'Proceedings of the meeting held at Calcutta on 14th October 1950 in connection with reinstatement of industrial labour' and other documents in CR 1I-18/53 (11-55).

[68] The West Bengal government could trace only 192 re-instated labourers out of over 8,000 names provided by the East Bengal government (CR 1I-18/53 (11-55)). The issue of re-instatement was on the agenda at the periodic conferences of the Chief Secretaries of the two governments, starting with the 18th conference in November 1950 (CR 1I-3/51 (11-53); see CR 3C1-2/55 (11-55). At that time it was clearly risky for industrial labourers from East Bengal to return to West Bengal to demand re-instatement on their own. Returning refugees were often jailed on suspicion of being spies. Even claiming arrear pay could end in disaster, as in the case of two labourers from Jessore who were arrested in Calcutta in 1951 on 'the pretext that they were Ansars' (CR 1A1-3/51 (2-54)).

had links with Pakistan immediately felt the repercussions.[69] A good example is the fate of 40 Muslim porters and gatekeepers (*darwans*) who had been employed by the Titagarh Jute Mills since 1937. While most labourers left quietly, they decided to go out with a bang.

> A few days before the Indo-Pak relation became strained over the Kashmir issue [in 1951], the mill-owners appointed a number of Hindu darwans. Very subtly estrangement was created between the old darwans and the newly recruited ones. As a result the Muslim darwans started to feel that it was no more possible to work with self-respect. They thought that the circumstances were against them. In order to escape retrenchment, they resigned in a body. They got 3 months pay and of these 40, 14 decided to return to their native place in Pakistan and they engaged a few drummers. In the evening of 10th August, they were arrested on their way. It was learnt that police permission was necessary to take out a procession in Titagarh and this they did not obtain.[70]

Industrial workers, like others, fell victim to the painful process of minority expulsion that followed Partition. Both religious community and place of origin were crucial markers in the early years. Gradually, the two coalesced as formal citizenship criteria became more important.[71] Little is known about the employment strategies

[69] Developments in industrial employment in East Bengal mirrored those in West Bengal. In June 1953 the *East Pakistan Labour Journal* published a speech by the Labour Minister in which he stated that in industrial concerns only Pakistan nationals should be employed and that the tea industry (where non-Muslim labourers from India had long been employed) must appoint a certain percentage of Pakistani Muslims (CR 3C1-3/54 (9-54)).

[70] *Shadhinota* (Bengali daily, Calcutta), 12 August 1951 (cf. CR 1A1-8/52 (7-54)). These labourers, who were not from East Bengal but from Punjab and the North-West Frontier Province, apparently had had their arrival accompanied by music as well. See Arjan de Haan, *Unsettled Settlers: Migrant Workers and Industrial Capitalism in Calcutta* (Hilversum, 1994), p. 174, n. 23.

[71] Although Pakistani/Bangladeshi labourers disappeared from the payrolls of the Calcutta jute industry, Muslims did not. In 1950, the number of Muslims in Victoria Mill decreased from over 1,700 to less than 800, and 'for years after that, no Muslims lived in the lines owned by the mill' (De Haan, *Unsettled Settlers*, p. 174, n. 23). In one jute mill studied by Fernandes in the early 1990s, 20 per cent of the labourers were Muslims. The labour force was overwhelmingly non-Bengali: 66 per cent was from Bihar, 15 per cent from Uttar Pradesh and only 7 per cent from West Bengal. Leela Fernandes, *Producing Workers: The Politics of Gender, Class, and Culture in the Calcutta Jute Mills* (Philadelphia, 1997), p. 64.

of displaced industrial workers from Calcutta. In East Bengal, many tried to join the new Pakistan armed forces and paramilitary outfits.[72] Others attempted to find jobs in the budding jute industries of the Narayanganj region. Very few appear to have followed the example of Mehbub's father who returned to an industrial job in Calcutta some years later.

If little is known about the employment effects of Partition on workers in urban industries, much less is known about the effects on industries in the borderland itself. That these could be devastating is attested to by a report on the handloom industry in the East Bengal/Burma borderland. Weaving had long been the mainstay of the Rakhain (Arakanese Buddhist) population of the southern Chittagong District. Partition cut them off from both their source of raw material and their market. They produced various silk textiles for the Burmese market which, because of new import and export restrictions, now became so difficult to reach that most producers had to abandon their trade. Many switched over to the production of cigars and cheroots, for which local tobacco could be used. This seemed to offer a solution until the Pakistan government decided to slap a double duty: 'once on raw tobacco and then on cigars and cheroots. . . . Due to this latter tax, the manufacture of cigars and cheroots by these people ha[s] stopped as they cannot find [a] market. The market is flooded with foreign cigars and cheroots which are sold at cheaper rates than the local products.'[73] As a result, 'being unable to cope with the changed conditions [the Rakhain] have already begun in hundreds to migrate to Burma against their will just in an attempt to save their lives'.[74]

It is often difficult to say whether cross-border migration was primarily due to political or economic causes. The industrial labourers from Calcutta fled targeted violence and ended up in reduced economic circumstances in East Pakistan. For them the

[72] Captain A. Ghani of the East Pakistan Recruiting Office reported that a crowd of more than five thousand gathered in front of the Noakhali Circuit House on 14 March 1950 in the hope of getting a job in the armed forces. 'The majority of the crowd comprised of the dislodged workers of Dunlop and Batta Companies due to communal riot' (Plt.3R-64/51 (3-52)).

[73] U. Chin, 'Report on the Migration of Arakanese Buddhists to Arakan' (1953), in CR 9M-14/53 (6-54).

[74] Ibid.

border was a political refuge. The Rakhain weavers migrating from East Pakistan to Burma took refuge behind the border for economic reasons, fleeing state policies which made it impossible for them to earn their living.

Regulating Cross-Border Work

The many forms of earning a cross-border living described above were predicated upon a curious time-lag in the imposition of effective restrictions on cross-border travel in the Bengal borderland. In this respect there was, for five years after Partition, a sharp difference between the two wings of Pakistan: 'Entry into Pakistan by permit is binding on those persons who wish to come to Western Pakistan. So far no permit is required for entry into East Pakistan.'[75] This meant that cross-border travel between India and East Pakistan and *vice versa* was almost completely uncontrolled. It was only in 1952 that citizenship in India and East Pakistan became more strictly regulated with the introduction of passports and visas. Monitoring cross-border population movement was a principal aim, and visas for citizens of the neighbouring country were different from those for other nationals. It was clear, however, that neither state was quite up to scrutinizing all movement across a 4,000 km borderline. In fact, India and Pakistan actually institutionalized the practice of cross-border commuting at this time: commuters were allowed special visas with which they could cross the border without being checked.[76] In order to get a

[75] Police P14M-167/49 (10-49).

[76] From 1952 Pakistan issued category 'A' visas for 'the following Indian nationals who live in Indian territory within ten miles of the East Bengal border and who normally earn their livelihood by working in Pakistan territory within ten miles of the East Bengal border:

(a) Cultivators who have to make frequent journeys in order to cultivate or supervise the cultivation of their own lands and their labourers and hired servants;
(b) Small artisans, such as blacksmiths, wood-cutters, carpenters, petty shopkeepers and petty traders; and
(c) Persons the only market for whose agricultural produce lie in Pakistan territory within ten miles of the East Bengal border.'

These visas were 'valid only for the village in East Bengal, including villages lying *en route*'. Holders could cross the border at any place within the villages specified (and not through an official Check Post) and as often as they wished. They were exempt from registration. The visas were valid for a

visa, one would of course need a passport but most people in the borderlands continued to cross without any official papers.

This arrangement did not take into consideration older systems of seasonal labour migration which had, after 1947, had become cross-border movements. For example, it had been common for labourers in Sylhet to harvest paddy locally and then move on to tea gardens elsewhere in Assam or Tripura. In 1947, Sylhet was detached from the rest of Assam and incorporated into Pakistan. The labour shortages in the Assam tea industry could not be met locally, however, and seasonal migration from Sylhet continued, although now the migrants, as Muslims and Pakistani citizens, were more vulnerable and faced the risk of being robbed on their way home.[77] In Tripura, labour contractors also continued to resort to recruitment from Sylhet. Suggestions were made to regulate this labour migration by means of permits, a recruiting centre, or a labour exchange.[78] The strained relationship between India and

---

period of up to five years. There were also category 'E' visas for Indian transport workers and businessmen. Ministry of Foreign Affairs, *Passport System to Regulate the Entry of Indian Nationals into Pakistan* (1952), in Plt. 2B-17/52 (3-53); cf. CR 8M-1/54 (1-55). See CR 1B1-4/53 (6-54); CR 3A-10/53 (8-54); CR 3I-436/53 (8-54); and CR 1B3-16/53 (11-54) for implementation of these rules at the border district level. In 1954, Pakistani officials estimated that the number of East Pakistanis holding visas of category 'A' was four or five times the number of Indians holding visas of that category (CR 8M-1/54 (1-55)). In addition, special arrangements were made for those who repaired telephone and telegraph lines on the border, members of survey parties engaged in demarcating the border, and contractors, workers and masons charged with constructing boundary pillars (CR 1B2-19/54 (7-54)).

[77] In March 1948, 'Asmatullah and others of Sylhet district were returning from Digari Tea Estate in Sib Sagar where they went to earn as day labourers, when the train reached between Lalting and Hatikuli, the checker checked their tickets and gave an indication to some Hindus, who attacked them, beat them, and took their belongings including their cash money amounting to Rs. 1128/10. The police and the public did not come to their rescue. They saw Muslims of Tippera, Noakhali and Sylhet, their co-passengers in other compartments being beaten and robbed of their money by the Hindus.' Matters for Consideration of the Conference of the Chief Secretaries at Calcutta on 10 May 1948 (CR 1I-16/48 (Part) (11-50)).

[78] In 1952 the East Pakistan Federation of Labour reported that 10,000 Pakistani labourers were working, under very bad conditions, on a new road that would link Agartala (the capital of Tripura) with the rest of India. 'The contractors have failed to proceed with out side labours recruited from Bharat,

Pakistan prevented the regulation of seasonal labour migration, and this may have contributed greatly to the permanent migration of settlers from East Pakistan to north-east India in the following period.[79]

Cross-border population movements between East Pakistan and its other neighbour, Burma, were even less formalized. In the colonial period there had been an important stream of internal labour migration from Orissa and Madras through Bengal to Arakan.[80] After 1947, however, following this trajectory meant crossing two international borders (from India to Pakistan and from Pakistan to Burma). Still, migration persisted, organized by commission agents in Akyab (Burma) and Chittagong (Pakistan). This gave rise, as far away as Karachi and Rangoon, to bureaucratic anxiety about 'surreptitious' and 'unauthorized emigration of Indian Nationals through East Bengal to Burma'.[81] In addition, harvesting Arakan's rich paddy lands had long been entrusted to migrant labour from the southern Chittagong District. This too

---

the Pakistani Labours have proved best worker with less payment . . . it is high time to consider, if Pakistani Labours should be allowed to complete [the] work of the Road in the enemy country. . . . If the Govt of Bharat [India] wants the services of these Pakistany Labours, it might be done in a regulated way with the knowledge & concent of the both the Dominions' (CR 3I-274/52 (3-53)). In 1950, the Federation had appeared to be in favour of continuing the system, but in a regulated way (CR 3T1-1/51 (5-53)).

[79] The issue of providing migrants with work permits resurfaced in the late 1990s in the context of debates in India regarding 'infiltration' from Bangladesh. See, e.g. Partha S. Ghosh, 'Illegal Immigration from Bangladesh–II', *The Hindu*, 12 August 1998; Anindita Ramaswamy, 'Govt Sees Work Permits as Solution to Influx Problem', *Financial Express*, 18 September 1998; Sanjoy Hazarika, 'Managing the Migrants in the Northeast', *Indian Express*, 29 January 1999; Sanjoy Hazarika, 'Turn Migration to India's Benefit', *Times of India*, 27 April 1999; Anindita Dasgupta, 'Thinking with the Head: Foreign Nationals in Assam', *The Daily Star*, 6 May 1999.

[80] Till 1937 this entire area was part of the colony of British India. After 1937, Burma (including Arakan) became a separate British colony.

[81] See correspondence between the Pakistan Ministry of Foreign Affairs and Commonwealth Relations (Karachi) and the Deputy High Commissioner for India in Pakistan (Karachi) in 1949 (Plt.7 F-1/49 (10-50)). According to the Pakistan Embassy in Rangoon, the Burmese Vice-Consul in Chittagong had been issuing temporary seasonal permits; there were no formal restrictions on seasonal labourers to the labour-deficient region of Arakan.

now became a cross-border movement and as entry of foreign labour into Burma became more difficult, 'the landholders of Akyab . . . encourage permanent settlement of those labouring classes who go there with their family. They are supplying food, shelter and land to these emigrants'. The Pakistan authorities estimated that about 10,000 people had migrated from Pakistan to Burma between March and June 1948.[82] That the flow of labour across the Burma–Pakistan border was not completely unregulated, however, is clear from the case of up to 50,000 Muslims from Arakan who fled to the Pakistan side in 1948. Three years later the All-Burma Rwangya Refugee Organization (East Pakistan) at the border settlement of Nhila used a visit by the Burmese consul to ask him to move the Pakistan government to introduce a 'permit system to facilitate their going to Burma for earning their bread'.[83]

In short, state regulation of cross-border work affected only a small proportion of those who earned a living on or near the border. In effect, except for the categories mentioned in the visa rules, the states of Pakistan and India did not attempt to regulate cross-border work at all but neither were they capable of stopping it. Since few cross-border workers cared to get the official papers which allowed them to work across the border—either because they did not know about the rules, had no money for passports and visas, made local arrangements with border guards, or simply took a chance—state regulation was even more marginal than the limited attempts indicate. After 1952, all kinds of cross-border work continued, now with the added, but in most cases remote, risk of getting arrested for trespassing.

[82] Answers by the Home Minister, Government of East Bengal, to questions in the East Bengal Legislative Assembly, 10 September 1948 (Plt. 12C-37/48 (12-50)).

[83] These Chittagonian-speaking Muslims from northern Arakan (later known as 'Rohingyas') were compelled to leave their ancestral homes as a result of a deliberate Burmese policy to remove them in an attempt to root out 'Muslim insurgents'. Massacres by armed forces occurred on 10 and 11 November 1948, and the military told surviving 'Rwangyas that unless they vacated Maungdaw and Buthidaung they would be tortured and butchered like animals and that they were appointed to wipe out the Rwangyas from Maungdaw and Buthidaung' (CR 1V-10/51 (5-53)).

Conclusion: Working Through Partition

The sudden creation of two new states, Pakistan and India, in 1947 is usually studied from the perspective of the resultant centres of state power and the symbolic creation of two nations. This essay has focused on another arena: the borderland where nations demarcate their imagined homelands and states define the margins of their territories and jurisdictions. This is where nations and states meet in geographical terms, and it is this physical confrontation which makes borderlands such essential sites for the study of nations and states, and, indeed, partitions.

The inhabitants of borderlands develop relationships with state organizations and national identities which are of necessity more ambiguous than in the territorial heartland: borderlanders are daily reminded of the reality, and the inherent opportunities and risks, of two competing political projects. In their social and economic behaviour, borderlanders have to find pragmatic solutions which frequently flout state rules. Hence they are often depicted as subversive, not only because they expose the weaknesses of state control but also because many illegal cross-border activities are only possible with the complicity of state agents.[84]

The inability of even the most powerful states to bring 'subversive' border economies under control is well documented, not least in the case of unauthorized workers.[85] For this reason, the study of labour in borderlands can be illuminating; it provides insights into the relationship between labour and the state which differ from those obtained from the more conventional sites of labour studies. And because bureaucrats and politicians worry about what goes on in borderlands, they tend to collect and preserve relatively much information on labour relations there.

In this essay we have seen how the struggle between states and borderlanders in search of a living unfolded in a *new* borderland, and how that struggle worked out for different groups of borderlanders. In the wake of state fragmentation, many found making a living hard whereas for others new opportunities opened up. The

[84] Hastings Donnan and Thomas M. Wilson, *Borders: Frontiers of Identity, Nation and State* (Oxford and New York, 1999), Ch. 5.

[85] The best researched, and most high-tech, case is the US–Mexican border. See Donnan and Wilson, *Borders*, pp. 96–100, and many contributions in the *Journal of Borderlands Studies*.

vignettes presented in the foregoing pages point to a host of questions about the relationship between Partition and borderland labour. To what extent did the character (rather than merely the personnel) of different labour arrangements change? Did Partition contribute to more contractual labour relations? Did workers move from agricultural to non-agricultural employment, or the other way around? How did workers get access to new sources of income? Did wage dependency figure more prominently in post-Partition household living strategies? How did Partition shape borderland workers' identities? And what role did these in turn play in the creation of subversive borderland economies which held state power at bay?

This essay began with a plea for a more thorough exploration of the landscape of knowledge and emotion known as 'Partition'. Studying how borderlanders worked their way through Partition opens up new perspectives with regard to the economic and social aspects of Partition, the living strategies of working people in periods of state fragmentation, and the role of such strategies in the formation of new states and nations. By connecting three dynamic but separate fields—Partition studies, labour studies, and borderland studies—the study of labour in the Partition borderlands can enrich each of these. For borderlanders, working through Partition was a challenge in the past. For students of labour, it is a challenge for the future as well as for the present.

5

Postmodern India

Peter van der Veer

The Indian Council for Social Science Research (ICSSR)—an institution comparable to the French CNRS but limited to the social sciences—is 'making a major effort to bring into the Social Science arena advanced information technology and the Internet through the Syama Prasad Mookerjee Information Gateway of Social Sciences' (from an ICSSR brochure). The effort to bring Information and Communication Technologies (ICTs) to Indian social sciences is laudable and much-needed, but who is or was S.P. Mookerjee? Before the Partition of the Indian subcontinent he was a leader of the Hindu Mahasabha and in 1951 one of the founders of the Bharatiya Jana Sangh, the predecessor of the Bharatiya Janata Party (BJP) which is currently the leading party in the Indian government under Prime Minister A.B. Vajpayee. Mookerjee, a Bengali intellectual and one-time Vice-Chancellor of Calcutta University, was known for a Hindu nationalism with a strong anti-Muslim and anti-Pakistan bias. It should not surprise us, of course, that the Hindu nationalists who are in power in Delhi today want to honour their heroes and leaders of the past. After Independence, Indian politics and Indian government was dominated by the Congress party which had a socialist ideology, supported by a more or less left-wing social science establishment. The right-wing Hindu nationalists in Indian society and politics had been marginalized for a long time and seized their chance to reverse the signs.[1] But why would one name the information

[1] About Hindu nationalism, see Peter van der Veer, *Religious Nationalism: Hindus and Muslims in India* (Berkeley, 1994).

highway after Mookerjee? What is the connection between ICTs and Hindu nationalism? One would perhaps have expected that agents of globalization, such as ICTs, would be vehemently resisted by these nationalists who emphasize the authenticity and superiority of Hindu culture and try to protect it from the 'vulgar' influence of the West. One would perhaps also expect that the scientists and engineers—and other highly educated professionals who form the cadre of the informational revolution—would feel little affinity with the cultural politics of the Hindu nationalists or would even resist it. If it is not a scientific spirit which underpins their work then it might be an innovative and entrepreneurial spirit. Descriptions of the computer industry emphasize the anti-hierarchical, anti-authoritarian culture of this group as well as a lifestyle which does not cherish ancient values but youthful experimentation. Especially the focus on 'newness' would seem to be incompatible with what is often seen as the traditionalizing, anti-modernist spirit of religious politics.

This paper begins—in a very tentative fashion—to explore some of the contradictions concerning the development of science and technology on the one hand and of religion and nationalism on the other. In its focus on migrant ('footloose') labour in the context of technological and industrial change, as well as in its critical understanding of nationalist politics in its relationship to world-economic processes, it is a tribute to the work of Jan Breman.[2]

The BJP government is extremely forceful in the promotion of the new ICT industry while, at the same time, its ideologues denounce 'foreign' (that is, Muslim and Christian) influences on Indian culture. To give one example: Ashok Singhal, leader of the Vishwa Hindu Parishad (a major ally of the BJP), has denounced the award of the Noble Prize to the economist Amartya Sen as a 'Christian conspiracy'. Sen's notion of the development of human capital through education (which, obviously, is a crucial factor also in developing the ICT industry) is seen as a threat to the inculcation of Hindu values in the curriculum.

The first section addresses some misunderstandings concerning the relation between science, technology, and religion. The second section examines that relation in the Indian context. The third

[2] Jan Breman, *Wage Hunters and Gatherers: Search for Work in the Urban and Rural Economy of South Gujarat* (Delhi, 1994) and *Footlose Labour* (Cambridge, 1996).

section explores the transnationalism of ICT-workers and its relationship with religion and Hindu nationalism. The last section draws some tentative conclusions about religious nationalism and ICTs.

The Information Revolution

The rapid development of ICTs is often called a revolution. These new technologies, so the argument runs, cause a complete transformation of the economy and society. The technological determinism, inherent in these arguments, resembles the claims made for the Industrial Revolution. Manuel Castells rightly rejects this determinism by arguing that 'technology is society, and society cannot be understood or represented without its technological tools'.[3] He thinks that what he calls 'the rise of the network society' is a societal revolution which requires a new sociological understanding. Robins and Webster doubt that one can even speak of a technological revolution and argue that it is a transformation in the management and control over information resources which is at issue.[4] In their view the role of knowledge structures and education is still the key political issue to be addressed, whatever the new technological possibilities.

Despite his emphasis on a new sociology, Castells slips, in the second volume of his impressive trilogy on the network society, called *The Power of Identity*, in an understanding of religion as a purely reactionary force. This perspective is precisely part of a discourse of modernity that was established in the nineteenth century in the wake of the Industrial Revolution and became dominant in the United States after the Scopes trial in the 1920s. This is therefore 'old' rather than 'new' sociological thinking. According to Castells, civil societies and national states are disintegrating under the influence of globalization and 'the search for meaning takes place then in the reconstruction of defensive identities around communal principles'.[5] Religion is therefore not

[3] Manuel Castells, *The Rise of the Network Society* [= Vol. 1 of *The Information Age: Economy, Society and Culture*] (Oxford, 1999), p. 5.

[4] Kevin Robins and Frank Webster, *Times of the Technoculture: From the Information Society to the Virtual Life* (London, 1999), p. 91.

[5] Manuel Castells, *The Power of Identity* [= Vol. 2 of *The Information Age: Economy, Society and Culture*] (Oxford, 1999).

anymore important as an apparatus in a Gramscian civil society, but has a new role as a communitarian, defensive project. Castells ignores mainstream institutions and focuses on religious fundamentalists, who are in the terms of the Chicago Fundamentalism Project 'always reactive, reactionary'. These religious groups resist globalization and its effects on the community and the family, just as in the nineteenth century they resisted modernization and its effects on community and family. The revolutionary world is, again, divided into progressive groups, who creatively respond to the new challenges of the time and give them a positive meaning, and the reactionary groups, who try to rescue old types of life and would, as the Luddites, prefer to destroy the agents of change, the new technologies.

Religion is portrayed as defensive and reactionary in this kind of argument, because there is an implicit assumption about religion under modern conditions that science and scientific reasoning marginalizes religion and religious reasoning. Religion can, therefore, not be progressive, because it stands outside of the progressive history of rational, scientific thought. First of all, there is the enlightenment view that religious absolutism hinders the growth of knowledge. The paradigmatic case is, of course, that of Galilei and his struggle against the Church, but there are many celebrations of the struggle of the powers of light, liberty, and rationality, against the powers of darkness and the Church, and the inevitable victory of the secular mind. Secondly, there is the notion that key discoveries by scientists have delivered a fatal blow to central religious doctrines. The paradigmatic case here is Darwin's discovery of evolution and the blow it delivered to doctrines of creation. In British history it is the victory of Huxley over Bishop Wilberforce in the 1860 Oxford Debate and the wonderful literary rendering of religious turmoil in Edmund Gosse's *Father and Son*, while in American history it is the 1920s Scopes trial which best illustrate the notion of a clash between Religion and Science.

The historical evidence shows, however, that instead of being a reactive and even reactionary force in the wake of the Industrial Revolution, religious movements and institutions have been exceedingly creative in shaping the transformation of society in which new scientific and technological knowledge was increasingly available.[6] Imperialism, the form of globalization that dominates the nineteenth century, with its new technologies of government, especially in the fields of education and leisure, was profoundly shaped by religion. And it is imperial culture which provides the infrastructure for scientific and technological progress. There have also been almost no attempts to stop the progress of scientific inquiry in the modern period on the basis of religious arguments. The debate in some societies, such as in the US, about the science curriculum in primary and secondary education is specifically about the role of evolution theory in it, but besides that there are very few religious claims which immediately clash with science. In fact, most of what happens in the natural sciences remains entirely beyond the comprehension of the uninitiated.[7] New technologies do, however, touch the life—world of the wider society, but they are in general (sometimes with a time-lag) readily accepted in most religious circles except for a few marginal groups. In fact, it is hard to discover a clash between science and technology on the one hand and religious doctrine on the other. That this is so may well be the result of the rapid declericalization of scientific research and the shift in power from the humanities (including theology) to the natural sciences. There is a large autonomy of scientific research which is not affected by larger religious or moral debate. The social environment in which this research takes place and in which researchers live is, however, in important ways, shaped by religious institutions. The development of these institutions determines the importance of religious or secular doctrine in society. The growth of scientific knowledge does not result in an automatic secularization of the mind.

The relative autonomy of scientific research would seem to depend on the separation of different spheres of life and what some sociologist have called the 'compartmentalization' of the mind. Jürgen Habermas (while referring to Hegel) summarizes the development succinctly:

[6] Peter van der Veer, *Imperial Encounters: Religion and Modernity in India and Britain* (Princeton, 2001).

[7] My stay at the Institute for Advanced Study in Princeton (which is dominated by mathematicians and theoretical physicists) in 1995 made that annoyingly clear to me.

In the process, the spheres in which the individual led his life as bourgeois, citoyen, and homme thereby grew even more apart from one another and became self-sufficient. This separation and self-sufficiency, which, considered from the standpoint of philosophy of history, paved the way for emancipation from age-old dependencies, were experienced at the same time as abstraction, as alienation from the totality of an ethical context of life. Once religion had been the unbreakable seal upon this totality; it is not by chance that this seal has been broken. The religious forces of social integration grew weaker in the wake of a process of enlightenment that is just as little susceptible of being revoked as it was arbitrarily brought about in the first place.[8]

Religion has thus developed in modernity from an all-embracing world-view to an autonomous sphere, like science and art, as Max Weber argued. This is, obviously, also a cornerstone of the secularization-thesis in modernization theory. In his celebrated essay 'Religion as a Cultural System' Clifford Geertz distinguishes a religious perspective from a scientific one 'in that it questions the realities of everyday life not out of an institutionalized scepticism which dissolves the world's givenness into a swirl of probabilistic hypotheses, but in terms of what it takes to be wider, nonhypothetical truths. Rather than detachment, its watchword is commitment; rather than analysis, encounter.'[9] In response, Talal Asad has argued that 'the optional flavour conveyed by the term *perspective* is surely misleading when it is applied equally to science and to religion in modern society: religion is indeed now optional in a way that science is not. Science and technology together are basic to the structure of modern lives, individual and collective, and religion, in any but the most vacuous sense, is not.'[10] Science and technology, then, are dominant, and religion is marginal. For Habermas the project of Enlightenment entails that the rationality of science and universal morality replaces religion in the organization of everyday life. He rejects the celebration of fragmentation in postmodernism, and sees the modernist project of Enlightenment

[8] Jürgen Habermas, *Philosophical Discourse of Modernity* (Cambridge, MA, 1987), p. 83.

[9] Clifford Geertz, *The Interpretation of Cultures* (New York, 1973), p. 112.

[10] Talal Asad, *Genealogies of Religion* (Baltimore, 1993), p. 49.

to restore some kind of unity as 'not yet fulfilled'.[11]

The notion that religion signified the unity and totality of life prior to modernity seems to me a stereotypical, romantic representation of the holism of 'pre-modern' life. It fits a sociological approach to society, as found in structural-functionalism, which sees society as a system with sub-systems. Sociological (and political) discourse about integration and about norms and values which hold a society together belong to this perspective. If we approach social phenomena and historical change from a history of power with an emphasis on the production of knowledge by movements and institutions (as Asad does), it seems clear that science and technology, as produced in universities and industries, have become very powerful in producing knowledge that affects people's lives and that churches and religious movements have no role anymore in the production of this kind of knowledge. This would imply that they can still be creative forces in shaping social life and creating religious dispositions, including responses to scientific and technological changes, but are not anymore the institutional sites for the creation of such changes. While this is definitely indicative of a marginalization of religious institutions in the production of important knowledge, it does not imply a marginalization in social and political life.

Let me illustrate this with the development of science and Christianity in contemporary US society. There is no doubt that the research institutions in the US are the major sites of the production of scientific and technological knowledge in the contemporary world. At the same time, a Gallup poll in the mid-1970s showed that over one-third of adult American (50 million Americans) described themselves as 'born-again', that is as having experienced 'a turning point in your life when you committed yourself to Jesus Christ' and felt 'that the Bible is the actual Word of God and is to be taken literally, word for word'.[12] Do these two facts—scientific productivity and religious fundamentalism—in one society conflict? No, they do not, except for the debate about

[11] Jürgen Habermas, 'Modernity—An Incomplete Project', *New German Critique*, 22 (1981), pp. 3–15. See also Jean-François Lyotard's response, 'Answering the Question: What is Postmodernism', in I. Hassan and S. Hassan (eds), *Innovation/Renovation* (Madison, WI, 1983), pp. 71–82.

[12] See Susan Harding, *The Book of Jerry Falwell: Fundamentalist Language and Politics* (Princeton, 2000).

creationism and evolutionism which is marginal to most science. Even the fact that so many Americans are biblical literalists does not seem to affect their participation in the scientific and technological activities in their society. Does this imply that there is a separation of spheres which are relatively autonomous? Only in the sense that laboratories and Churches are different sites of the production of knowledge and that these knowledges have different effects, but not in the sense that they can be reified as separate spheres. The relative irrelevance of science for religious doctrine and *vice versa* does not marginalize the public role of religious institutions and movements in the US. Jerry Falwell's Moral Majority was perhaps the most important political movement in the US in the 1980s. The support it gave to the military–industrial complex in its Christian patriotism has been of crucial importance to the funding of scientific research for military purposes and that includes the development of the Internet. The development of the new ICTs has been and will be overwhelmingly dependent on military research.[13] Moreover, the Moral Majority made ample use of the technological advances in communication and consumption (telemarketing, television, theme parks) to bring the message of the literal truth of the Bible. This continued in the 1990s with the full use of the new ICTs by these movements. What is particularly striking is the extent to which these movements occupy the same terrain as secular humanist movements and with a similar flexibility and versatility. They are not outside modernity, but are fully apart of it.

Hindu Science and ICTs

Compared to the USA India is definitely not at the cutting edge of scientific and technological production. It is a relatively poor country with low literacy rates and low life expectancy. It does not have the wealth which would be required for huge investments in research. Nevertheless, from the nineteenth century onwards, there has been in India, as in the rest of the modern world, a continuous development of modern science and technology. Moreover, there can be little doubt of the centrality of science to the Indian nationalist project in its various incarnations, including the Hindu one.

[13] See Robins and Webster, *Times of the Technoculture*.

Even more than elsewhere, the Indian nationalists' idea is that science and religion belong together. One of the questions posed by Hindu nationalists was how it happened that modern science and technology had not been developed in Hindu civilization, superior as it was. This question had also been persistently raised by the British and answered by them in terms of an essential difference between Indian backwardness, mainly ascribed to Hinduism, and British forwardness, mainly ascribed to a combination of rationality and Christian morality. The British could not get enough of stories about the bewilderment of natives upon seeing the railways or telegraphs. They mixed this view of the *naïveté* of the common people with the quite Protestant view about Hindu priests who had misled the common people with false knowledge. The response to this notion of Western and Christian superiority naturally was one of Hindu superiority. Hindu scientists searched for and found an archaic Hindu science in the Vedas and other sacred scripture. Some of the assertions were simply that rituals had results which could be scientifically demonstrated or that certain technological inventions were already mentioned in ancient scriptures. Others were more sophisticated in their use of scientific experimentation to show some basic philosophical points of Hinduism, such as the research done by J.C. Bose (1858–1937), the renowned physicist, who used his work on electric waves to explore consciousness in plants in order to prove Hindu monism. Perhaps the most important and lasting effort to connect Hinduism and science can be found in the field of health practices, from Ayurveda, an indigenous system of doctrines and practices concerning health, and Unani, its Islamic counterpart, to the system of yoga which unites notions of Hindu spirituality with disciplines of the body to create *mens sana in corpore sano*. The extent to which Allopathic (Western) medicine is combined in India with Homeopathic and Ayurvedic medicine and not seen as conflicting systems is quite striking till the present day.

Modern science then was not rejected, but embraced and creatively translated in Hindu civilizational terms. The idea of scientific rationality was used both by secular modernists, like Nehru, to nationalize science and to marginalize religion and by Hindu nationalists to nationalize religion and appropriate the 'scientific spirit' and apply it in the reform of certain Hindu customs. Science is a field that both secularists and religious nationalists wished to take away from the imperialist project and celebrate as truly their own. This was done with such fervour that science and technology came to be the hallmark of Indian civilization for all members of the Indian intelligentsia whatever their political views, except for Gandhi and the Gandhians who remained radical outsiders in this regard. All this is, obviously, quite contrary to the popular view in the West that the Indian civilization is mystical, focused on renouncing the world and instrumental rationality.

For Nehru especially, it was quite clear that the spirit of science had to be harnessed to the project of modernizing India. He did not see science and technology as in themselves solving the basic needs of life, unless it was harnessed to a more superior morality than that available in imperialism. In *The Discovery of India* (1946) Nehru showed that Indian civilization possessed great moral resources which would help it to appropriate modern science for the common good.[14] Gandhi, on the other hand, could easily be portrayed as a Luddite with his spinning-wheel. But, as Gyan Prakash has pointed out, he was not against technology as such, but against the enslavement that industrialization had brought India.[15] Only if one could resist the capitalist drive which was destroying the world one could use technology appropriately. Both Nehru and Gandhi, then, had (often opposite) visions of the use of science and technology, but they agreed that they should be embedded in a civilizational morality and that India was superior to the West in this regard.

While there was some lip-service paid to the Gandhian philosophy of appropriate technology in the post-Independence period (ironically described in V.S. Naipaul's *A Wounded Civilization*, 1977), Nehru's views dominated the scene for several decades. Nehru cared less for the growth of pure science than for the rational planning of India's development. Science (and especially the science of Economics) and technology (especially, technology applied in heavy industry) would be instrumental to a social change

[14] I take here Gyan Prakash's interpretation in his *Another Reason: Science and the Imagination of Modern India* (Princeton, 1999), p. 213.

[15] This follows an argument, generally accepted, by Indian nationalists of all persuasions that Britain's industrial ascendancy (the Industrial Revolution) had been accomplished by ruining the Indian economy. This thesis had been brilliantly formulated in R.C. Dutt's *Economic History of India* (1901–3) which became a nationalist classic. Its argument is very close to the 'development of underdevelopment' thesis formulated in the 1960s by Andre Gunder Frank.

which would be scientifically planned and executed. It is immediately clear why engineering had such an importance for Nehru. He gave full support to the education of scientists and engineers; this is a major reason why engineering colleges especially (as well as medical colleges) have flourished in Independent India.

Transnational Engineers and Hindu Nationalism

The very top of the education pyramid in India is formed by the Indian Institutes of Technology, which have a competitive selection that can only be compared to the top echelon of American institutes such as MIT and CalTech. Below that one finds a whole range of engineering colleges of varying quality. This system of higher education depends on a system of pre-college education in which mathematics and science are considered to be important topics. In interviews with Indian engineers that I held in the US, an often-heard view was not only that education was of prime value, but that Indian education was superior to American primary and secondary education, especially in the fields of mathematics and science. Some of them wanted to send their children back to India for that very reason. Even when one considers that we are dealing here with an elite group that can afford private schooling in India, this remains a striking observation about Indian education.

Thanks to this high level of education for the most gifted (and socially best positioned) in India there has been a longstanding tradition of Indian students pursuing higher research, education, and training (at the Ph.D. level) in Western universities. It has been observed that Graduate Schools of Engineering in the US in the 1970s would have had to close because of too little interest in engineering careers in the US population, if it were not for the influx of Chinese and Indian students.[16] This coincided with the Immigration Act of 1965 in the US which allowed for a much larger quota for immigration for highly trained and educated professionals. The Immigration and Nationality Act of 1990 tripled the number of visas granted on the basis of occupational skills and thus further enhanced the immigration of engineers. These new laws made it also possible for Indian students to stay on in the US. The earlier preference for going to the UK was replaced with a

[16] Between 1985 and 1996 62 per cent of all the doctorates in science and engineering granted to foreigners in the US were given to Chinese and Indians.

craze for 'green cards'. Nehru's vision of an Indian modernity which would be created by Indian engineers and scientists and would allow India to be fully self-sufficient ironically laid the basis for the emergence of a transnational cadre of Indian engineers who would be instrumental in creating wealth in the West.

The informational revolution, if it is a revolution, is being created, primarily, by engineers, many of whom are Indian. A recent study of Chinese and Indian entrepreneurs in Silicon Valley by Saxenian shows that between 1975 and 1990 US the foreign-born population of the region doubled to almost 350,000.[17] According to the 1990 US census, more than half of Asian-born engineers in the region were of Chinese or Indian descent. In 1998, 24 per cent of the high-tech firms started in Silicon Valley were run by a Chinese or Indian CEO. Together they employed more than 58,000 workers. A difference between Chinese-run and Indian-run firms is that the former are more concentrated in computer and electronic hardware manufacturing and trade, while the latter are in software and business services. Saxenian relates that to the superior English language skills of Indian immigrants.

The transnational migration of what are sometimes called 'knowledge workers' has economic effects on both the country of immigration and on the country of origin. Saxenian's study demonstrates clearly that the politically motivated fears in California about Asian immigrants who take jobs away from native workers are false, because these Asians have massively created new jobs. There is a clear awareness in the American business community that the arrival of Asian engineers and scientists has been a great blessing for the American economy. The effects of the departure of these professionals on the Indian economy have generally been captured under the negative term 'brain-drain'. Clearly many more Indian professionals stay on in the US, after having benefited from Indian education, than return. In short, India's brain drain is the USA's brain gain. The effects of this can be probably calculated in terms of investments in education versus remittances, but the issue is more complex and interesting than that. Binod Khadria distinguishes financial resource flows, technological resource flows, and human resource flows back to India

[17] The data on Silicon Valley are based on Anna Lee Saxenian, *Silicon Valley's New Immigrant Entrepreneurs* (San Francisco, 1999).

and comes to a very sceptical assessment of the benefits for India thus far.[18]

The negative effects on the Indian economy and society from the emigration of scientists and engineers could, however, be reversed by the 'death of distance' inherent in the new ICTs which makes it in principle possible that the work done by Indian ICT specialists in the US (and elsewhere in the developed world) is also done in India itself. The rise of high-tech sites in Bangalore and Hyderabad, as well as in a number of other cities in India, mainly initiated by US-based or US-returned Indian entrepreneurs, may bear that possibility out. This development has great potential which is already clear in the effects of this industry on the Indian economy, but the real issue is whether this industry which is still by-and-large providing low-grade, low-wage, low value-added services to the global market can develop into a more upgraded software industry. Transnational networks of Non-Resident Indians (NRIs) and their India-based counterparts would be essential for such a development. The social field created by transnational migration would then really grow into a decentred economic field, enabled by ICTs.

What could motivate NRIs to return to India and/or invest in its development? My suggestion would be that the historically established notion of the superiority of Hindu culture and the prominent place of science and technology in it is crucial here. These notions are not only inculcated in the upbringing of Indian migrants who were born in India, but also actively propagated by the Vishwa Hindu Parishad (VHP), the religious ally of the BJP. The VHP is a movement that is very active globally and one of the prime agents of the globalization of Hinduism. In the USA it has been active since 1974, following sizeable immigration from India. The anti-Muslim politics which is central to its activities in India, does not make much sense in the USA. Anti-globalization rhetoric is conspicuously absent from VHP propaganda in the US and rightly so, since its supporters there are strongly in favour of the liberalization and globalization of the economy.[19] As NRIs they

[18] See Binod Khadria, *The Migration of Knowledge Workers: Second-Generation Effects of India's Brain Drain* (New Delhi, 1999). I am grateful to Jan Breman for bringing this book to my notice.

[19] Arvind Rajagopal, 'Transnational Networks and Hindu Nationalism', *Bulletin of Concerned Asian Scholars*, 29, 3 (1997).

have also direct personal advantage in the free flow of capital. The focus of the VHP in the US is, as with many religious movements globally, on the family. The great fear of Indian migrants to the US is not so much the threat to the patriarchal nature of the Hindu family (as one would expect from Castells's analysis), since many of these migrants are well-educated professionals, and depend on two incomes. Rather, it is the struggle to reproduce Hindu culture in a foreign environment in order to socialize their children in the hybridity of Indian-Americans. The fear is often that the children will lose all touch with the culture of the parents and thus, in some sense, be lost to them. Both Internet-chat-groups and youth camps are organized by the VHP to keep Hinduism alive among young Indians in the US. As Arvind Rajagopal rightly observes in his insightful article on the VHP in the US, the VHP needs different tactics, different objectives in different places in order to be able to recruit members. In India it is a nationalist movement, but in the US it is a global religious movement. Arjun Appadurai's work on globalization has reminded us how important it is to keep these disjunctures and differences in global flows in view.[20]

Even with all this cultural politics it would still be difficult for Indian entrepreneurial engineers to be interested in India economically if the state would not encourage them. This it has been doing to some extent already under the Congress governments from 1985 onwards. The global economic ideology of liberalization and privatization has affected India in a major way. In India this was introduced by Rajiv Gandhi's government in 1985 in terms of 'bringing India into the twenty-first century' and with a major effort to bring ICTs into India. The favourite themes of the Rajiv Gandhi administration were the introduction of advanced technology, imported from outside of India, and the replacement of the old ethos of authartic asceticism with a new ethos of Westernized consumerism. It is crucial to realize that ICTs not only made consumerist identities more viable, but also became a new *avatar* of a technological nationalism, reminiscent of the Nehruvian pride in the great hydraulic works and heavy industry of the 1950s, but differing from it in its stress on individualism instead of collectivism.

[20] See Arjun Appadurai, *Modernity at Large: Cultural Dimensions of Globalization* (Minneapolis, 1996).

In 1991 the technological enthusiasm for ICTs, depending, as it is, on the lifting of import restrictions, was further enhanced when the government agreed to implement a comprehensive liberalization and reform package negotiated by the International Monetary Fund (IMF). Already, much earlier, the Indian government had made special arrangements for the remittances of that hyphenated social category: the Non-Resident Indian. The Foreign Exchange Regulations Act of 1973 includes in this category: (1) citizens of India living abroad for the purpose of carrying on a business or career, but declaring their intention to stay in India for an indefinite period, and (2) persons of Indian origin holding a passport of another country. One is of Indian origin if one has held an Indian passport, or if either of the parents or grandparents was Indian. The wife of a person of Indian origin is held to be of Indian origin too. Neither citizenship nor residence is thus the criteria for deciding on this category, but 'origin' is and in that sense it has much in common with the German genealogical definition of belonging to the German nation and having the right to return to Germany. The main reason for the Indian state to create this category is to raise foreign exchange, since NRIs are allowed to deposit money in Indian banks with competitive, guaranteed rates of interest. Transnational investment and the cultural capital of 'belonging' go hand in hand here.[21]

Some Final Observations

Science and technology are central to conceptualizations of Indian modernity, both in its secular and its Hindu variants. The Enlightenment notion that there is an opposition between science and religion has been an important element in sociological theories of modernity and secularity, but cannot be historically justified. It has been an ideological notion in particular secularist movements, especially in Western Europe, but has to be sociologically recognized as such. It is quite striking how provincial the sociological understanding of modernity often has been.[22] In societies as diverse as India and the

[21] See the interesting argument by Arvind Rajagopal, 'Transnational Networks and Hindu Nationalism'.

[22] I think here in specific of the work of the late Ernest Gellner, but I single him out only for his extraordinary combination of extreme clarity and wrongheadedness.

USA 'Enlightenment fundamentalism' (to use Gellner's term) has only played a very marginal role.

There is no reason at all to expect Hindu engineers and scientists to 'lose their religion' and become secular. Hindu modernity includes an ideological valuation of science and technology. The empirical question is rather to explore what religion does for them; what kind of specific needs it produces or addresses. The globalization of production and consumption, including the flexibility and mobility of labour, is addressed by movements like the VHP and is a major element in their nationalist politics of 'belonging'. The idea that 'symbolic analysts' (to use Robert Reich's term) are rootless because they are highly mobile misunderstands the imaginary nature of roots. To have roots requires a lot of work for the imagination (dreamwork). One element of that dreamwork is that pride in one's nation of origin is important in the construction of self-esteem in the place of immigration. It gives a different feeling to admit that one is from a country ravaged by famines and floods than to say with pride that one is from a superior civilization that is also very good in high-tech developments.[23] The coherence of a Hindu modernity tied to the sovereignty of India's past and territory is gradually giving way to a postmodern bricolage of deterritorialized and dehistoricized discourses on family values and cyber-spirituality which is very hard to capture. Contrary to what their opponents think, these movements are not 'outside of modernity', they were very much part of it and are now moving beyond it.

Science and technology are instrumental in the transformation of the lifeworld and therefore have a considerable impact on religious communication and on religious notions of the self and of belonging. The mediation and virtuality involved in the new technologies of communication, like the Internet, may have a profound impact on religious communication. Religion is not only mediated, but is also crucially concerned with the forms and practices of mediation. According to William James, religion is founded on the subjective experience of an invisible presence. This may be true, but we only have access to that subjective experience through the mediation of concrete practices, such as speaking,

[23] See Peter van der Veer (ed.), *Nation and Migration: The Politics of Belonging in the South Asian Diaspora* (Philadelphia, 1995).

writing, acts of worship, while, at the same time, these acts may be considered to produce the experience. There is a whole range of activities which induce religious dispositions and which are about the relation between human subjects and, what I would like to call provisionally for lack of a better term, 'the supernatural'. Crucial in that mediation is the relative invisibility of the supernatural or, perhaps better, its virtuality. There is always in religious mediation an ambivalence about the addressee and about the arrival of the message which is connected to epistemological uncertainty. I cannot explore this here, but it is clear to me that this is an area of substantial interest if one wants to understand religious transformation.[24] To give one example. One of many websites with the word *prarthana* ('prayer') in it is E-Prarthana, where one can 'click a deity' and address Hindu deities in more than 450 temples in India.[25] This might be interpreted as just a technological advance to prayer by mail and money-order, but the communicative possibilities are much larger.

In order to assess the relative centrality or marginality of religious discourses and practices in society, one has to examine processes of state formation and the dynamics of religious institutions and movements. For Nehru the state was central to the project of modernity. His entire conception was tied up with the idea of engineering and naturally scientists and engineers played a dominant role in that. This kind of view of the role of the state has been entirely discredited since the 1980s almost everywhere and also in India. The transnational class of IT engineers is obviously a carrier of the ideology of deregulation, privatization, and economic liberalization. It is individual entrepreneurship which they have learned to celebrate in California, not the Planning Commission. With that they have become postmodern in the sense that they will not accept Nehru's socialist vision that modernization can only be brought about by the State. Contrary to what one sometimes thinks, however, the tremendous transformation of Indian society required to develop the IT-sector requires not less state, but a different state. The process of regionalization which has developed quite rapidly in Indian politics in the 1980s and 1990s seems, to give one example, to be precisely one of those

[24] See also Peter van der Veer, 'Religious Mediation', in Enrique Larreta (ed.), *Media and Social Perception* (Rio de Janeiro, 1999), pp. 345–56.

[25] I am grateful to Sudeep Dasgupta for pointing this site out to me.

processes of State formation which are required for the development of certain cities in certain regions for the IT-sector. Hindu nationalism is the major force which counterbalances these centrifugal developments and it operates exactly in this field of tension between territorial and cultural unity. Before our eyes the spectacle of a postmodern India seems to emerge in which ICTs enhance regionalization, in which religious soaps on TV transform Hinduism, in which the huge problems of spatial mobility and transport might be partly undercut by the electronic highway, in which house prices in Bombay are higher than in New York, in which Hindu nationalists support ICTs, but try to boycott the Miss World contests.

Asia

6

Labour and Capital in Asia's Transformation: On Dichotomies, Continuities, and Linkages

K.P. Kannan and Mario Rutten

Globalization and economic liberalization are often seen as phenomena that will dominate Asian societies during the first decades of the twenty-first century. An accelerated movement of capital and information seems to determine the agenda of the research community and policy-makers today. Studies on economic liberalization, capital flows, and the new international economy in Asia reflect this trend. The human aspect of this transformation of societies has not received as much attention as it should.[1] Labour as an important player of Asia's transformation, its mobility within Asia, and its position within the emerging world economy are largely ignored. While labour was one of the central issues in the social science debate at the end of the nineteenth century, it was relegated to an obscure position at the end of the twentieth century and is hardly considered relevant to understanding Asia's transformation at the beginning of the twenty-first century.

The Asian financial and economic crisis of 1997 seems to have only further marginalized the position of labour in the process of

[1] This does not mean that there are no attempts, notably by such international agencies as the United Nations Development Programme, to focus attention on the human aspects of development in the context of a liberalizing world economy. But except for the human-development approach of Amartya Sen and his school of thought, research and policy today is more dominated than ever before by the concepts of liberalization and globalization as laid down by the interests of global capital. Even the paradigm of human-centred development offers very little space for studying the dynamics of labour and capital in the development process.

capitalist transformation in this part of the world. Some see lack of control over capital flows as the cause of the crisis, while others have emphasized the close interaction between government and capital in these countries as the main reason for the economic crisis. The consequences of the crisis for the position and condition of labour are hardly prominent in the discussions. The need to understand the condition of labour in the Asian societies, particularly in South and South-East Asia, as a result of the process of liberalization and globalization is not being adequately recognized. The lack of political power makes labour 'invisible' for policy-makers and researchers alike.

In order to bring back labour in this discussion it is necessary to have a long-term perspective. However, current discussions of labour in Asia are dominated by the agenda of globalization in which the inclusion of labour under World Trade Organization agreements has become a contentious issue between rich and poor countries. This has, in our opinion, sidelined the core issue of the role of labour in Asia's transformation. It is our understanding that the phenomenal growth in income in Asia, first in East Asia, then in South-East Asia followed by South Asia, has been largely the result of the important contribution of labour without any corresponding returns, either in terms of income or better conditions of life. This has thrown up formidable theoretical challenges concerning the role of labour in economic development. Following the European experience it was thought that more and more labour would find regular and secure employment in the so-called formal sector, thereby reducing the sphere of the informal sector in the process of economic growth and development. On the contrary, the so-called informal sector has remained strong in most Asian countries; in many societies the share of the formal sector is in fact quite low. Viewed in a historical perspective this is in sharp contrast to the earlier experience of Europe and North America. The implications of such a phenomenon, we feel, have not yet been properly appreciated.

One scholar who has, throughout his research career, not only dealt with the problem of transformation of Asian societies but also sought to highlight the issues from a labour perspective is Jan Breman. His writings have contributed, in our opinion, to clearing away rigid typologies and notions about labour and capital in contemporary developing societies. Specifically, he has pointed out forcefully that neither labour nor capital are homogeneous categories, nor do they lend themselves to clear-cut dichotomous divisions such as rural and urban, agriculture and industry, or formal and informal. Basing ourselves on this broad theme, we would like to raise a few issues in this paper that we think are important for an understanding of capitalist transformation in Asia from the perspective of labour, especially those at the bottom of society.

Multi-layered Categories of Labour

Since the early 1970s, the notion of labour in developing countries has been dominated by a dichotomy between formal and informal sector workers. One of the first scholars to question and critique this labour dualism was Jan Breman.[2] As he showed, the dualistic concept of labour may lend some simplicity to the discussion but it betrays a lack of understanding of the complexity of multi-structural societies in Asia. There is certainly a minority of labour working under conditions of job security and regularity of employment with formal relations in a small number of organized activities. However, a sizeable section of labour finds itself at the bottom of society without any kind of job security or regularity of employment. While these workers have to work long hours without much productivity-enhancing skill or technology, they remain by and large extremely poor in terms of basic subsistence as well as a dignified human existence. Their position at the bottom of society is reinforced by strong social segmentation such as caste or community identity in these societies. At the same time, this underclass of labour is integral to the process of accumulation in both rural and urban settings. This is because its members work not just in subsistence activities but also in a variety of commodity-production activities such as urban construction, garment, leather products, diamond cutting and other forms of light industry, which are often producing for export. This underclass of labour is not confined to urban areas alone but is also present in several sectors of rural production, be it in the processing of cotton, jute, cashew, coir, or marine products or the production of sugar, tea or coffee, most of which are also exported to markets in high-income

[2] Jan Breman, 'A Dualistic Labour System? A Critique of the "Informal Sector" Concept', *Economic and Political Weekly*, II (1976), pp. 1870–6, 1905–8, 1939–43.

industrialized countries. Much production of food such as rice has also become commodity production in many Asian countries, for the domestic as well as world markets.

Following the lead given by Breman, one of us had an opportunity to study the composition of labour in a largely agrarian economy in south-west India, i.e. the state of Kerala. Doing research on the working class in this very politically conscious part of India, we found that labour was not amenable to a rigid, dichotomous classification. Plantation labour in the rural hinterland co-existed with casual wage labour in rice cultivation in the villages. Many of these casual agricultural labourers also worked in small rural workshops to process coconut fibre when employment in crop cultivation was scarce. Not far away from the villages but not in clearly delineated urban centres were large factories that processed high value cashew nuts for export to the international market but with wage levels that were hardly different from agricultural labourers.[3] Breman's close association with the study led him to remark that

> the conceptualization of rural proletariat negates the conventional distinction made between town and countryside, industry and agriculture, as separate spheres of life and work. There seems to be no better place to illustrate this point than Kerala where spatial and sectoral segmentation are so markedly absent.[4]

In most of his work on labour relations in Asia, Breman has characterized what may be called labour status as a continuum with one segment at the top and the other at the bottom. In between these two extremes there is a class of labourers who may not be at the bottom of society but still may have a low status, toiling in farms, workshops, and factories as semi-skilled workers who also do not enjoy much security or regularity in employment. There is also a large class of so-called self-employed workers whose earnings are largely dependent on what may be called self-exploitation. Some of them may own some semblance of capital in

[3] K.P. Kannan, 'Evolution of Unionization and Changes in Labour Processes under Lower Forms of Capitalist Production: A Study of the Cashew Industry of Kerala', in Arvind N. Das et al., *The Worker and the Working Class: A Labour Studies Anthology* (Delhi, 1983); Kannan, *Of Rural Proletarian Struggles: Mobilization and Organization of Rural Workers in South West India* (Delhi, 1988).

[4] Foreword to Kannan, *Of Rural Proletarian Struggles*.

the form of simple tools and equipment, others may have a share in a borrowed asset, such as a piece of land or a handcart or cycle rickshaw, but all of them by and large have to struggle for survival by creating opportunities to eke out a living by using their only asset, that is labour power.[5]

Here again, one of us had an opportunity to apply a methodology 'to understand the structuring of the urban labour market which goes beyond the dualistic conception and instead emphasises a greater diversity of components'.[6] This study was carried out in an urban setting in southern India. The idea was to apply the concept of vulnerability within the labour status approach by examining the elements of *protection* and *regularity* in wage labour and the availability of capital among the self-employed. By applying this set of criteria for quantification, we distinguished between the labour status at the top called 'protected and regular' and the status at the bottom called 'unprotected and irregular'. More important, however, we found that in between the top and the bottom there were many categories such as 'unprotected but regular workers', 'unprotected workers with short-term contracts', 'independent waged workers', 'self-employed workers with some capital' and 'self-employed but marginal workers'. These intermediate categories made up more than half of the labour force. The study showed that an analysis of these intermediate categories was of great value, not only for a thorough understanding of the structure of the labour market, but also because it is critical for effective labour market interventions and policies.

In official surveys, sectors of labourers are associated with certain occupations or jobs. This is reinforced by a system of data collection in which a worker has to identify with a main occupation. However, it is often the case that people are constantly in search of some job or the other, which compels them to work in one occupation or another with different levels of skills and intensity of work. Thus, multiple jobs are a characteristic feature

[5] Jan Breman, *Of Peasants, Migrants and Paupers: Rural Labour Circulation and Capitalist Production in West India* (Delhi, 1985); Breman, *Wage Hunters and Gatherers: Studies of Urban and Rural Labour Markets in South Gujarat, India* (Delhi, 1994); Breman, *Footloose Labour: Working in India's Informal Economy* (Cambridge, 1996).

[6] John Harriss, K.P. Kannan and Gerry Rodgers, *Urban Labour Market Structure and Job Access in India: A Study of Coimbatore* (Geneva, 1990), p. 107.

of significant sectors of the labouring poor, not just in urban areas but in many rural contexts as well.

In this constant search for jobs as part of a struggle for survival, another category of labour emerges, which is often referred to as migrant labour. This is because these workers do not seek employment in a fixed location but have to be constantly on the move to find work. Labour migration has been a feature of Asia's transformation for many centuries already,[7] but it has accelerated further during recent decades. Migration of labour in Asia has, therefore, always involved a dual mobility: across space and across occupations or jobs. Jan Breman characterized this first as labour circulation but later chose to call such labour, somewhat dramatically but more provokingly, 'wage hunters and gatherers'.[8] In his latest work that sums up, verbally and visually, the findings of his research work in India, Breman observed:[9]

> There is in fact a continuum in the workforce, ranging from the miserable ragpicker to the relatively well-off organized sector high-tech factory worker. In fact, by making pertinent but simplistic dichotomies, we tend to lose sight of multiple identities and ambiguities in the vast landscape of labour. There are of course many differences across the spectrum of various forms and types of labour but it is also important to note the commonalities and essentialities of labour, particularly in these 'post-industrial' times in a 'globalized' world.[10]

Occupational multiplicity—doing as many jobs as can be available, and often simultaneously—and cyclical mobility—moving from work sites to work sites almost seasonally—are, in any event, prominent features of the life of the working poor. However, the combined process of urbanization and factory-based industrialization that over a time span of about

[7] Jan Breman, *Labour Migration and Rural Transformation in Colonial Asia* (Amsterdam, 1990).

[8] Jan Breman, *Wage Hunters and Gatherers: Studies of Urban and Rural Labour Markets in South Gujarat, India* (Delhi, 1994).

[9] In this publication, Jan Breman joined hands with the late Arvind Das, himself an outstanding scholar who has contributed much to the study of the labouring poor in India (see, e.g. Arvind N. Das (ed.), *Agrarian Movements in India: Studies on Twentieth Century Bihar* (London, 1982); Das et al., *The Worker and the Working Class*). Together with the perceptive photographer Ravi Agarwal, Das also focused on the 'down and out' who are 'labouring under global capitalism'.

[10] Jan Breman and Arvind Das, *Down and Out: Labouring under Global Capitalism* (Delhi and Amsterdam, 2000), p. 16.

two centuries transformed the character of Western societies, seems to take a different shape in Third World countries such as India. Here even migration is a two-way process. When people go away, they do not necessarily stay away: there is a circulation of labour. Most resourceless workers are pushed out of the village only to be pushed back again after several months or a couple of years in a repetitive drift. Besides, the nature of production itself makes the village a point of arrival as well as departure. Against those who are driven out there are others who are driven in to work as sugarcane cutters employed by agro-industries or in other rural-based industries such as stone quarries or brick kilns.[11]

If there is a streak of despair in what has been reported by Breman on the basis of four decades of sustained research, it is not without foundation in empirical, stark reality. Thus he observes:

> The picture of labour demolishes the myth of duality and does suggest that there exists a labour continuum. However, it also implies that it is a dismal scene at the bottom of the heap, a scene that can only evoke despair. That is true to a large extent. There is vulnerability, irregularity, insecurity and indignity of living at the bottom. Often the only escape for the poor is by passing out in a state of drunkenness. Even this outlet is, however, available only to men. Women cannot afford to opt out because of their reproductive role. They have the dual burden of looking after their families after doing paid work outside.
>
> The image of the pyramid should suggest no grandness. Despite the fact that labour of this sort is essential to sustain the kind of society that obtains, the prevailing image of labour is that of a nuisance. It is one of unwelcome filthy people, stinking from sweat and despair, illegally squatting on land and being evicted from time to time. It is one of dirt, disease and squalor. Hence, often enough the municipal authorities attempt to 'clean up' cities by removing the working poor out of sight.[12]

In such a scenario, the conventional notion of labour mobility in the sense of improving one's job prospects from a lower job to a higher one takes a beating, because the mobility is often horizontal. In times of crisis it is more likely than not that workers fall into a lower level of earnings, thus experiencing increasing vulnerability. Such a characterization of labour presents formidable challenges for social researchers in their attempt to understand the larger process of transformation. Asia perhaps presents the most formidable challenge because of its not merely economic, but also social

[11] Ibid., pp. 19–20.
[12] Ibid., pp. 138–40.

and cultural, complexities. One of the most recent and telling experiences of vulnerability of labour at the bottom has been provided by the economic crisis in Indonesia. Based on village-level field research in Java, Breman reported the expulsion of the labouring poor from urban Jakarta, their sense of vulnerability when they returned to villages which had only meagre resources to support them in agriculture, their expectations of returning to the urban labour market, and the sense of helpless that gripped the labour households at the bottom.[13] This once more shows the untenability of the dichotomous division of labour employed in most of the literature: many of the labouring poor in Asia have no choice but to be highly mobile, and to move regularly in search of work between the village and the city and between agriculture and industry.

Multi-layered Categories of Capital

The characterization of capital also poses equal challenges. Quite often, the notion of capital is highly influenced by the Marxian paradigm, in which a capitalist is the owner of the means of large-scale industrial production in an urban setting, who employs the labour power of workers, gives them only subsistence wages, and appropriates the surplus. This of course is a realistic characterization in Asian societies, though only to a very limited extent. In fact, Asian economies largely consist of a wide variety of capitalists, ranging from farmers who operate as agrarian entrepreneurs to owners of modern industrial enterprises; and from small businessmen with some capital, employing wage labourers for commodity production, to large owners of means of production, such as factories, plantations, business conglomerates, and multinational companies. In terms of numbers, the in-between category is perhaps the largest on the Asian economic scene. These middle-level capitalists consist of owners of capitalist farms, shops, trading companies, small-scale factories, workshops, and agro-processing industries.

Following the emphasis placed in Breman's work on the interaction between developments in agriculture and industry, one of us had the opportunity to study the economic behaviour and

[13] Jan Breman, *The Impact of the Asian Economic Crisis on Work and Welfare in Village Java* (The Hague, 2000).

way of life of rural capitalists in the western Indian state of Gujarat. This study showed that there are many similarities in the style of management and pattern of investment between large farmers and small-scale industrialists in the Indian countryside. The surplus accumulated by these rural capitalists is substantial. Part of it is reinvested in their farms or factories, resulting in an increase in capital-intensity and in the scale of agricultural or industrial operation. Part of the accumulated surplus is invested outside the agricultural or industrial sector, resulting in a move towards diversification of economic activities by these families. These rural capitalists in agriculture and industry share not only common economic characteristics but also common social characteristics. The lifestyle of both large farmers and rural industrialists is characterized by an emphasis on leisure and consumption, withdrawal from manual labour, and an increase in expenditure on education. Their socio-political behaviour is characterized by the pursuit of specific economic interests and by a tendency to widen their social and political networks away from local and family ties to regional upper class linkages. Therefore, the dichotomy between agricultural and industrial capital does not hold as one was led to believe by received theory. It is the interaction between the two sectors that explains the emergence of a rural capitalist class in this part of India.[14]

Going one step further, we also found that it was extremely difficult to make the distinction between 'rural' and 'urban' capitalist classes, as suggested by Lipton.[15] Drawing on the theme of linkages between the rural and urban sectors of the economy, as proposed by Breman,[16] we found that rural capitalists in Asia often use part of their profits to establish enterprises in the urban setting, while urban-based traders or industrialists invest part of their surplus in agricultural or agriculture-related activities in the countryside. Just as the workers in the casual labour market are characterized by multiple jobs as a means of survival, the small capitalists are also characterized by multiple activities in production and services as a

[14] Mario Rutten, *Farms and Factories: Social Profile of Large Farmers and Rural Industrialists in West India* (Delhi, 1995).

[15] Michael Lipton, *Why Poor People Stay Poor: A Study of Urban Bias in World Development* (London, 1997).

[16] Breman, *Of Peasants, Migrants and Paupers* and *Wage Hunters and Gatherers*.

means of accumulation. As we already demonstrated in the Indian context, our research on rural capitalists in Indonesia and Malaysia indicates that capitalists in South-East Asia also cannot be identified with either rural or urban or agricultural or non-agricultural activities. Rural capitalists in different parts of Asia are usually well connected through social relations and business contacts with members of entrepreneurial families in regional towns, and *vice versa*. The possibility of economic diversification is at the core of the strategy of intermediate capital in Asian societies, which breaks down the neat divisions of rural/urban or agriculture/non-agriculture. As a result, the differentiation between 'urban-industrial' and 'rural-agricultural' is not at all clear-cut. In fact, it is the interpenetration of these sectors that exercises an important influence upon class formation and is the key to explaining the internal dynamic of the rural economy in Asia.[17]

Scholars studying Asian capitalists point to the predominance of economic diversification as evidence of a specific Asian business strategy of 'commercialism'. One can question, however, whether this is a specific Asian phenomenon, or has a wider relevance even for advanced capitalist countries, both at present and in the past. The findings of an earlier study by one of us show that plurality of interests was also common among the European entrepreneurs during the early phase of industrialization. It has been pointed out that men of capital in eighteenth- and nineteenth-century Europe were frequently interested in several enterprises of different kinds. Industrial and commercial wealth was invested in land, while landowning and commercial wealth flowed to mining and industry.[18] A similar process of economic diversification is visible among contemporary businessmen in Europe.[19]

Research has shown that the development of enterprises is not a linear process. Small family capitalist enterprises are not a stage on a path that leads to large corporate businesses. The size and weight of the small business sector remain of great significance in the Asian context, both in terms of employment generation and capital

[17] Mario Rutten, *Rural Capitalists in Asia: A Comparative Analysis on India, Indonesia, and Malaysia* (Richmond, forthcoming).

[18] Mario Rutten, *Asian Capitalists in the European Mirror* (Amsterdam, 1994).

[19] Mario Rutten and Carol Upadhya (eds), *Small Business Entrepreneurs in Asia and Europe: Towards a Comparative Perspective* (Delhi, 1997).

accumulation. The predominance of family enterprises in Asia is often held responsible for the lack of economic development in specific countries because they are thought to hinder Asian entrepreneurs from becoming large-scale industrialists who are able to compete with their Western counterparts. Our findings on capitalist entrepreneurs in India, Indonesia, and Malaysia show the untenability of the view that the presence of family and wider kinship ties inhibits economic growth. Extended ties of family, kin, and caste have obvious advantages, not only in raising private capital but also in maximizing trust, loyalty, and in long-term planning over generations, as well as in motivating entrepreneurs. Far from inhibiting the growth of the economy, family enterprises and wider caste or kinship groups often turn out to play a critical role in commercial and industrial activities in Asia.[20]

Therefore, the predominance of small family enterprises in Asia does not imply stagnation in economic development, but a process of dynamic change characterized by both growth and the decline of such small capital. What this implies from the viewpoint of Asian transition is also the vitality of entrepreneurial skills in Asia manifested in different forms and on different scales in both rural and urban areas. Such entrepreneurial talent has been crucial in the export-led industrialization of Asian economies such as Taiwan and Thailand. In bigger Asian countries such as India and Indonesia, entrepreneurial skills of small-scale capitalists in such industries as agro-processing, textiles, leather goods, diamonds and jewelleries, and a variety of light engineering products have contributed significantly to export diversification. For example, official statistics in India point out that the small-scale sector contributed as much as 35 per cent to the country's exports during the 1990s.

These findings on the predominance of small family enterprises in Asia are in line with studies on European entrepreneurs, which show that small family businesses have been important in the rise of industrial entrepreneurs in Europe, both at present and in the

[20] Rutten, *Farms and Factories*; idem, 'Business Strategy and Life-Style: Owners of Combine-Harvesters in North Malaysia', *Kajian Malaysia: Journal of Malaysian Studies*, XIV, 1–2 (1996), pp. 112–50; 'Cooperation and Differentiation: Social History of Iron Founders in Central Java', in Rutten and Upadhya, *Small Business Entrepreneurs in Asia and Europe*, pp. 173–207.

past. During the early phase of industrialization in Europe, external supplies of capital were less important than personal and family funds. The power of heredity and the vitality of the family as an economic group stand out whenever we examine the history of pioneering manufacturers in Europe. Judged by the size of the unit and the amount of fixed capital, the vast majority of the manufacturing firms in England, for example, continued to be family businesses in the mid-1880s.[21]

This use of small and family forms of business organization in Europe in the past is also reflected in studies on contemporary European entrepreneurs. An overview of the studies on small businessmen in Europe indicates that the most important characteristic of these enterprises is that they are family affairs.[22] Italy's industrial districts are the classic example of the 'flexible specialization' mode of industrial organization, in which a large number of small firms, engaged in a highly specialized activity, are interlinked by elaborate relations of subcontracting. In these industrial districts, entrepreneurs trust and help each other, both informally and through formal institutions.[23] Therefore, collective forms of business organization such as family enterprises are also an important aspect of the business strategy of entrepreneurs in Europe today.

Drawing on the theme proposed by Breman, our study of capitalists in various parts of Asia indicates the complexity of capital in Asia's transformation. The oft-repeated dichotomies between agriculture and industry, between rural and urban, and between small family businesses and big corporate enterprises turn out to be a simplistic characterization of Asia's reality. Moreover, earlier research has shown that this complexity is not a specific Asian phenomenon, but holds to a large extent for entrepreneurial developments in Europe as well, both at present and in the past.

[21] Rutten, *Asian Capitalists in the European Mirror*.

[22] Jeremy Boissevain, 'Small European Entrepreneurs', in Rutten and Upadhya, *Small Business Entrepreneurs in Asia and Europe*, pp. 301–23.

[23] Michael Piore and Charles Sabel, *The Second Industrial Divide: Possibilities for Prosperity* (New York, 1984). For a discussion of the flexible specialization debate and its relevance to the Asian context, see Philippe Cadene and Mark Holmström (eds), *Decentralized Production in India: Industrial Districts, Flexible Specialization, and Employment* (Pondicherry, 1998).

Labour and Capital: Overlapping and Interlinked Categories

The reality is not just a continuum of labour statuses or grades of capitalists but also an overlapping one, which in our opinion is central to an understanding of transformation in Asian societies. In an earlier context, Chayanov had already drawn attention to the self-exploiting peasant.[24] But in the modern context one can identify a class of people who may own some capital but strive to generate an income through intensification of their own labour as well as hiring labour with the same or greater degree of intensity. The picture, for example, of an automobile repair shop owner is perhaps a typical one in the Asian context. Engaged in this 'double exploitation' of one's own labour as well as that of others, he cannot increase the price of his service because of intense competition, nor can he restrict competition in the market. Therefore he turns to the only input where he can reduce the price: that is, his own wages as well as those of others hired by him.

Such a category may encompass a variety of activities, from agriculture to processing of agro-products, trading, services, small-scale manufacturing, and so on. The theoretical as well as analytical significance of this category is quite important. Here is a significant mass of working people, who are neither workers nor capitalists in a Marxian sense. Sometimes they behave in a capitalistic fashion and sometimes they behave like workers. This poses theoretical challenges because of the dynamics of this category in the process of economic and social change. The conventional Marxian wisdom is that they will dissolve over time into the ranks of the proletariat as the concentration of capital progresses. But this has not happened and there are no signs that this is what will happen. Asian capitalism has successfully incorporated this category as a convenient one in avoiding a sharp polarization between capital and labour. This, no doubt, is a reflection of the demographic as well as multi-structural character of Asian societies. The presence of such a category, therefore, poses challenging but interesting issues for the political economy of development of Asian societies.

One may point out that studies on household manufacturing

[24] A.V. Chayanov, *The Theory of Peasant Economy*, eds Daniel Thorner, Basile Kerblay and R.E.F. Smith (Homewood, IL, 1996).

and, later on, micro-enterprises have taken note of this category in the literature. These studies no doubt have provided much empirical data on its dynamic character in the process of economic change. We must note, however, that these studies are not set in the context of the dynamics of labour and capital in societal transformation. They are often studied as a category in itself without much attention to the historical context. What is important from the perspective of transformation is their positioning and relationship *vis-à-vis* other categories of capital and labour on the one hand and the role of the state in the larger context of the political economy of development on the other. Analytically, this overlapping category of labour and capital poses challenges for an understanding of labour market situations with regard to employment and unemployment. There is no neat division between wages and profits. Much unemployment could be concealed by the pervasive presence of such a category as one finds in many Asian societies.

The complex nature of labour and capital in Asian societies certainly poses serious challenges to researchers engaged in understanding the nature of the transformation. Our own view is that generalizations based on either capital or labour do not necessarily give a proper understanding of this transformation. The study of labour implies, even if implicitly, the active presence and response of capital. Conversely, the focus on capital has to be tempered with an understanding of the complex nature of labour. Therefore the challenge is one of coping with the interrelationship of labour and capital. This has indeed been a central theme of much of Jan Breman's work. Similarly, a focus on one section of labour or one section of capital, without reference to the other categories and the interrelationship among them, is also likely to impede a proper understanding of transformation, even from a labour or capital perspective. Our own limited research has sought to underline these relationships, for example the dependence of small capitalists on big ones and the continuum of labour statuses in urban/rural labour markets. This has also alerted us to the critical importance of transcending one's own narrow disciplinary background and internalizing an interdisciplinary approach to the study of social reality.

In the context of the current process of globalization, which we think is qualitatively very different from the previous one characterized by colonial subjugation, studying labour and capital in the context of societal transformation has been further complicated by advancements in technology and communication. Often the presence of capital, especially of international big capital, is not even felt, and nonetheless it is central to the exploitation of cheap labour in Third World countries. For example, the dismantling of old forms of organization of production in textile industries has given rise to innumerable small-scale production centres with the overlapping characteristics of labour and capital. They produce the goods (e.g. garments) for unknown buyers located abroad through the intermediation of an exporter, while the product design, quality, and other aspects are strictly dictated. They have no idea who this capitalist is or where he is located. Such invisible but powerful forms of exploitation of labour across space have been a characteristic feature of the so-called miraculous growth in many Asian economies. This again poses serious theoretical as well as analytical challenges for the social researcher.

Role of the State

Our reflections so far have been confined to some of the critical notions in understanding labour and capital in Asian transformation. The role of the state has been kept out of the discussion. We must however mention that just as in the case of labour and capital, the state, especially its role in economic development, has also been often understood in a dichotomous fashion. The state is conceptualized either as a barrier to economic growth and development or seen as the prime mover. The reality in Asia, as indeed in other parts of the world, is quite different. In the post-colonial situation the state assumed the role of the leader in economic development in some of the Asian countries following successful political revolutions. That led to a denial of a *raison d'être* for the existence of capital, not to speak of an active role. That did not last long, and what we see now is a conscious attempt to bring capital back into the process of economic development. This shows that the state is not only aiding but also accelerating capitalist transformation in some of the Asian societies.

On the other hand, the state in some other Asian societies pushed for economic growth and development by relying, assisting, and collaborating with capital, both domestic and foreign. East Asia took the lead in this process with relatively less reliance on foreign capital and markets, but later South-East Asia followed with a much greater degree of reliance on foreign capital and markets. The state in many of these countries is facing a crisis of legitimacy as a result of the challenges posed by people's protests that are, broadly speaking, sparked by the sufferings as well as the aspirations of the mass of the labouring poor. A telling example is that of Indonesia. The capital-friendly state is being compelled to respond to the economic and political aspirations of labour through the emerging mobilization of the broad mass of the people. In this way, the state has been getting inextricably linked with labour and capital in determining the nature and pace of much of the transformation in Asia in the latter half of the twentieth century.

Implications

An understanding of the complexity of labour and capital is not only relevant to research, but also has important policy implications. This is particularly so in this age, when issues of labour standards and working conditions are discussed from a legal point of view in both national and international contexts. One of the most challenging issues for trade unions has been the organization of workers who are outside of what is called the formal or organized sector, without much legal protection. Both ideologically grounded Marxian theory, as well as the theory of economic development deeply influenced trade unions into believing that the process of economic growth would cause an increasing marginalization of workers in the informal sector and the dominance of the formal sector. However, the actual Asian experience as well as that of other developing countries has been quite different.

By and large, trade unionism remained strongly influenced by this conventional wisdom until recently, when trade unionists realized that the informal sector need not necessarily be a transitional category. A large majority of workers in the informal sector still remains unorganized due to both ideological and structural reasons. However, there are examples of overcoming these limitations. One important example studied by one of us is the case of Kerala, where most workers in the informal sector are as strongly organized in trade unions as workers in the formal sector, if not more. Innovative strategies of organizing the informal sector workers can also be witnessed in the self-organization of poor women workers in Ahmedabad in the state of Gujarat. This is the case of the now well-known Self Employed Women's

Association (SEWA). While such isolated examples of 'organizing the unorganized' abound, there are very few regions where such organization is the norm and not the exception. International organizations such as the International Labour Organization have taken cognizance of this emerging phenomenon and have been extending their sphere of activity beyond the conventional tripartite mechanism of governments, employers' organizations, and trade unions in the formal sector. An increasing amount of literature has also been generated to understand the problems and organizational challenges of workers in the informal sector. The plight of the labouring poor may often evoke a sense of despair, especially for sensitive social scientists, but reality is not devoid of hope. The examples of Kerala and SEWA in India are indeed inspiring ones, but we assume that there are other cases. We believe that this research agenda of studying the emergence and functioning of organizations and movements of the labouring poor ought to receive much more attention than they receive today. Research could give hope and hope in turn could change reality.[25]

One of the challenges to state policy concerns the social security requirements of unprotected labour outside the organized/formal sector. This is an area that has not been adequately addressed, either by researchers or the state. The notion of social security is still very much linked to jobs in the formal sector. Given the size of the workforce in the informal sector, as well as its contribution to both national income and exports, there is no reason why innovative measures should not be designed to provide a modicum of social security.

The issue of social security, as it is generally understood, is closely related to jobs in the formal sector. The very meaning of social security is likely to change once it is extended to the informal sector, because of the close linkage between security in work and workplace with the wider notion of secure livelihood. It is here

[25] The SEWA experience is described in a number of papers, including Ela Bhat, 'SEWA as a Movement', in Ruddar Datt (ed.), *Organizing the Unorganized Workers* (New Delhi, 1997). The book contains a number of cases of 'organizing the unorganized' in India. For a study of a recent experience of fish workers, see K.P. Kannan and T.T. Sreekumar, 'Rural Labour Movements and Organization in India: A Case Study of Fishworkers' Struggle in Kerala', *Labour and Development*, 3, 1–2 (July 1997–June 1998), pp. 24–64.

that the notion of social protection becomes relevant. This could encompass social provision of such basic needs as food security, housing, education, and health care. Given the policy biases and quite often anti-labour policies of governments, researchers will have to recognize the need to explore a wider set of strategies for social protection. This is of course an aspect of public policy and public action, in which the state, as well as non-state institutions such as the trade unions, voluntary development organizations, communities, and local governments, can become active players. Here again we would like to underline the experience of the state of Kerala in India, which has demonstrated that such social security can indeed be designed and provided as part of public policy.[26] It also goes without saying that in countries with socialist regimes the social protection afforded to the labouring poor distinguishes them from regimes that are primarily capital- and market-friendly. But the agenda of social protection has begun to be addressed in the emerging context of all-round liberalization and globalization, irrespective of the political nature of governance. This means that there is a vast area to be explored in looking for collective care arrangements that would transcend the narrow meanings attached to social security and/or state assistance.

Labour market functioning is characterized by biases against women workers, especially those who are poor. Only a very small minority of women workers are in the formal sector in Asian countries, as in other developing countries. To some extent, such a bias is also characteristic of labour markets in rich countries. Women are, therefore, more vulnerable in the labour market in a variety of ways, including job and wage discrimination, casualization, and absence of social protection. The invisibility of women in many economic occupations adds to the complexity of the problem, because very often their labour is unaccounted, unpaid, or both. While there is an increasing recognition of the specific nature of problems faced by women workers, there are very few policy responses as yet. The role of women workers in the transformation of Asian societies, although studied on its own, demands more attention in terms of their manifold contributions, especially with regard to the coping mechanisms of the labouring

[26] K.P. Kannan, 'State-Assisted Social Security for Poverty Alleviation and Human Development' in Mahendra S. Dev et al. (eds), *Social Security in India* (forthcoming).

poor in these societies. It is for that reason that such studies will have to be included in broader studies of societal transformation rather than being compartmentalized into specific gender/women studies.

The complex reality of gradations of labour and capital, and within it the specific position and role of women workers, are already posing challenges to conventional labour–capital relations in terms of organized labour and big capital. The gradations of labour and capital, cutting across the rural–urban divide, and the overlapping nature of some of the categories present a much more complex reality in studying labour and capital in long-term transformation. What is increasingly evident is the power of global capital and the different ways in which it incorporates local capital. The capitalistic nature of this transformation is becoming clearer, despite the absence of neat categories of labour and capital. The basic economic nature of this transformation cannot be understood by relying only on the discipline of economics. It calls for a broader application of social science theories and methodologies in order to lay bare the social, cultural, and political underpinnings of this economic process.

7

The Politics of Domination and Protest in Indonesia: 'Marsinah' and Its Aftermath

Ratna Saptari

Introduction

The 'labour question', whether in colonial or post-colonial conditions, has never been only a matter of guaranteeing and regulating a supply of cheap and compliant labour. It has also been a matter of contending moralities regarding economic development, stability, social order, and social justice. In looking at how this labour question is played out and resolved one has to examine the politics of domination and resistance within a particular historical moment. However, if in the past we have tended to use a broad brush in examining the politics of class by dichotomizing the colonized and colonizers, the rulers and the ruled, currently we have learned to be more attentive to the ambivalencies within each category and to the shifts in alliances different segments make within a particular moment in time.[1] Jan Breman's *Koelies, planters en koloniale politiek*, which illuminates the realities of north Sumatran plantations and the debates among Dutch policy-makers regarding the 'Coolie Question', shows how political issues may thrive or dwindle according to the particular conjuncture in Dutch politics under which such issues emerged.[2] Even though concerns

[1] Frederic Cooper, *Decolonization and African Society: The Labor Question in French and British Africa* (Cambridge, 1996); Cooper and Ann Laura Stoler (eds), *Tensions of Empire: Colonial Cultures in a Bourgeois World* (Berkeley, 1997).

[2] Jan Breman, *Koelies, planters en koloniale politiek: het arbeidsregime op de grootlandbouwondernemingen aan Sumatra's Oostkust in het begin van de*

regarding the condition in the colony had been voiced since the late nineteenth century it was only in the early twentieth century, with the emergence of liberalist ideas, that questions were raised in the Dutch parliament regarding the conditions of the indigenous population and some action taken to respond to these criticisms, if not to alleviate the suffering of the colonized.[3] Therefore, when van den Brand's pamphlet *De millioenen uit Deli* came out, the political reverberations in the metropole were strong enough to endorse an investigative mission to the colonies.[4] This eventually resulted in the establishment of an investigative mission conducted by J.T.L. Rhemrev to the Sumatra East Coast, which in general corroborated van den Brand's allegations.[5] However, the politics of that particular moment in history also shaped the way this question was 'resolved'. Despite the large publicity this whole process invoked, not much else happened to improve the plight of the workers in that area apart from the establishment of a Labour Inspectorate in Deli[6] and the proliferation of police troops in the

---

twintigste eeuw (Dordrecht, 1987). The English translation of this book, *Taming the Coolie Beast: Plantation Society and the Colonial Order in Southeast Asia* was published in 1989 by Oxford University Press, India, and does not include Van den Brand's *De millioenen uit Deli* and the Rhemrev report which became the basis for the debates on the labour question.

[3] More than twenty years earlier, an account of the situation in Deli had already been given by Valck, a government district head in Deli who, in a letter to the Governor-General, wrote that 'the situation is as bad as it can be and this is the result of a policy pursued for years of leniency *vis-à-vis* the planters (Ann Stoler, 'Perceptions of Protest: Defining the Dangerous in Colonial Sumatra', *American Ethnologist*, 12 (1985), pp. 124–43, quoting Valck 1876). This letter written in 1876 never received any public response.

[4] Prior to the distribution of this pamphlet a public debate was held by the local branch of the Indische Bond in Medan to facilitate the presence of a parliamentary member of the socialist opposition, Henri van Kol, to form an opinion regarding the situation in the plantation region of East Coast Sumatra. This was then followed by a pamphlet written by Van den Brand, a practising lawyer, which attacked Dutch colonial policy by condemning the Coolie Ordinance on moral grounds.

[5] On 8 June 1903, Rhemrev, a member of the Council of Justice in Batavia arrived in Medan to investigate the conditions in the plantations and to verify the allegations made by Van den Brand against the plantations in East Sumatra and the Netherlands Indies government. Breman, *Koelies, planters en koloniale politiek*, 3rd revd edn (Leiden, 1992), p. 266.

[6] It was only later that labour inspectorates were established in other parts of the Netherlands Indies.

plantation areas to prevent acts of misconduct by planters and workers alike. As Breman has shown it was particularly the strength of the planters' power and authority that blocked possible intervention of the colonial state into the daily running of the plantations. Workers' collective resistance emerged only in the early 1920s which meant that the planters' authority remained unchallenged for some time.[7]

History has shown us that relationships between the state and corporate capital, between different sections of the ruling elite and different groups of workers are extremely complex and produce different kinds of outcomes. Therefore, it would be erroneous to infer that if the state had been able to intervene or the workers' movement had been stronger in the plantation belt of north Sumatra, labour relations in the plantations would have been improved. The convergence of the ruling elite and the strengthening of colonial power which occurred in the 1920s did not necessarily mean a quiescence of the labour movement.[8] Also, if in the 1950s and 1960s, the nationalist Indonesian post-colonial state was more sympathetic to organized labour, by the early 1970s it was strongly hostile to it. While in the 1920s organized labour was mainly concerned with workplace issues, in the 1940s their rhetoric was embedded in nationalist ideals and by the 1970s they were only allowed to channel their grievances in the structures that the New Order state had created for them. The post-Suharto period (after 1998) provides a different backdrop altogether, as the contemporary rhetorics of reform, decentralization, and democratization colour the politics of labour.

The fact that shifts in priorities and orientation occur in different periods of history and often do not follow any linear trend should be recognized if we are to understand the dynamics of any particular labour dispute and conflict. The discussion below is not about the colonial past but about the post-colonial present. It is about how debates on labour issues have been forged at national and local level, using the 'Marsinah case' as an entry point. This

[7] Breman, *Koelies, planters en koloniale politieke*, 3rd revd edn, p. 189.

[8] It was in this period that labour organizations under the aegis of Sarekat Islam and the Central Federation of Labor (*Persatuan Pergerakan Kaum Boeroeh*) emerged. Everett D. Hawkins, 'Labor in Developing Countries: Indonesia', in Bruce Glassburner (ed.), *The Economy of Indonesia* (Ithaca, NY, 1971), pp. 196–250.

incident occurred almost ninety years after Rhemrev's report, and concerns a labour dispute in a factory in East Java resulting in the murder of a worker. This occurred when for some thirty odd years Indonesia had been going through a period of state authoritarianism, when freedom to organize and freedom of expression were severely curtailed and when state involvement in labour affairs meant also military intervention in disputes occurring in the workplace. Not unlike the colonial period, any incident perceived to undermine the goals of profit accumulation and political stability may be dismissed or dealt with under the guise of 'the communist threat' or subversion.[9] The difference between this incident and the Deli case mentioned above is that corporate power and disputes in the workplace have become more 'open' to public pressure and received much attention from the international world. Yet again, as we will see, the outcomes are never to be predicted in advance, even by the main architects of the labour scenario.

This chapter examines the rhetoric surrounding the case of Marsinah, a woman worker activist in a watch factory in Sidoarjo, East Java, and how this rhetoric influenced and was influenced by the politics of the moment. Marsinah was found raped and murdered on 9 May 1993 in a paddy field in Porong, East Java. Her death and the public attention it received pushed the 'labour question' into centre stage and produced multiple areas of debate. Examination of the debates that emerged, of the claims and counter-claims made, shows how what was initially a workplace dispute, culminating in a two day strike, became within a few days time a case of obstruction of 'peace and order'. Where initially the target of opposition was the company management, it shifted very swiftly to the military apparatus. What was initially a locally-based workers' issue soon shifted into international condemnation of human rights violations. The conflict of interest between the

[9] The involvement of the military in civilian matters was already officially sanctioned in the colonial period. In September 1914 an Ordinance was enacted allowing the use of the military on civil functions 'for the preservation of public order or the maintenance of essential services in the public or private sectors' (*Staatsblad*, 1914/614, see John Ingleson, *In Search of Justice: Workers and Unions in Colonial Java, 1908–1926* (Singapore, 1986), p. 71). However the government at this time was relatively 'neutral', not overly reactive to labour disputes and only intervening when the situation was considered to 'get out of hand'. See Hawkins, 'Labor', p. 198.

state and capital in this case became quite clear when eventually, in order to find scapegoats, the local military apparatus detained nine company staff members, and interrogated and tortured them. The power of the military seemed to be indisputable and yet the direction in which the incident took eventually was neither planned nor desirable for all sides. It was a product of the developments concerning the labour question, but has also influenced subsequent campaigns.

This focus on the Marsinah case provides a window not only on the various forces in play which defined the boundaries of 'the labour question' but also on the way in which this question has been phrased. It allows one to examine how the rhetoric of labour can be appropriated and used by different contending parties, and critically brings into question the issue of workers' subjectivities and 'working-class consciousness'. Despite the large degree of public attention given to this case, eventually the labour dispute itself became forgotten and hidden. As Weix has cogently shown, the Marsinah affair both revealed and concealed various aspects of labour relations and also their gendered dimension.[10] On a broader scale, the Marsinah case will be juxtaposed with other labour campaigns conducted after the incident to trace the different emphases, the overlap of interests, and the tensions with the dominant classes.

Many scholars of the Indonesian labour movement have focused on the rise in workers strikes and protest actions, which is considered to herald the emergence of working class consciousness as a logical consequence of the 'deepening' of industrialization.[11] In focusing on the events surrounding the Marsinah case and its aftermath I would like to critically examine the links between workers' collective action and the nature of working-class consciousness. More specifically, I would like to show how relations of production and state–labour relations in and outside the workplace as well as the involvement of workers in public collective action became the basis of working-class consciousness.

[10] G.G. Weix, 'Resisting History: Indonesian Labour Activism in the 1990s and the "Marsinah" case', in Brenda Yeoh et al. (eds), *Gender Politics in the Asia-Pacific Region* (London, 2002), pp. 221–51.

[11] Ed. Aspinall, 'Democratization, the Working Class and the Indonesian Transition', *Rima*, 33 (1999), pp. 1–32; Vedi Hadiz, *Workers and the State in New Order Indonesia* (London, 1997).

However, the ways demands are formulated and articulated are highly contingent on the different interests framing their claims and therefore on the rhetoric used to bring up the labour issue in the public sphere.

The debates around Thompson's use of the class concept provide a useful point of reference. Thompson's view that the formation of class consciousness is constructed on the basis of the interface between workers' structural position and their 'lived experiences' has brought much critique by scholars influenced by the linguistic turn in social science in that Thompson draws too direct a line between one's economic position and one's lived experiences.[12] They argue that language and discourse (and through these, other systems of power and domination such as gender, race, and ethnicity) mediate one's lived experiences. As a result according to these scholars, workers may have a consciousness of class, but rarely a class consciousness.[13] The Marsinah case shows indeed the importance of rhetoric in shaping the direction of workers' struggles. However, it also highlights the way rhetoric can be an instrument through which certain struggles can be expressed. Therefore, the way in which demands are brought up and framed has to be balanced with a critical reading of the structural factors underlying particular debates and struggles as well as the components involved in the struggles.[14] This event shows that even

[12] Such as Joan Scott, Gareth Stedman Jones, Patrick Joyce.

[13] Jones for instance argues that workers' shared consciousness was founded on a critique of the corrupt ruling order and not so much directed at capitalists or an economic system. (Gareth Stedman Jones, *Languages of Class: Studies in English Working-Class History, 1832–1982* (Cambridge, 1983).) Joyce also shows that popular languages of labour focused neither on exploitation in production nor deprecated capitalism as necessarily evil but emphasized reciprocal rights and duties of trade membership (Patrick Joyce, *Visions of the People: Industrial England and the Question of Class* (Cambridge, 1991)). For a critique of these views, see also Marc Steinberg, 'Talkin' Class: Discourse, Ideology and their Roles in Class Conflict', in Scott G. McNall, Rhonda F. Levine and Rick Fantasia (eds), *Bringing Class Back In: Contemporary and Historical Perspectives* (Boulder, CO, 1991), pp. 261–84.

[14] Katznelson has argued that the tendency to infer working-class consciousness through collective action is unsatisfactory. Since class is a juncture term, any class analysis should examine the points of connection between structure at the macro-economic level, workers' lived experiences, their dispositions, and their instances of collective action. Ira Katznelson,

though the language used may not be of class, the interests of sections of the labour movement making the claims are class based. It also shows that the struggles of the working class may be based on multi-layered framings and reflect different alliances. Although the Marsinah case shifted from a labour dispute into a murder case, different groups within the labour movement, as well as the general public, used the event in different ways. From the side of the status quo, 'Marsinah' also became a useful instrument for speaking the language of democracy and justice without necessarily having to go into more deap-seated reforms.[15]

Below, we will first focus on how the labour dispute came about and how it progressed. This is followed by a discussion on how the labour dispute and the death of Marsinah have been reconstructed and the official versions challenged. A discussion on how the Marsinah case has affected and has itself been influenced by the labour politics of the particular moment in history is given in the section after that. This brings us then to reflect on the meaning of these events in changing the lives and consciousness of the workers affected by these events, directly or indirectly.

The Construction of a Labour Dispute

The murder of Marsinah was brought to the foreground by the media and by Indonesian columnists.[16] But this gives only a scattered notion of the sequence of events and the evolution of the labour dispute, the findings of the court proceedings, and most importantly the views of the various actors themselves. Based on the bits of evidence provided by media coverage and workers' and company staff testimonies compiled by the Institute of Legal Aid in Surabaya and Jakarta, Alex Supartono wrote a comprehensive report surrounding the Marsinah case. This report details the events based on testimonies of the workers, of the detained

---

'Working Class Formation: Constructing Cases and Comparisons', in Ira Katznelson and Aristide R. Zolberg Katznelson (eds), *Working Class Formation: Nineteenth-Century Patterns in Western Europe and the United States* (Princeton, NJ, 1986), pp. 3–41.

[15] The latter was typical of the SPSI, the government sanctioned trade union who nominated her as 'the workers' hero'.

[16] See Weix, 'Resisting History' for a concise overview of the 'discourse' around the Marsinah case.

company management, newspaper clippings, and other documents.[17] Although this report can be read as a narrative in itself, most of the discussion below is based on this report.

The labour dispute which later culminated in 'the Marsinah case' (*kasus Marsinah*) originated in a strike action carried out by workers in a watch factory located in the industrial estate of Sidoarjo, East Java, beginning on 3 May 1993. The Catur Putra Surya company (CPS, originally called PT Empat Putra Watch Industry) was initially geared towards production for the domestic market. In 1991, it expanded into its present 14 units sprawled over 10 hectares of land, with 70 per cent of production geared towards export markets. Five hundred workers were involved in production, among them two hundred women. With production reaching quite high levels, workers were divided into three 7.5 hour shifts. The workers, who were differentiated according to length of employment and wage status, were unified in their grievances regarding the working conditions in the factory and the manner in which production was organized. As with many other industries, the tools of production were subsidized by the workers themselves.[18] Gloves, working masks, polishing equipment, production 'machines'—all had to be rented by the workers for Rp 1,425 per hour. A system of fines was also put into practice: whenever workers could not meet the specified targets, the remaining work would be carried over to the next day. Sick leave was not known so that part of the wage packet would be deducted when workers were sick and absent. Health insurance was not known, neither was there a factory clinic.[19]

One of the factors that brought matters to a head was the decree issued by the Governor of East Java, Basofi Sudirman, stating that workers' basic wages should be increased by 20 per cent starting from April 1993. Much earlier, the Minister of Manpower had issued a decree, to be enacted on 1 March 1993, stating that workers' wages should reach the minimum level of Rp 2,250

[17] See Alex Supartono, *Marsinah: Campur Tangan Militer dan Politik Perburuhan* (Jakarta, 1999).

[18] For a similar situation in the cigarette industry, see Ratna Saptari, 'Rural Women to the Factories: Continuity and Change in East Java's *Kretek* Cigarette Industry' (Ph.D. thesis, University of Amsterdam, 1995).

[19] Supartono, *Marsinah*.

which meant a 30 per cent increase.[20] Despite the fact that the governor's decree brought minimum wages to a level lower than that stipulated by the minister's decree, the statement was sufficient to spark off workers' collective action against the company. Workers met on Sunday 2 May 1993, to discuss the situation and to formulate their demands to the management. That they would go on strike seemed beyond doubt; the question was how high their demands should be. Marsinah's role at this point was to find out the regulations concerning the Basic Minimum Wage. Having a relative working in the Justice Department in Surabaya gave her access to the bureaucracy and allowed her to obtain the regulations regarding minimum wages.

It is not clear, in reading the report, *when* exactly these workers initially started to organize. However it is known that since the late 1980s, student groups and NGOs together with workers' groups have been active in various industrial estates in Jakarta, Surabaya, and Medan. One finds traces of the general pattern and strategy commonly deployed by these groups in the workers' terminology. In the workers' testimonies recorded in the report, mention was made of the involvement of workers in 'discussion groups', the procedures of making an 'inventory of problems' found within the factory, discussion of the strategies to deal with management, channels to be used, etc. These terms and tactics are commonly found in workers' discussion groups in other parts of Indonesia.[21]

On the first day of the strike, workers assembled at 6.00 a.m. on the road heading towards the factory. As they walked they recruited more workers to join the strike. It is also not clear in the report how many workers were involved on this first day. However it was enough to induce the manager of CPS, Yudi Astono, to invite the local military, the district police, officials from the Ministry of Manpower, and the Sidoarjo branch of the SPSI (*Serikat Pekerja Seluruh Indonesia* [All Indonesia Workers Union])

[20] A similar situation was found in the case of Cosmas Batubara's announcement of a wage increase in the late 1980s. See Saptari, 'Rural Women to the Factories'.

[21] Unlike the period of the late 1970s and early 1980s where workers' organizations and the involvement of students and NGO activists were still seldom if not non-existent, the early 1990s was a period of general political activity in various industrial centres in Java and in North Sumatra.

to come to the factory precincts to deal with the situation.[22]

Rather than bringing forth specific demands, the main goal of this first strike was primarily to bring workers' discontent to the streets and, thereby, to public attention.[23] However this tactic very quickly brought a chain of responses which were eventually beyond the control of the company management itself. How far out of control it was to become was not yet to be read in the events on the first day of the strike. The fact that the whole paraphernalia of the state apparatus came down on the workers and became also involved in the dispute was in itself nothing new. The procedures taken to gain control of the situation were also not new. As soon as the workers voiced their discontent on the streets and the strike became a public event, two parallel processes occurred. One was the negotiations that the CPS company management conducted with the workers themselves. The second was the investigations that the police and military officials conducted in order to weed out the 'masterminds' behind the strike. Although in other cases both processes usually occur too and have the same ultimate goal, namely to contain workers' insubordination, in this case the contradiction between the two interests was so great that it resulted in

[22] The role of the military in labour relations is recognized by the government and strengthened by the Ministerial Regulation No. 342/1986 ('Guidelines for Mediating Industrial Labour Disputes, Especially those Regarding Overtime, Strikes, Contract Labor, Dismissals and the Change in Status or Ownership of Companies'). Among others it was stated that the security apparatus (at different levels of the administrative structure) in collaboration with the local government, company officials and 'labour mediators' were authorized to be involved in dispute settlements to prevent the occurrence of strikes and physical destruction by workers. In many cases the security apparatus was not only to prevent physical destruction but also to intervene in labour disputes, even if those did not at all involve strikes or physical destruction. 'Monitoring' involved the presence of the military apparatus in negotiations between workers, management and the Ministry of Manpower. Danu Rudiono, 'Kebijaksanaan Perburuhan Pasca Boom Minyak', *Prisma*, 1 (1992), pp. 61–80, here p. 65.

[23] As Asef Bayat shows: 'the street in this sense serves as the only locus of collective expression for, but by no means limited to, those who structurally lack any institutional setting to express discontent . . . though [the actors] do not know each other, they may act collectively because common space makes it possible for them to recognise their common interests and identity'. Asef Bayat, *Street Politics: Poor People's Movements in Iran* (New York, 1997), p. 15.

a situation where one became subordinated to the other. Prior to any process of negotiation in the workplace, the *Muspika* official[24] requested the company manager, Yudi Astono, to submit the names of ten workers who he thought had masterminded this strike. The Koramil (district military command) official that same day went to one of the persons whose name was on the list, namely Yudo. Inopportunely, at the time Yudo was in the middle of a workers' meeting and therefore all the eighteen workers who were at that time in his house were also hauled to the military command office. The workers were questioned and at the same time given a lecture. One official is reported to have said: 'You are all obstructing other people's good intention to go to work! That is sabotage! Those are PKI [Communist Party] tactics!'[25]

These intimidations did not daunt the workers however, since the next day (4 May 1993) the workers went on strike again. This time Yudi Astono from the management was willing to sit at the negotiating table with the workers but staff from the Ministry of Manpower and the DPC SPSI (*Dewan Pimpinan Cabang* or district level organization of the SPSI) were also requested to join the negotiations. When the meeting began the workers' representatives were divided into those representing the official trade union SPSI and those representing 'the workers'. The former consisted of nine persons and the latter of nineteen, one of whom was Marsinah.[26] Twelve demands were brought up by the workers, namely, increase in wages (to the level recommended by the Minister); inclusion of overtime pay; adjustment of menstruation leave with minimum wages; health care facilities in accordance with the Regulation No. 1/1992; inclusion of workers in the workers' insurance scheme (*Asuransi Tenaga Kerja* or ASTEK); provision of the thirteenth month wages; increase in food and transport allowance; disbanding

[24] Gathering of District Level Heads (*Musyawarah Pimpinan Tingkat Kecamatan*) consisting of District Head, Military Command, and Police Chief.

[25] Supartono, *Marsinah*. This is similar to the plantation situation in colonial Sumatra. As Stoler points out the 'politicization' of workers' economic grievances by the planters and the colonial state, 'deflected attention away from investigation of labour conditions per se and placed it on events that were at once both external to the estates and within the anticolonial movement' Stoler, 'Perceptions of Protest', p. 652.

[26] This separation reflected the division among the workers regarding their view on the role of the government-sanctioned union, SPSI, but it did not seem to ultimately colour the way workers confronted management.

of the SPSI factory union; payment of wages during maternity leave at the given time; equalization of payment of workers' wages who have finished training with those who have worked for a year; no annulment of attained rights; and no retrenchments, mutations, or intimidations after the strike. As a result of the negotiations the company conceded to most of these demands. However these were phrased in conditional terms and made it possible for the company to breach them should the conditions not be conducive for such improvements.[27] A collective agreement was then signed by twenty-four workers' representatives, among them Marsinah.

At this stage however, the situation was not considered to be just about collective bargaining or what officials regarded as an issue safely within the confines of 'the economic'; it was viewed also as a 'security' problem (*masalah keamanan*) and as such the company management was therefore no longer in a position to decide the course of events. Despite the fact that a collective agreement had been achieved, the military district office (*Komando Rayon Militer* or Koramil) was still attempting to get to the 'core' of the matter by searching for the culprits who had led the strike. Yudo was summoned again by the military and interrogated. The direction of the questions, according to the testimony of Yudo himself, focused on two points: (a) to make him acknowledge that he was the mastermind (*dalang*) behind the strike; (b) to make him relate how the whole process started and how this led to the formulation of those demands.

On the day the collective bargaining (4 May) took place, 13 workers (12 men and 1 woman) received a letter from the village head summoning them to meet with the local military police. Not all these people had signed the original agreement, and among them was only one woman, Sumarah.[28] Marsinah's role at this stage was

[27] The basic minimum wage would increase but would be linked to the workers' length of employment; overtime pay would not change—since it was considered to have followed the Ministerial Regulation; wages during menstrual leave would be paid; registration into ASTEK would have to wait; the thirteenth month salary would be paid according to the company's abilities; food and transport allowance was already included in the wage bill; the presence of the factory-based SPSI union would still be acknowledged; on the last two demands, the company's response was open-ended.

[28] Of the 24 signatories, only 5 were women: these were: Marsinah, Masiáh, Mutmainah, Lilik Indarsih, and Endang Widiati.

already crucial but she maintained a low profile, helping to prepare the workers to face the interrogation with the Kodim (District Military Command). Her intentions were to go to her uncle at the Justice Department in Surabaya if the workers were brought to trial by Kodim.

Following the chronology given in Supartono's report we are able to discern how new categories were being constructed by the interrogators, within the private confines of the military headquarters. In these interrogations, outside the public sphere, the military at a certain moment were able to use vocabulary which somewhat deviated from the public transcript. Categories of race were used to portray the employers as exploiters who 'treat our people like dogs'. As the company was owned by domestic Chinese capitalists, and racial sentiments against the Chinese are inherent in Indonesian history, they manipulated this narrative to create the boundaries between 'we' and 'them'. Concomitantly, they portrayed themselves as the protectors and providers of better opportunities. As one official stated: 'Such treatment is insulting to "us" Indonesians as a nation (*sebagai bangsa*). Rather than be treated like that you should ask for resignation. I will write you a memo so that you can find jobs in other companies.'[29]

However, the workers' did not seem to be influenced by this offical transcript. Instead they sought alternative terms within the sanctioned language of industrial relations characteristic of the New Order:

—'Even though I may have made a mistake I will correct that mistake. I still want to work, Sir!'

—'But we already have a KKB here![30] There is already an agreement that the management will not make any dismissals, no mutations, no transfers, etc. KKB has already been acknowledged by the Ministry of Manpower and Dewan Pimpinan Cabang, so then the matter should already be settled!'[31]

[29] Supartono, *Marsinah*, p. 23.

[30] The KKB (*Kesepakatan Kerja Bersama*) is a watered down version of the PKB (*Perjanjian Kerja Bersama*) which is the Collective Labour Agreement. The change in term from *perjanjian* (promise, agreement) to *kesepakatan* (consensus) highlights the stipulation on consensus which tends not to have any legal consequences for the management when they violate the agreement.

[31] Supartono, *Marsinah*, p. 23.

These responses reflected the terms sanctioned by the government, namely (a) the right to work and (b) the institutional channels through which workers were allowed to bring their demands, i.e. the KKB. By framing their response in this way the workers were deploying 'public transcripts' to legitimize their own actions.[32] The commanding officer then became more impatient and angry and threatened to take them all to court with the allegation of having held a secret meeting (*rapat gelap*), having conducted sabotage, having intimidated other workers who wanted to work, and being equivalent to the PKI. The terms under which this conversation took place were also revealing. Occasionally, the workers spoke high Javanese, and the interrogators spoke low Javanese revealing the boundary-making process based on status hierarchies.

Letters of resignation, already prepared in advance by the military interrogators, were then shoved in their faces. At this stage all the thirteen workers became frightened and agreed to resign—although some were more reluctant than others. After the tense exchange between the military personnel and the workers had taken place, a number of the company staff arrived at the military headquarters in the afternoon, bringing with them the severance payment, already in envelopes.[33] One company official, according to the workers' reports, hinted that this was not his doing but the will of the 'security people' (*pihak keamanan*).

The next day, 5 May 1993, three of the thirteen workers who were among those forced to sign, still attempted to redress their situation by going to the office of the Ministry of Manpower (Depnaker) in Surabaya to lodge complaints on the way their case had been handled both by the company and by the military officials. The response of the Depnaker official reflected a partial distancing from the case when he heard that the district military was involved. 'Well, if that is the case, then we cannot interfere. I suggest, but do not say this comes from me otherwise we will have problems of the district military (Kodim), you do have your people's representatives, so you should bring your case there'.[34] During this interaction members of the DPC SPSI came by, and the Depnaker official suggested also that they bring their case to the

[32] James C. Scott, *Domination and the Arts of Resistance: Hidden Transcripts* (New Haven and London, 1990), p. 157.

[33] Each person was given Rp 170,000. The total amount was Rp 2,200,000.

[34] Supartono, *Marsinah*, p. 31.

DPC SPSI. The workers then went there, and were given examples of letters of complaint to be submitted to the Manpower Office in Sidoarjo so that they could air their grievances on the unilateral dismissals (*PHK sepihak*) undertaken by the company. However before any further steps could be taken, a new round of dismissals came about.

On 7 May 1993, another summons was issued by the District Military Command to eight other workers. The same set of questions were asked as the day before, and as agreed upon among themselves they all said that they were just *ikut-ikutan* ('following the others'). The person in charge of the interrogation, Sugeng, asked whether during the meetings prior to the strike there had been anyone involved from outside (the factory). One of the workers, a woman named Mutmainah, answered:

> No sir, we discussed this only among ourselves (*musyawarah*). The demands came up from our meetings in the sections. From the suggestions from my friends when we had a meeting with the SPSI at that time, we then tried to check these points with the company regulations as stated on the pinboards in each department. We found then that the rules were not implemented by the company. And from there we compiled our demands and discussed them together.[35]

Sugeng then became angry and turned on her:

—'You are stupid, you talk too much (*bawel*)! What is your religion?'
—'Islam.'
—'Then you are a hypocrite (*munafik*). You are the mastermind (*dalang*) behind this strike!'
—'Whatever you say sir (*bapak*)—the most important thing is I don't feel that I am a *dalang*. I don't feel that I have incited my friends to go on strike.'[36]

Sugeng then started hitting the table with his fist and threw an ashtray on the table—the pieces hitting Mutmainah's face and causing her chin to bleed. 'If you were a man, I would have killed you by now! Get out of here, I don't want to see you again.'[37] This scene illustrates how Mutmainah again used the officially sanctioned terms of *musyawarah* and regulations enacted by the company as the base for her defence. The military official brought

[35] Ibid., p. 32.
[36] Ibid., p. 33.
[37] Ibid.

up her religion as a means to point out that lying involves a huge sin in Islam. The allusion to her gender insinuated that he was showing kindness to her because she was a woman. The intimidations ultimately forced the workers to give in. From the eight workers who were summoned, five then resigned.

In the meantime, in their continuing frustration with the way the whole process was developing, twelve workers went to the provincial parliament (the DPRD) and the Manpower office in Sidoarjo on 10 May. They were accompanied by the Branch Representative of the SPSI Sidoarjo and received by the vice chairman of the DPRD in Sidoarjo, Harun Al Rasjid. The workers stated that the most frightening aspect of this whole affair was the involvement of the Kodim 0816 of Sidoarjo. The vice chairman of the DPRD promised to arrange a meeting with the company and security officials to clarify why the workers' strike should be settled by the military. When a *Surabaya Post* reporter asked the Kodim 0816 personnel about their involvement in the workers' strike he received the answer: 'Oh we are only helping to find a solution to the case.' This is because the demonstration that ended in dismissals had been reported by the company as being preceded by a 'secret meeting' (*rapat gelap*).[38]

In the various situations where the security apparatus was attempting to weed out workers who were considered rebellious and a threat to workplace and public order, alternative transcripts were employed to bring these elements under control, namely the language of communist threat and religious extremism, thus politicizing what was originally an 'economic' issue.[39] In most of these instances, workers attempted to work through the official channels using public trancripts endorsed by the government to

[38] Ibid., quoted from *Surabaya Post*, 10 June 1993.

[39] The use of 'the communist threat' as potentially inherent in labour conflicts is common among the ruling elite of any capitalist state. In a revealing report written to the United States Trade Representative in November 1992, almost three decades after the New Order was established, and when Suharto's power was still strongly entrenched, it is mentioned that: 'One possible inroad for communist subversion is through worker unrest. The Government especially fears that the communist ideology might be attractive to young people who did not live through the national distress of the 1960s and many of those young people can best be reached on the job through labor disputes.' *Asiawatch*, 1993, 1–2, quoted in Saptari, 'Rural Women to the Factories', p. 63.

bring up their claims.[40] Thus, as we have seen, the workers repeatedly referred to the agreements they had made under the collective agreement, to consultations with the government-sponsored trade union SPSI and to their need 'to continue working', when they were faced with threats of dismissal. In the private confines of the military headquarters, such public transcripts were less effective, as the military would use other points of reference. However, the tactic employed by the workers was meant to increase the legitimacy of their struggles.

Reconstructing Marsinah's Death

Workers' protest and collective action had already been highly visible a few years before the incident. However, Marsinah's death gave an extra impetus and broader coverage to the workers' movement because of the media attention and the dramatic nature of the case (which, as explained below, involved also kidnapping and torturing of the employers). At the same time it has also been deployed for various other agendas which cover a broad spectrum of economic and political demands. After the death of Marsinah, one can broadly classify the overt forms of protest into three sometimes overlapping strategies. The first strategy has basically viewed the case of Marsinah as a murder case, viewing the military as the perpetrators; the second strategy emphasizes the struggle for workers' rights, i.e. their institutional rights, namely the right to organize, freedom of speech, and the right to strike. The third strategy presented the case as part of the general struggle for political and economic change. Before we embark on a discussion of the way in which the rhetoric has evolved in this case, it is worthwhile to reflect briefly on the concealment of gender. The women's organizations such as *Solidaritas Perempuan* and *Yayasan Perempuan Mardhika* who were involved in the meetings and campaigns to bring up the case had earlier brought up the case of sexual violence, but since the Marsinah case happened at a time when Suharto's authoritarian regime was still more or less intact,

[40] As Scott has argued, 'the theatrical imperatives that normally prevail in situations of domination produce a public transcript in close conformity with how the dominant group would wish to have things appear' (Scott, *Domination*, p. 4).

such voices were gradually overpowered by the louder voices of anti-militarism.[41]

Although Marsinah died in early May, it was only in early June 1993 that her case received public attention. Until one month after the body was found the police were still trying to determine the cause of Marsinah's death, eventually resulting in a statement by the head of the East Java police that Marsinah did not die a natural death.[42] However even then there was still no clarity on who killed her and a special team had to be established to investigate the murder. The heads of the police and military had warned the public not to make any judgements on the death, let alone link her death with the labour dispute that she was involved in. However this did not stop them from drawing their own conclusions, as in August 1993 when both Kapolda (Head of Police) and Pangdam (Head of Military) were saying that the death of Marsinah was a purely criminal case, so that no one should connect it with the strikes occurring prior to her death.[43]

Within the following weeks, various opinions regarding why she was murdered and who murdered her, were expressed. One columnist wrote that there could be a number of possible motives associated with her death. Firstly, that it was a family affair and involved a case of inheritance conflicts. However, this assumption could not be upheld for long since Marsinah came from a poor family and there was, therefore, no question of a division of property. Secondly, the East Java police wanted to bring up the classical motive of a triangle relationship. It was said that Marsinah was actually married but separated from her husband and that she had a relationship with a secret lover. However, again this motive was quickly dismissed because neither the 'husband' nor the lover were ever found.[44] The third motive was that her death was linked to the demonstrations and strikes that occurred prior to her death. However, this motive was squarely rejected by the police.

It was only found out later, at the time when the media was

[41] Personal observations and communication with Tati Krishnawati and later on with Yuniyanti Chuzaifah, both from *Solidaritas Perempuan*. It was also a point in time when women's organizations were still marginally involved with the political issues of the day.

[42] Memorandum, 11 June 1993, quoted by Supartono, *Marsinah*, p. 35.

[43] Supartono, *Marsinah*, p. 35.

[44] Supartono, *Marsinah*, p. 36, quoting *Tempo*, 30 October 1993.

covering the debates and controversies surrounding the death of Marsinah, that nine people had been detained, tortured, and forced to admit that they were behind the murder of Marsinah.[45] According to the official version the whole issue started with a letter that Marsinah had written to the company management. Because of this letter it was said that the management held a meeting. This letter was of crucial significance because Marsinah mentioned that she had an ace card against the company as she knew about the illegal activities that the company was involved in, namely producing fake watches with famous brand names. From the factory, Marsinah was allegedly brought to the house of Yudi Susanto in Surabaya. After being held for three days in Yudi's house, Marsinah was executed and the body was ditched in Nganjuk.[46] The Polda (*Kepolisian Daerah*, Provincial Police) Jatim felt that they had handled the case as well as possible and even invited those who were not happy with the results to bring the case to court.[47]

On 11 November 1993 a member of the police searched the CPS factory in Porong. The police report stated that watches with various famous brand names such as Christian Dior, Citizen, Rado and Cartier were found. However, campaigns conducted and organized by the Solidarity Committee for Marsinah (*Komite Solidaritas Untuk Marsinah*) challenged this official version.[48] The committee was actively coordinating a number of campaigns and activities to bring the Marsinah case to public attention, such as visiting Marsinah's grave in Nganjuk, organizing cultural events

[45] It was reported that they had a letter of detention signed on 30 September 1993 and an arrest warrant on 2 October 1993. The detained persons only signed their warrants for arrest two weeks after they were taken away. The nine detained persons gave their testimonies to the legal aid team and said that they were hit, forced to crawl naked on their knees, eat grass, and lick the floor clean with their tongues. The manager of CPS, Yudi Astono was forced to acknowledge that he had raped Marsinah. When he refused to do so, Yudi's mouth was gagged with cloth used to clean a kerosene stove. When he vomited he was forced to wash his face with the vomit. Electric shocks were also applied to his private parts. At the end of this he finally followed his captors' scenario. Ibid., pp. 42–7.

[46] Ibid., p. 71.

[47] Ibid., p. 59, quoting *Suara Karya*, 28 October 1993.

[48] Which was primarily initiated by the Surabaya branch of the Legal Aid Institute who had followed the case closely and passed this on to the Jakarta office.

with plays and poetry reading focusing on the life of Marsinah. The Committee argued that the watches had been produced under licence. What Supartono's report found peculiar was that the police did not at all deny this, or try to revise their version of the story. The Legal Aid Institute also argued that the involvement of the military (Kodam V Brawijaya or the Provincial Military Command of East Java) in this case was legally unwarranted. Even by 1999, not one person within the military had been brought to the military court.

Protest centred around the legal procedures: the process in which the persons accused of having been involved in the murder of Marsinah were detained was highly suspect. Questions were also raised as to the role of the provincial police. Parallel with the whole debate regarding her death were also public acknowledgements of Marsinah as a symbol of workers' rights. Various institutions granted her posthumous awards: the regent of Nganjuk awarded her the Good Citizen Award, while other organizations nominated her for the Yap Thiam Hien Award and the Young Patriot's Award.[49]

The Marsinah incident has coloured the debates regarding Labour Day, even years after her murder. However, what one can observe is the shift in the emphasis as Marsinah's case and symbolizations were put to the fore. If in 1994 until prior to the fall of Suharto the focus of the opposition groups was on viewing 'Marsinah' as the military's Achilles heel with which the military could be toppled, after Suharto's resignation the accent was less on viewing it as a murder case and more as one illustration out of the many violations of workers' rights. This is done in the context of the growing visibility of workers' protest and students' involvement in workers' and other social issues. Among others, since 1999 there have been various rallies demanding that Labour Day be commemorated and recognized as a public holiday. However, as crucial a question as the recognition of Labour Day as an official holiday was the choice of the date on which it should fall. The Government's view was that 20 February had already been chosen as the Indonesian Employees' Day (*Hari Pekerja Indonesia*), since 20 February 1973 had been the day trade unions were all merged under one umbrella by the then Minister of Manpower.[50] This day

[49] Weix, 'Resisting History'.

had been legally recognized by a Presidential Decree and prior to that a Ministerial Decree.[51] In 1999, however, in a situation where political struggles questioning New Order ideology became widespread, several views challenged this official version. Some suggested that Labour Day should fall on the day when the Republic first enacted its Labour Law. Others stated that it should fall on the day the first large strike occurred in Indonesia. Yet others demanded that the day of Marsinah's death should be regarded as Labour Day.

The rallies organized around 'Marsinah' have also used Labour Day to remind the public of the unsettled murder case of Marsinah and the collusion between the military and the local government in covering up and masterminding the incident. A rally on 9 May 2000 organized by *Serikat Buruh Kerakyatan* (People's Labour Union), where almost 100 workers and non-governmental organization (NGO) activists assembled in front of the Local Military Headquarters (Mapolda), brought up three issues: the dubious role of the police in the whole investigation ('*1993–2000 kami dibohongi polisi*'),[52] the demand to hang Marsinah's murderer and the appeal for the prevention of any more killings by the state

[50] It was particularly after the appointment of Sudomo, in 1983 as Minister of Manpower that comprehensive changes were made to the vocabulary of labour issues parallel with the thorough reorganization of labour-related institutions. Sudomo was formerly Chief of Staff of the Navy (1969–73) and head of the Operational Command for the Restoration of Security and Order or widely known as the KOPKAMTIB (1973–83).Because the term 'labourer' (*Buruh*) itself was still considered too reminiscent of the old communist propaganda, in 'Pancasila Industrial Relations' workers were not to be coined as *buruh* anymore but as *pekerja* or *karyawan* (employee); *pemecatan* (dismissals) was replaced by *pemutusan hubungan kerja* (termination of work relations); and *mogok* (strike) by *unjuk rasa* (expressing feelings); while *Perjanjian Perburuhan Bersama* (Collective Labour Agreement) was changed into *Kesepakatan Kerja Bersama* (Collective Work Agreement). Since the emphasis was on the family spirit and mutual cooperation, anything connoting a one-sided action or non-cooperative tone should be erased from the vocabulary. Workers were portrayed as 'black ants' (*semut hitam*) symbolizing the hard work they were meant to do. Saptari, 'Rural Women to the Factories', p. 63.

[51] Presidential Decree No. 9, 1991 and Ministerial Decree of the Ministry of Manpower, Transmigation and Cooperatives No. 43/Men/1977.

[52] Meaning: '1993–2000 we were lied to by the police'.

apparatus. They stated that the investigation had only concentrated on the company management and hadn't yet touched the military.[53]

The SPSI officials also made use of these rallies and demonstrations surrounding the Marsinah case, but on a somewhat different platform than the non-SPSI groups. Thus, around 8,000 workers from 150 companies went on a long march on 28 May to commemorate the death of Marsinah. The 'Marsinah' element in this case was invoked simply as a means of publicizing their existence since they were aware that the SPSI in public opinion is considered to be non-functional as a labour institution. This rally started from the East Java SPSI headquarters in Surabaya and ended at the SPSI branch office which was also located in Surabaya. This march was also integral to the preparations for the Fifteenth National Sports Week (*Pekan Olahraga Nasional*).[54] The participation of the Mayor and the head of the SPSI in the rally to commemorate Marsinah, and their physical presence among the workers ('*disela-sela buruh*') underline the function of this public gesture to show their 'people-oriented' leanings while simultaneously appropriating the symbols of the opposition.[55]

Why has the Marsinah case been given such prominence, although hers was by no means the only case of a worker killed after a protest action?[56] It seems that Marsinah's death coincided with a general crackdown on labour unrest, following a period of slight slackening of state repression and controlled openness (*keterbukaan*).[57] This crackdown was a culmination of military

[53] *Jawa Pos*, 9 May 2000; *Surya*, 9 May 2000.

[54] The Mayor of Surabaya was also involved in symbolically seeing the head of the SPSI of East Java off to join the workers' march.

[55] *Surya*, 29 May 2000.

[56] Other recorded deaths are: Rusli in Medan 1994, Udin in Yogyakarta 1996, Lasimo in Sidoarjo 1998, and Solikah Anam in Malang 1998. Rusli was a worker of the rubber factory, PT Industri Karet Deli, located in the Medan Industrial Estate, North Sumatra. His body was found in the Deli River. He was involved in a strike held on 11 March 1994 by thousands of workers of three companies, Industri Karet Deli, Cipta Rimba Jaya, and Gunung, Gahapi Sakti, all of them based in this industrial estate. Another wave of strikes occurred in Medan during 14–16 of April which culminated in the death of another person, this time a Chinese company director, Yuli Kristianto. Bergerak [NGO Information and Communication Media], No. 24 (1994), pp. 23–5.

aggravation towards the large-scale strikes that occurred in the early 1990s, and Marsinah's case was the first that came to the attention of NGO activists at a moment when public outrage of military involvement in daily affairs had reached its peak. It also coincided with the APEC summit and the US threat to suspend the General System of Preference because of workers' rights violations.[58] The cases that happened afterwards were overshadowed by the Marsinah incident.

However, in the course of time, although 'Marsinah' is still commemorated every year the centrality of her presence has become much more subdued and secondary if placed in the broader context of workers' collective campaigns. Particularly after the fall of Suharto, there has been a resurgence of labour protest, often involving thousands of workers each time. The nature of these collective actions has also shifted through time, following the politics of the moment. To place these actions within the changing scenarios, the section below reviews the general pattern of the politics of protest after Marsinah's death. As with the Marsinah case, workers' protest and state dominance have shown different and sometimes contradictory dimensions when faced towards the national platform and when localized in the vicinity of the workplace.

The Rhetoric of Protest, 1993–2001: The Workplace and Beyond

Large-scale strikes, already an emerging feature of the years prior to the Marsinah incident, have continued unabated. In the last quarter of 1994, one report estimated that there were 213 cases of worker protest, mainly in Java, but with some cases also in parts of Sumatra (Riau, Aceh, Lampung, Medan) and also in Irian.[59] In the second quarter of 1995 there were 308 cases; and in the last quarter there were 173 cases.[60] Although the percentages vary

[57] This was largely a response to foreign, and especially US pressure towards Indonesia to liberalize its economy and therefore its labour situation also. Hadiz, *Workers and the State*, p. 182; Aspinall, 'Democratization', p. 10.

[58] Human Rights Watch 1994, quoted by Weix, 'Resisting History'.

[59] *Index Pelanggaran Hak Asasi Manusia*, 1995.

[60] *Index Pelanggaran Hak Asasi Manusia*, 1996, Nos. 5 and 7.

slightly, the largest percentage of the strikes were about wages and payment of wages followed by protests against dismissals. Other issues included working conditions, collective labour agreements, and company violations against the proper functioning of factory-based unions or their leaders. Most of these cases start with strikes and demonstrations at the workplace or industrial site, but if the cases are not dealt with satisfactorily, they end up at state institutions such as the office of the Ministry of Manpower, the parliament, the SPSI office, or the local police or military headquarters.[61] Collective actions dealing with workers' issues on a national platform usually do not focus on single factory cases but merge a number of issues together, thus consolidating a larger group of workers.[62] The rhetoric of these protest actions, although some of them did not neglect to incorporate the Marsinah case, is strongly influenced by the broader resentment against state violations and military repression blended with the politics of the moment.

During the period 1997 until late 1998, workers' protests and strikes decreased whereas the wave of demonstrations and rallies conducted by students and various elements within the civil society grew.[63] Although the reasons for this need further examination, one can assume that it reflects the focus of civil-society activists on combating central state authorities on the eve of Suharto's fall, as well as the public attention to independence movements and ethnic conflicts in various parts of Indonesia. Unlike the revolutionary period in 1945 when labour unions were involved in nationalist and anti-colonial movements, this period of transition did not result in a coalition of labour and other social forces in society to bring down the Suharto government. This may be because workers were hit by the economic crisis and had to struggle for survival. Various reports have also shown that companies attempted to reduce production costs in response to the crisis not so much through mass dismissals but through gradual and prolonged temporary lay-offs.[64] With the history of mass strikes in the

[61] Ibid. 1995 and 1996.

[62] Therefore not focused on a specific workplace issue.

[63] See also Aspinall, 'Democratization', p. 10.

[64] See Indrasari Tjandraningsih, 'Krisis Ekonomi dan PHK: Maknanya Bagi Perempuan', *Jurnal Analisis Sosial*, 4 (1999), pp. 61–74, for a discussion on women workers and the crisis. Also see Ratna Saptari, 'Isu Perempuan

preceding years, companies were to some extent more careful not to provoke such actions. Only since 1999 when the first jolts of 'the crisis' had abated somewhat, has there was an increase in workers' large strikes again. The First of May has become a crucial rallying point for these broad and large-scale protest actions. Although these actions basically demanded the recognition of the first of May as 'the Day of the Worker' (*Hari Buruh*) and that it should be considered a public holiday, this was usually merged with other issues, both economic and political.

The rallies are always held at crucial public sites, to attract attention and obtain a prominent place in the national and local media. In these public expressions of collective protest, tensions between different groups of workers can often not be avoided. These tensions usually revolve around problems such as who should represent the workers or who has the right to claim certain public spaces. One group took over the People's Assembly Building in Jakarta, and demanded that other groups support their group. Others preferred to create their own, possibly less spectacular, public spaces, and conducted a march from the National Monument to the Hotel Indonesia Roundabout (*Bundaran Senayan*).[65]

Perceptions of Workers' Activism and the Nature of State Concessions

After the crackdown on worker activism in the mid-1990s, some loosening up of control occurred as a result of both international and internal pressures, in which the Marsinah factor was a strong component. The increasing pressure on the military by the civil society in general and workers in particular made them more careful in handling labour disputes.

On 18 January 1995, Abdul Latief, the then Minister of Manpower, revoked the regulation that permitted military intervention in industrial disputes.[66] When Habibie came into power in 1998, he immediately ratified various International Labour

Dalam Agenda Gerakan Buruh di Indonesia', *Jurnal Analisis Sosial*, 4 (1999), pp. 89–113, for a case study in Surabaya which looks at workers' and companies' responses to the monetary crisis. This latter case study was based on research done by members of *Humanika* based in Surabaya.

[65] *Surabaya Post*, 2 May 1999.

[66] Weix, 'Resisting History'.

Organization (ILO) Conventions, namely No. 105, 1957 (Abolition of Forced Labour); No. 111, 1958 (Anti Discrimination in Work and Position); No. 138, 1973 (Minimum Age for Admission to Employment); No. 87, 1948 (The Right to Assemble and the Right to Organize); and No. 98 (the Right to Collective Bargaining) in quick succession.[67]

Despite the fact that dozens of unions and labour organizations have mushroomed as a result of national level concessions, the existence of these unions has not gone unchallenged by the companies and state authorities. This has taken the form of either enacting regulations that cancel out or contradict each other, or by undermining the liberal policies at a lower level. For instance, in some companies workers who have started to register their independent union with the Ministry of Manpower providing the names of their members, would find themselves blacklisted from the company and eventually dismissed.[68]

The increasing frequency and visibility of labour protests in the public arena has also provoked responses from the middle classes quite often, confirming their ideas of the working classes as rude and uncouth trouble makers. For instance, 4,000 workers of Kong Tai Indonesia went on strike and caused a traffic hold-up. One of the newspapers covering the event showed a photograph of a pregnant woman who had to be carried away from the blocked toll road, thus suggesting that the protest action inconvenienced the public.[69] When after a few months their demands were not heard they went to stay for a number of weeks at the parliament building, washed their clothes there, and used the public toilets, but still got no response from the parliament members. The reaction from the vice chairman of the parliament was that the men and women staying there were illegal occupants and 'since they all slept together there is a possibility that they are conducting immoral acts'.[70] Some even complained that workers' actions were obstructing governments attempts to revive the economy which

[67] 'Labor Situation of Indonesia', *LIPS News*, April–July 2000.
[68] Saptari, 'Isu Perempuan Dalam Agenda Gerakan Buruh di Indonesia', p. 97; Saut Manalu, 'Kebijakan Perburuhan di Masa Krisis', *Jurnal Analisis Sosial*, 4 (1999), pp. 1–23, here p. 17.
[69] 'Labor Situation of Indonesia', *LIPS News*, April–July 2000.
[70] *Suara Pembaruan*, 9 May 1999.

according to these critical observers is supposed to be 'the main instrument by which human rights can be achieved'.[71]

Conclusion

What has the Marsinah case meant for our understanding of the labour question, labour politics, and working class consciousness in Indonesia? As we have seen, the state's goal is not just to safeguard capital accumulation. At a general level, political stability is indeed a necessary condition for foreign investment but political stability is also much more than that—it is part of the nationalist cause and by extension, of the military's justification for their existence and power. In many examples in Indonesian history, capital or certain sections of capital have been subordinated to this cause. In the reports and pamphlets written by people such as Valck, Rhemrev, and Brand, we can observe the strength of capital in deflecting state power away from the business of running their enterprises. However, the Marsinah case has exemplified the role of the state (or the military) in interfering in the affairs of management. At the level of the state, we can also see the contradictions between the regulations that are promulgated (which are often formulated in such a way as to aim at the wider public, at international and national levels) and the practice at local level. The tensions within the ruling class itself reveal cracks in the hegemonic project which has often been viewed as impregnable. The essence of the opposition movement for the last fifteen years has been to identify these cracks and pry them open to expose the faulty workings of the repressive and corrupt state. These tensions themselves emerge also because of challenges coming from civil society, in this case spearheaded by the labour movement. Workers' and students' collective actions have forced officials to rephrase their public rhetoric which generally allows for more commonality of language.

It is within this historical environment that we should understand 'Marsinah'. The labour movement does not operate in a political and cultural vacuum. Whatever the origins of Indonesian workers' discontent in recent years, this general atmosphere has helped to broaden the scope of workers' collective action, at the same time

[71] *Kompas*, 2 May 2000.

as it has widened the framing of their actions. Particularly since the 1990s, as large scale demonstrations and strikes have become more widespread, public spaces became sites of contestation. Regardless of how individual workers identify with the struggle, the common use of space and the responses directed at them make it possible for them to recognize their common interests and identity. However, as we have seen, the contestations and struggles of workers occur at two levels. What is played out in the streets and in public may not necessarily be replicated at the workplace or local level, where behind closed doors the language of authority and subordination and the exercise of power may be more blatant than in public where repressive authority can become more contested.

Therefore, what we have seen is a play with words both inside and outside the workplace. Using the same public transcripts or at times rejecting certain sections of them through adopting others, workers are able to challenge the hegemonic power of the state. But a concentration on public (or hidden) transcripts has its limitations. Attempts to read the nature of workers' consciousness and lived experience from their use of language would be a complicated procedure, since as we have seen there are different transcripts invoked for different purposes. Workers' protest in public spaces can be interpreted as a manifestation of their consciousness, though we cannot see the shifts and ambivalences colouring this consciousness as workers go back to their communities and families or when competing demands influence their identities in the long run. In these collective actions and the rhetoric surrounding them there is much that is revealed but at the same time much that is concealed, and it is to these gaps that we should turn in our future research.

8

Landlord Credit in Philippine's Rice Cultivation, 1920s–1930s

Willem Wolters

Introduction

In the extensive literature on landlord–tenant relationships in developing countries, much attention has been given to the insurance aspect of these ties. Sociologists and anthropologists have done this by emphasizing the patron–client character of sharecropping relationships, with landlords and tenants in the role of patrons and clients respectively. Patrons are supposed to give financial support and protection to their clients, while clients look for this kind of enduring personal relationships. Social scientists often depict a transition in time, whereby the traditional benevolent landlord–tenant relationships in the past give way to more exploitative relationships in later periods. Economists have rarely used the patron–client concept, but instead have emphasized the insurance aspect of credit. In developing countries, risk and uncertainty are substantial, while insurance markets are non-existent or poorly developed. Economists have stated that under these conditions, access to credit can be considered to provide a close substitute for insurance.[1]

[1] A general study on patron–client relations is Stephen Schmidt et al. (eds), *Friends, Followers, and Factions: A Reader in Political Clientelism* (Berkeley, 1977). For India a landmark study is by Jan Breman, *Patronage and Exploitation: Changing Agrarian Relations in South Gujarat, India* (Berkeley, 1974). For the Philippines, Benedict J. Kerkvliet, *The Huk Rebellion: A Study of Peasant Revolt in the Philippines* (Berkeley, 1977). Economic studies on the insurance function of credit are: Hans P. Binswanger and Mark R. Rosenzweig, 'Behavioral and Material Determinants of Productive Relations

These elements can all be found in the literature on landlord–tenant relationships in the Philippines, particularly in the sector of rice cultivation since the beginning of the twentieth century. The sharecropping contract was viewed as a form of cooperation between a landowner and a labourer, called the *kasamà* system, whereby the harvest was divided, according to a certain formula, between land and labour. Contemporary observers were quick to recognize the element of personalism and dependency in the sharecropping contract. The economist Hugo Miller has hypothesized that the *kasamà*-share system in the Philippines was a survival of the ancient Malay institution of serfdom based on the control of labour through debt. In the beginning of the twentieth century there were still bonded debtors of whom two classes could be discerned, viz., household servants and labourers and they were indicated with specific names, such as *alila* or *bataan* in Tagalog and other names in the other languages in the islands. Often the servants were young people or children whose parents had pledged their services to a rich family for debt. However, Miller remarked: 'Bonded debtors as decribed here are disappearing in a good many communities; there are fewer of them to-day than during the Spanish administration.'[2]

In the 1920s, the typical *kasamà* or sharecropping contract in rice cultivation had the following features. The landowner furnished the tenant with land, seed, and an advance for production costs, while the tenant furnished the labour and the draught animal. After the harvest, the seed and the advance payment was deducted and returned to the landlord (these costs were thus equally borne by both parties). The crop was then divided equally between the landlord and the tenant. The tenant was indentured by a debt called *bugnos*, which was never settled, but which the landlord regularly recalled as the obligation holding the tenant family upon the land. If the family left without paying the debt, the insular constabularies and the local police could be called upon

---

in Agriculture', *Journal of Development Studies*, 22 (1986), pp. 503–39; J-Ph. Platteau and A. Abraham, 'An Inquiry into Quasi-Credit Contracts: The Role of Reciprocal Credit and Interlinked Deals in Small-Scale Fishing Communities', *Journal of Development Studies*, 23 (1987), pp. 461–90.

[2] Hugo H. Miller, *Economic Conditions in the Philippines* (Boston, 1920), p. 308; idem, *Principles of Economics Applied to the Philippines* (Boston, 1932), p. 53.

to bring the people back to the land. In addition to the production costs the landlord gave advances and credit to the tenant for daily subsistence, partly in the form of interest-free advances of rice and cash, partly as credit at higher and often usurious interest rates.[3]

Agricultural economists who studied the economic aspects of the sharecropping relationship in the 1930s concluded that the contract was equitable and just, taking into account the actual money value of what each party had put into the business. The landlord should receive the normal return on his or her capital investment (land and money), at the then current rate of interest (about 7 per cent), while the tenant family should be compensated for its labour on the basis of current wages. When the returns are calculated in accordance with these principles, the ratio of the factors land and labour then is almost completely in accordance with the 50–50 division of the crop.[4] However, one of the agricultural economists gave this conclusion a conditional twist when he wrote that the tenancy contract was fair and equitable, 'when stripped of implied agreements on loans'.[5]

Contemporary observers considered the advances and interest the most important aspect of the tenancy contract, 'because they are the means by which the tenants are oppressed'.[6] Another author observes: 'It is through advances, interest and debt that the planter often controls the actions of the tenant and holds him to the land.'[7] What made the landlord–tenant relationship exploitative and oppressive, in the eyes of contemporary observers, was the widespread use of credit at usurious interest rates. Credit tied the tenants to the land, and caught them in unfree and dependency relationships. Landlord credit, or the obverse, tenant indebtedness, locked the tenants in a life of unfreedom, peonage, and drudgery. For the landlord, credit seemed to be a source of power as well as additional income.

[3] Miller, *Principles of Economics*, pp. 388–90.

[4] Evett D. Hester et al., 'Some Economic and Social Aspects of Philippine Rice Tenancies', *The Philippine Agriculturist*, 12, 9 (1924), pp. 367–444; José E. Velmonte, 'Farm Tenancy Problems in the Philippines with Particular Reference to Tenancies in Rice-Producing Regions', *The Philippine Agriculturist*, 27, 7 (1938), pp. 515–29.

[5] Velmonte, 'Farm Tenancy Problems', p. 525.

[6] Amando M. Dalisay, 'Types of Tenancy Contracts on Rice Farms in Nueva Ecija', *The Philippine Agriculturist*, 26, 2 (1937), pp. 159–98.

[7] Miller, *Principles of Economics*, p. 394.

It was only in the 1960s and 1970s that social scientists characterized landlord–tenant relationships in terms of patron–client relationships. The political scientist Kerkvliet who had interviewed older respondents in his research area in Central Luzon, was told by the farmers that landlords had been benevolent during the 1910s and 1920s, but had become mean and oppressive during the 1930s. Other researchers have also reported statements from respondents praising the generosity of previous generations of landlords.[8]

However, this picture of oppression and almost total dependency of the tenants is not entirely correct. In a general study on tenancy the economist Clive Bell analyses the landlord–tenant relationship as a principal–agent interaction. He argues that if a principal (landlord) does not face a perfectly elastic supply of agents (tenants) it is arbitrary to assume that the terms of contract are decided unilaterally by the landlord. It is more reasonable to assume that the terms are arrived at through bilateral negotiations with each side having some bargaining power.[9]

The question is then whether and to what extent landlord–tenant relationships in the Philippines did have an insurance aspect, in other words whether landlords were able to protect their tenants from risks. In general, people face two distinct types of risk: individual or specific risks which are uncorrelated with the risks facing their neighbours, and area-wide risks faced by all the people in a certain area. Insurance can deal with individual risks (sickness, death), with the usual instruments of premium payment and risk pooling among a larger group of people. However, area-wide risks or covariant risks cannot be insured by a local insurer, as the disaster hits all the people and the claims exceed the insurance fund.[10]

This paper analyses landlord–tenant relationships in the central Luzon plain in the 1920s and 1930s, with a brief excursion to the 1950s and 1960s, at both the macro- and the micro-levels. At the

[8] Kerkvliet, *Huk Rebellion*.

[9] Clive Bell, 'A Comparison of Principal–Agent and Bargaining Solutions: The Case of Tenancy Contracts', in Pranab Bardhan (ed.), *The Economic Theory of Agrarian Institutions* (Oxford, 1989), pp. 73–92.

[10] David M. Newbery, 'Agricultural Institutions for Insurance and Stabilization', in Bardhan, *Economic Theory of Agrarian Institutions*, pp. 267–96.

macro-level the wider context imposes constraints on individuals, both tenants and landlords. An important factor is the human ecology of the Central Luzon plain with its long dry season, which creates among sharecroppers the need for credit as an insurance substitute (discussed in the next section). The underdeveloped and distorted markets for land and for capital and credit limited the possibilities for extensive support for sharecroppers (discussed in the third section). The next step is to analyse the interaction between landlord and tenants in terms of the principal–agent model, but with the additional aspect that the landlord plays the game of selection, favouritism, and exclusion with the tenants and to apply this analysis to the development of landlord–tenant relationships in the Central Luzon plain between the 1920s and 1960s (discussed in the fourth section). The main hypothesis, that the tenancy system combined with low productivity in Central Luzon was the cause of widespread poverty and low purchasing power is supported by data on per capita merchandise sales (the fifth section). The last section draws together different lines in the argument (the sixth section).

Ecological Risks and Constraints: The Need for Credit in Semi-Arid Regions

The Philippine islands show considerable variety in climatic conditions and this diversity lies at the basis of the development of agricultural specialization in the regions. The most important climatic element in the humid tropics is rainfall, for it is the most variable in a spatial, seasonal, and temporal sense. Rainfall distribution is the regulator of crop occurrence. The general climate system distinguishes four climate types, with on the one hand a climate type with two pronounced seasons, dry and wet, and on the other a climate type with no dry season, and having rainfall throughout the year but with a pronounced maximum during the north-east monsoon. The two other climate types fall in between these extremes, with varying lengths of the dry and wet seasons.[11]

The different climate types form the basis for very different ecological systems. In areas with a long dry season, farming

[11] Robert E. Huke, *Shadows on the Land: An Economic Geography of the Philippines* (Manila, 1963), pp. 44–51.

families can harvest only one rice or corn crop per year. Agriculture is not very diversified, as few, if any, crops can be grown during the dry season, in the absence of irrigation. Under these ecological conditions, farming families need bridging mechanisms to survive the lean months between the time when the old supplies are depleted and the new harvest comes in. Common bridging mechanisms, in the semi-arid climate type, are animal husbandry (hogs, cows), engaging in local wage labour, seasonal migration to urban areas, and borrowing. In this agrarian system, money and credit play an important role. Rice is both a subsistence and a cash crop, and farming families often have to sell part of their rice crop immediately after the harvest in order to meet pressing household expenditures.

Such a semi-arid region is found in the inner part of the Central Luzon plain, with a long six to seven months dry season. Aside from this regular pattern of a long dry season, the climate brings several risks. One of these was that the dates of rainfall onset and recession are variable in the islands, particularly in the leeward side of the mountains, such as the Central Luzon plain. Late onset of the rainy season, long dry spells, and an early recession can reduce the harvest significantly. The typhoons passing the islands during the months of August through December, with heavy winds and much rainfall, can severely damage the crops. Finally there are extensive draughts, once in three to five years, as a result of the El Niño climatic disturbance, ravaging the crops. These climatic conditions warrant the characterization of the Central Luzon plain as a risky environment.

Originally the area was a vast tropical rainforest with extensive swamps and lakes and some grasslands as a result of shifting cultivation, and it was opened up from the middle of the nineteenth century till the 1920s. Tagalog settlers migrating from the south and Ilocano settlers from the north cleared forest and grassland and turned it into rice fields. Wet rice cultivation requires more labour than other crops, the initial field preparation is time-consuming, and cultivation and harvesting require much labour. The pioneer farming families cultivated fields of three to five hectares. During the first decades of the twentieth century, parts of the Central Luzon plain, particularly the provinces Bulacan, Tarlac, Nueva Ecija, and Pangasinan, developed into a rice monocrop region, while Pampanga and part of Tarlac were largely devoted to sugar cane cultivation.[12]

The settlers who had carried out the monumental task of clearing the land, were robbed of the fruits of their work. The system of land laws in the Philippine islands consisted of a mixture of Spanish and American regulations, managed by a small bureaucratic apparatus. Under this system registration of land titles was very difficult and tedious. The system favoured large land claims over small ones. The result was that large parts of the land which had been opened up and cultivated by small holders were claimed and appropriated by politically powerful landlords. From the mid-1910s onward, this process of massive landgrabbing led to the emergence of large haciendas and scattered landed property in the Central Luzon plain. Both the haciendas and the large landholdings were cultivated under the sharecropping system, in which the sharecropper cultivated a family farm of around three hectares.

Agriculture in the Central Luzon plain was mainly rainfed. A few irrigation systems were constructed during the 1920s and 1930s, providing irrigation water to relatively small areas. These systems mainly functioned to regulate the flow of water during the rainy season. Storage tanks or lakes to provide water during the dry season were not constructed. It was only in the early 1970s, with the construction of the Pantabangan dam and reservoir, linking up with an extensive system of canals in the plain, that dry-season irrigation was made possible.

From the 1920s onward rice production in the Central Luzon plain increased steadily, mainly as a result of acreage expansion. The Central Luzon plain became the rice granary of the Philippines, exporting increasing amounts of rice via Manila to other parts of the country. And this meant that substantial money payments flowed to the rice producers.

However, productivity (production per hectare) did not go up between the 1920s and the early 1960s. For the Philippines as a whole, average production was around 1,000 kg of paddy per hectare per harvest; for the province of Nueva Ecija in the Central

[12] M.S. McLennan, *The Central Luzon Plain: Land and Society on the Inland Frontier* (Quezon City, 1981).

Luzon plain, the figure was about 1,800–2,000 kg of paddy.[13] There was not much that could be done to increase productivity, except the basic measures of proper farming methods. Fertilizer did not increase the yield of traditional varieties. The application of fertilizer would only result in the plants making more leaf, not more grain. More leaf would cause more lodging as the tall droopy-leafed tropical indica rice varieties would become top heavy with leaf, and then catch more wind and fall down. Mutual shading of heavy leafed plants would also reduce yield by restricting photosynthesis. It was only the modern high-yielding varieties, which appeared on the scene from the late 1960s onward, that were responsive to fertilizer and particularly to nitrogen. From that time on productivity curves showed an upward trend.[14]

Traditional rice cultivation was subject to serious harvest risks. Typhoons and floods during the rainy season could cause significant damage to the crops in the field. As the traditional indica varieties were photoperiod sensitive, which means that their growth duration varied with the length of the daylight period, they had fixed harvesting dates independent of the planting date. The early varieties had to be harvested in the beginning of November, the common varieties were harvested by the end of November, and the late varieties were harvested in late December or early January. The middle season varieties had their pollination period in the first half of November, with the risk that a typhoon would disturb that process, resulting in a much lower paddy yield.[15]

Under the system prevailing in the Central Luzon plain both landlords and tenants were constrained by the seasonal cycle. For the large landlords, investment possibilities in the Central Luzon plain were limited. They could try to acquire more land, but by the late 1920s the region had lost its frontier character and there was hardly any wasteland left. Landlords who had acquired hundreds and sometimes thousands of hectares of rice land had to provide their tenants with loans, not only during the planting season, but

[13] Percy Hill, 'The Rice Industry', *The American Chamber of Commerce Journal* [hereafter: *ACCJ*], 6, 7 (1926), p. 22.

[14] I gratefully acknowledge information and advice given by Dr Brian Fegan, 18 November 2000.

[15] Percy A. Hill and Kilmer O. Moe, 'The Cultivation of Rice', *A Handbook of Rice Cultivation* (Manila, 1917), reprinted in *Journal of East Asiatic Studies*, 9, 4 (1960), pp. 90–134.

also during the following months, to tide them over to the next harvest season.

The sharecroppers were confronted with a long season with virtually no income, as well as serious harvest risks. The rice harvest took place in November–December, at the beginning of the six-months dry season. If the harvest was good, the farming family still had rice supplies for daily subsistence, during the first few months, but after the planting season had started in June at the beginning of the wet season, supplies ran low. The months of August till October, just before the new harvest came in, were months of scarcity and starvation. It was during these months that the sharecropping families were crucially dependent upon credit as a bridging mechanism.

Limited Development of the Financial System

Generally speaking, a monetary economy consists of two sectors or complexes, viz., the exchange system, in which goods and services are transacted for money, and the financial system or pure-money complex, in which transactions are performed in terms of time and money. The financial system is a set of institutions that perform the function of making money available to transactors in the economy, and providing markets for the various monetary instruments used in that particular economy. These institutions have been developed in the course of time, and during the twentieth century one finds among them banks, stock markets, and markets for negotiable instruments. It is not sufficient to define money solely as a means of exchange, and to characterize an economy as an exchange system. The financial system is an essential function of any economy and the exchange economy is subordinate to the pure-money complex.[16]

In the Philippines, the financial system was put on a new footing when the American government created a new monetary system based on the principle of a gold-exchange fund, with the theoretical gold peso as the unit of account. The peso was linked to the American dollar, at a fixed rate of two pesos to the dollar. This system put an end to the confusing monetary situation in the islands where various silver coins of different value circulated, and which could not be controlled by the government. The new

[16] Thomas Crump, *The Phenomenon of Money* (London, 1981).

monetary system was state controlled and this opened the possibility for a more flexible money system, which could respond to the fluctuating demands from business in this monsoon ecology. As the colonial state guaranteed the gold exchange system, the currency could be fiduciary money, with silver peso coins, treasury and bank notes, and bank deposits. In principle the system allowed for the creation of credit on a much larger scale than the previous silver bullion system.

In the capitalist core countries in the Western world and in international trade, credit had expanded enormously since the sixteenth century with the use of negotiable instruments, such as bills of exchange and promissory notes. With these modern business practices a debt was no longer a personal relationship between the creditor and the debtor, but became a piece of paper which could circulate for some time and function as money. The increased use of credit with the help of these instruments was not only an adjustment to the needs of business, but it became a production factor in its own right. The use of negotiable instruments is only possible when there is enough trust among business people that promises will be honoured and that the bills will be generally accepted.

In this new monetary system the institutions of the pure-money complex were located in Manila with adjuncts in secondary harbours, and the complex itself functioned primarily at the service of the export and import economy, the national government agencies, the world of banking, and the higher strata of the urban bourgeoisie. The institutions, and particularly the banking services, were not extended to the countryside. The reason for this can be explained as follows.[17] In the rural areas the income of the population, and the per capita amount of money circulating are so low, that the transaction costs for a modern banking institution are very high. The costs of extending the institutions of the national pure-money complex into the rural areas is prohibitive. Informal moneylenders can survive because they do not have the same overhead costs as banks and they are content with a lower annual income than bank officials.

Economists are expressing this view when they say that in developing countries the markets for capital and credit are

[17] Ibid., pp. 221–4.

underdeveloped, inadequately formed, or incomplete. Pranab Bardhan has pointed out that inadequately formed markets are characterized by the absence of prices and interest rates for loans and services, while implicit interest rates often differ between different loan transactions. Bardhan argues that this causes high transaction costs, and that the solution to this problem is often found in personal ties between the transacting agents. In other words, inadequately formed credit markets bring about personal ties and dependency relationships in the labour market. The reason why capital and credit markets have remained incomplete for a long time is that the basic institutions on which contracts in these markets depend have not been developed. In this respect we can think of institutions such as a system of well-defined and enforceable property rights, a court system for the enforcement of contracts, and bankruptcy laws which guide the demise of failing firms. In other words, the state does not enforce the law and among the population there is a general atmosphere of distrust, unless specific persons engage in a personal relationship.[18]

During the period under discussion the Philippines fitted this description. The Philippine economic system gave considerable scope for all kinds of opportunistic behaviour (cheating, shirking, moral hazard) that was difficult to monitor and control. A tradition dating from the Spanish period still exerted some influence on loan repayment. The laws of the Indias stipulated that no Filipino could be held liable for the repayment of any loan above 25 dollars. Originally the law intended to protect the natives from falling into the hands of rapacious moneylenders. In practice, the system was counterproductive because it prevented the loaning of money to Philippine agriculturists, because moneylenders were reluctant to lend money to people who could invoke the law of the Indias to evade repayment. During the Spanish regime, pleas to have the laws repealed were without result, as the religious orders successfully resisted all attempts at amendment.[19] During the 1880s, several foreign merchant houses collapsed because they had lent money to producers who invoked the law of the Indias to dodge their obligations. During the 1870s, it was reported that European

[18] Pranab K. Bardhan, *Land, Labor, and Rural Poverty: Essays in Development Economics* (New York, 1984), p. 159.

[19] Antonio M. Regidor y Jurado and J. Warren T. Mason, *Commercial Progress in the Philippine Islands* (London, 1905), p. 25.

traders were not interested in starting plantations for the cultivation of cash crops, because it was well-known that labourers who had been given advance money, would not show up for work and that the Spanish government was unwilling to exert pressure or to punish workers who failed to fulfil their contracts.[20]

Negotiable instruments were used in the sector of trade and commerce. The few banks that were around during the late Spanish and early American administration granted loans to traders on the basis of supplies of export products. A trader who had stored agricultural produce in a warehouse for a couple of months could get credit from the bank on the basis of the warehouse receipt, called *quedan*, from the first words of the sentence '*Queda en nuestro poder la cantidad de . . .*' ('there remains in our possession the amount of . . .'). These *quedan* were negotiable and could circulate among the business community. The American administration regulated the use of negotiable instruments by law in 1911, by recognizing four types of promissory notes, viz., bank notes, certificates of deposit, bills of exchange, and government bonds. There were markets for these negotiable instruments, but they were restricted to the Manila area.[21]

As the use of negotiable instruments was limited, and business firms remained privately owned, credit could only be provided in the form of loans to individuals. This means that special mechanisms had to be designed to ensure contract enforcement and trust enhancement. A general mechanism is to create personal relationships between lender and borrower, based on mutual obligations. Personal ties to some extent offset the asymmetry in the relationship. Personal ties are most effective when they are multi-stranded, i.e. when they are built on several pre-existing social bonds, such as kinship, friendship, political coalition, etc. A similar mechanism can be observed in the more recent phenomenon of interlinked contracts, i.e. the creation of a bundle of contracts that reinforce each other, and prevent opportunism on the side of the debtor. For instance, a paddy trader may engage in an interlinked contract with a farmer, combining a labour or sharecropping contract with a credit relationship whereby the trader supplies the fertilizer and

[20] J.A.B. Wiselius, *Een bezoek aan Manila en omstreken* (The Hague, 1876), pp. 58–9.

[21] Frank Hindman Golay, *Face of Empire: United States–Philippine Relations, 1898–1946* (Quezon City, 1997), pp. 215–17.

other inputs on credit, and the farmer promises to deliver the crop after harvest to the trader.

Before the Pacific War the largest part of credit extended to the trading community was in the form of bank loans, on the basis of real estate titles as collateral. But granting this kind of commercial credit was a risky operation. In Europe and the United States, a system of laws and regulatory agencies protected creditors from fraudulent borrowers. In the Philippines, the laws existing on this point were weak and they were rarely implemented. Bank officials complained that commercial borrowers had the practice to defer payment as much as possible, with delays ranging from a few days to several months. Each of these delays caused a chain of late or non-payments through the commercial system. A system of credit information was absent. The agencies involved with credit, such as banks, mercantile firms, and government bureaus, were disinclined to share information with each other. The Chinese business community preferred to keep most of its business activities secret. In the mid-1930s, a ledger exchange bureau was established with the purpose of compiling reports by member agencies on the payment reputation of their clients. However, the bureau had few members and was therefore not efficient.[22]

For a long time the banking system was only interested in providing support to agricultural sectors producing export crops. From the early 1920s onward the Philippine National Bank (PNB) had extended huge loans to large firms in the sugar business for the construction of centrifugal sugar mills. The PNB and other private banks had always financed trade in export products and they also financed coconut processing factories. It was only in 1933 that the PNB started to look at the rice sector and initiated a programme for small-scale agricultural loans. For this purpose the bank opened agencies in the various provinces. These agencies were allowed to lend money to small farmers on the basis of land as security for the loan. Within a few years a large number of agencies had been established all over the country. However, during the 1930s the coverage was still very small, with less than 1 per cent of the farmers reached.[23]

[22] Rufino Manotok, 'Credit and its Importance', *The Philippine Journal of Commerce*, 16, 3 (1936), pp. 11, 12, 24.

[23] Pablo N. Mabbun, 'Farm Credit in Aparri, Cagayan', *The Philippine Agriculturist*, 25, 6 (1936), pp. 493–506.

It was only in the 1950s and 1960s that private rural banks were established in the rural areas, usually on the initiative of local landowning families. The purpose of these banks was to attract savings in the local setting and to provide loans to farmers. In the course of time these banks have provided credit to landowners, on the basis of strict collateral requirements, but never on a large scale. Although by the early 1980s the number of rural banks had grown to almost 1,000, most of these banks have never been very successful, often as a result of mismanagement and fraud, and in 1986 policy-makers had to draw the conclusion that most of these banks were no longer financially viable.

The economists Binswanger and Rosenzweig have pointed out that banks in rural areas exhibit a structural weakness for two reasons.[24] The first one is the problem of seasonality and synchronic timing: if depositors and borrowers are both engaged in agricultural production, the depositors will bring their money to the bank after harvest time, at the beginning of the dry season when the banks cannot lend it out, and they will withdraw their funds at the beginning of the new growing season for production purposes, that is at the time that borrowers will want to borrow for production purposes as well. The second reason is that co-variance of yield risk leads to covariance of default risk. If the crop fails in one year, most depositors will find that they have low incomes and will want to withdraw their deposits. But at that time most borrowers will find it impossible to repay their loans. Rural banks can only function well when they are part of a larger system, with an apex bank at the top, and when they can draw upon funds available from regions with a different agricultural cycle or from central government resources. In the Philippines, an apex system for rural banks never got off the ground.

A more important source of credit for agriculture was traders' credit, not only in the export sector, but also in the food crops sector. During the 1920s Chinese rice traders extended credit on a significant scale to rice producers in the central plain. These loans were not given for production purposes, but were provided to farmers who deposited their paddy in the warehouses of Chinese millers and traders. The purpose of the millers was to have ready supplies at hand to keep their rice mills busy throughout the year.

[24] Binswanger and Rosenzweig, 'Behavioral and Material Determinants', p. 516.

In the town of Cabanatuan, the largest shipping point for paddy and rice in the plain, rice traders spent an amount of more than 7 million pesos to purchase the harvest from January till April. Of this total amount, about 2–3 million pesos was provided in the form of credit against paddy deposits in the warehouses.[25]

The economist Amar Siamwalla has argued that the relationship between credit and marketing ties is often misunderstood. It is often thought that because the advance of credit is temporarily prior to to the marketing of the crop, the credit tie must be the cause of the marketing tie between the farmer and the middleman. However, the causation is the reverse, the marketing tie comes first. It is only when the middleman has acquired control over the marketing operations of the farmer, that he or she is willing to extend credit to the farmers. The credit tie is a consequence of the marketing tie.[26]

This holds true for the Chinese traders in Central Luzon. Chinese rice millers operated in a number of towns in the region, and they were supplied by a wide network of collection traders. During the 1920s the largest part of the rice export from the plain was transported by railroad to Manila, where it entered the rice-trading centre at Tutuban Station, the terminal of the Manila, Railroad, which was controlled by Chinese merchants. From Manila, Chinese wholesalers despatched a large part of the rice to rice-deficit areas in the other islands.[27] The Chinese merchants were also engaged in the importation of rice from Indo-china. In the words of Miller: 'the Chinese have built up a large commercial organization consisting of importers, wholesalers, middlemen, retailers and buyers, and a credit system extending through all of these'.[28]

The Chinese credit stopped in 1930, when the Philippine government enacted the Bonded Rice Warehouse Law, a system whereby a number of licensed warehouses owned by non-Chinese were authorized to receive paddy deposits and to issue warehouse receipts (*quedan*) which could function as negotiable instruments

25 Percy A. Hill, 'The Rice Industry', *ACCJ*, 3, 3 (1923), p. 18; idem, 'The Rice Industry', *ACCJ*, 12, 2 (1932), p. 33.

26 Amar Siamwalla, 'Farmers and Middlemen: Aspects of Agricultural Marketing in Thailand', *Economic Bulletin for Asia and the Pacific*, 24, 1 (1978), pp. 38–50.

27 Miller, *Principles of Economics*, p. 198.

28 Ibid., pp. 544–5.

and could serve as security for bank loans. The purpose of this system was to protect the interests of the farmers and to allow them to borrow money, so that they would not be compelled to sell their rice right after harvest when the supply is abundant and the prices low. The PNB was supposed to provide loans, but did so only on a small scale and at 9 per cent interest. When this system started to operate, the Chinese rice millers stopped their credit operations and from then on, only bought paddy supplies on a cash basis.[29]

The basic reason for this lack of interest on the part of capital owners in the food crop sector was that rice cultivation and rice trading were not profitable undertakings. During the 1920s and 1930s several authors have pointed out that the costs of production in Philippine rice cultivation were high and profit margins consequently small. With fluctuating and, during the early 1930s, declining prices, the costs were sometimes higher than the revenues from rice farming. In other words, farmers who sold their supplies immediately after harvest incurred financial losses. Rice trading yielded limited profits as well. The agriculturist and farmer Percy Hill compared paddy farmgate prices in Central Luzon with rice retail prices in Manila, taking into account the costs for milling, transportation, handling, and marketing, and estimated that net profits for intermediate traders was 3 per cent. He wryly adds the following comment: 'If people want to invest their capital in the industry for 3%, less merchants tax, the way lies open to all.' Apparently only Chinese rice millers and traders were willing to operate on such small profit margins.[30]

Landlord Credit to Tenants

Under these conditions the landlords who had acquired claims and property rights to large tracts of land, and who had to employ sharecroppers to till the land, mainly had to rely on their own resources to finance their tenants. They had income from their share of the paddy harvest, which they could store in the warehouses of Chinese millers, waiting for the higher prices after the harvest. They could avail themselves of loans from Chinese

[29] Percy A. Hill, 'Rice and the Warehouse Law', *ACCJ*, 9, 12 (1929), p. 11; idem, 'The Rice Industry', *ACCJ*, 12, 2 (1932), p. 33.

[30] Percy A. Hill, 'The Rice Industry', *ACCJ*, 11, 7 (1931), p. 23.

warehouse traders, on the basis of their supplies, for relatively short periods of time. They had to provide credit to their tenants, not only for productive purposes, but also for consumption, as the tenant family's income from the harvest share and from additional labour was insufficient to maintain a family with a few children, throughout the year.

Landlords charged interest rates varying from 0 to 200–300 per cent, depending on the period of the agricultural cycle. During the period between preparing the seedbed and planting the fields, the landlord gives an interest-free ration of rice to the family, to be repaid after harvest. Between the time of planting and the harvest, advances of rice or money bear heavy interest. A *terciahan* arrangement requires the payment of four sacks of paddy for every three sacks borrowed, implying a fixed interest rate of 60–117 per cent on a yearly basis, depending on the maturing time of the loan. The *talindua* arrangement requires the payment of three sacks for every two sacks borrowed, implying an interest rate of 48–156 per cent. The *takipan* loan arrangement requires the payment of two sacks for every sack borrowed, implying an interest rate of 155–238 per cent. The *takalanan* arrangement is a cash loan, to be repaid after the harvest with paddy, at an agreed price, usually a fraction of the real market value, implying a 'hidden' interest rate. It should be pointed out that these interest rates apply to the period of a few months until the next harvest.[31]

In the literature on landlord–tenant relationships in the Philippines, these loans have usually been looked at as the salient characteristic of an exploitative and oppressive landlord class. However, Miller has argued that the loans were often a burden to the landlords:

> This advance-and-debt system seems at first sight advantageous to the landlord, since he receives a large rate of interest and is able to hold his tenants. It is really, however, disadvantageous to him, since it compels him to invest all his money in agriculture. Were the hired labourers and the tenants independent of these advances, the landlord classes could invest their money in other enterprises and increase general business activity in the Philippines.[32]

[31] Miller, *Principles of Economics*, pp. 388–9; Orlando J. Sacay, Meliza H. Agabin and Chita Irene E. Tanchoco, *Small Farmer Credit Dilemma* (Metro Manila, 1985).

[32] Miller, *Principles of Economics*, p. 404.

The Central Luzon landowning families had alternative uses for spending the income from their landholdings. The first option was to spend for the education of their numerous children, who were sent to schools in Manila or abroad. A second alternative for spending money was to invest in real estate in Manila, which became fashionable for wealthy and middle class families from the rural areas, from the 1920s onward. A third alternative for spending, viz., investing in urban business enterprises, was probably of limited importance for landowners from the rice-producing areas.

Looking at the landlord–tenant relationships in the Philippines over a longer period, from the 1920s till the 1970s, it is clear that the financial capabilities of the landlords changed over time and fluctuated with the economic conjuncture. For instance, paddy prices were relatively high in the first half of the 1920s, but started to decline in the second half, and reached very low levels during the Depression years in the first half of the 1930s. In the 1950s, prices showed a downward trend again, only to move upward again in the 1960s. From the 1950s onward, new sources of agricultural financing came into existence, providing credit to landlords as well as tenants. These changing conditions influenced the patterns of lending in the rice sector.

In general we can hypothesize that the low productivity in the rice sector in the Philippines, combined with often low prices for paddy and rice in the markets, limited the capability of landlords to provide much credit to their tenants. This general proposition can be tested with data on incomes and prices.

We can make a rough calculation of the incomes of landlords and tenants in Nueva Ecija in the mid-1930s, using a detailed model of costs and yields, presented by an anonymous Philippine agriculturist.[33] We can eliminate the size of the landlord holdings, by focusing on the landlord's income per tenant family. We then postulate the following assumptions. A typical tenant family consists of six persons, both adults and children, which is in consumer terms equivalent to 4.4 units of adult equivalent consumers. The tenant family cultivates 3 hectares of rice land (the average in Nueva Ecija), yielding one rice crop per year, which is shared on a 50–50 basis with the landlord. The average yield is

[33] 'Relations of Landowner and Tenant', *The Philippine Journal of Commerce*, 16, 4 (1936), pp. 14, 15, 18.

46 sacks (of 44 kg each) of paddy per hectare, or slightly over 2,000 kg of paddy (the average for Nueva Ecija). We further assume that the price of one sack of paddy is 2.50 pesos (normal year 1936). The costs of production are estimated at 18.13 pesos per hectare for the landlord and 12.50 pesos for the tenant.

The income for the landlord then can be calculated as follows. Landlord's share per hectare is one half of 46 sacks, that is 23 sacks of paddy, at 2.50 pesos per sack, yielding a total of 57.50 pesos. Expenses at 18.13 pesos should be deducted, leaving a net result of 39.37 pesos. For the 3 hectare tenant farm the landlord's income is 118.11 pesos per year. It can be pointed out that if the landlord would have sold the land (value 300 pesos per hectare) and put the money in the bank at 6 per cent interest, his interest would have been 18 pesos per hectare, and for the 3 hectare tenant holding 54 pesos. This means that the landlord's administrative or management earnings are 118.11 pesos minus 54 pesos, which is equal to 64.11 pesos.[34]

The tenant family's income per hectare from the farm, is 23 sacks of paddy at 2.50 peso per sack, i.e. in total 57.50 pesos. Expenses per hectare are 12.50 pesos, leaving a net result of 45 pesos per hectare or 135 pesos for the farm. Aside from this income from the farm the tenant family often earned income from wage labour, estimated at about 70 pesos, making a total family income of about 200 pesos per year.

Costs of living for a tenant family include rice consumption, calculated at 4.4 consumption units, each consuming three sacks (at 57 kg) of clean rice per year (168 kg of rice is the standard consumption of an adult), at a price of 6 pesos per sack, making a total of almost 80 pesos per year. As the farm does not produce other agricultural products, food has to be purchased at local stores. In addition there is the need for clothes, education, the purchase or repair of household utensils and farm implements, etc. It is estimated that these additional expenses amounted to 200 pesos per year,[35] or a total of 280 pesos per year for the whole family. This means that the average tenant family had a negative balance or deficit of at least 80 pesos per year. As the tenant family did not have other sources of income it had to borrow this amount, or part of it, during the year.

[34] Ibid., p. 18.

[35] Kerkvliet, *Huk Rebellion*, pp. 12–13.

However, if we look at the landlord's income from this 3 hectare tenant holding, it is doubtful whether the landlord would have had the means or the willingness to lend to the tenant family the total amount of its deficit. The landlord's total income from this holding was 118 pesos, while the tenant family's deficit amounted to 80 pesos. It would be realistic to assume that the landlord would not be able and willing to spend of his 118 pesos an amount as large as 80 pesos to give credit to the tenant family.

This is the picture for Nueva Ecija in the 1930s. Nueva Ecija had the highest average yield per hectare in the Philippines, viz., 46 sacks of paddy, or 2,000 kg. Elsewhere the yield was at a much lower level and the average for the Philippines as a whole was about 25 sacks of paddy, or 1,000 kg of paddy. If we make the calculation above for a region with a much lower production per hectare, we get lower incomes for both landlord and tenant. As the tenant family still has the above-mentioned parameters, in terms of income pattern and consumer units, the deficit is higher than the 80 pesos in the example above. The landlord, with a much lower income from the tenant holding, is less capable of financing the deficit.

It should be noted that landlord credit was graded. Production loans were provided free of interest, but the burden was shared equally between both parties. Also part of the consumption loans was given free of charge, during the first few months of the cultivation period. After that period higher interest was charged for consumption loans until harvest time. Contemporary observers considered these exorbitant interest rates as a form of usury and saw them as exploitation and oppression. Later authors supposed that moneylending was an additional source of income to the landlords.

The high interest rates on credit have drawn the attention of policy-makers, economists, and practitioners, both during the colonial period and after Independence. The popular view contends that interest rates are high because informal lenders are a powerful group able to make monopoly or usury profits. This is the hypothesis of the moneylender's *monopoly power*. The lender is supposed to be perfectly exploitative, in total control of the situation, and therefore able to charge whatever interest rate he or she likes, and able to collect both the loans and the charges. This hypothesis has been refuted on both logical and empirical grounds. The Indian economist Kaushik Basu has pointed out the logical and theoretical contradiction of this statement: a market with a perfectly exploitative lender is efficient, and this feature would attract outside capital and the market would become competitive. But a competitive market would not allow the creation of monopoly positions. Moreover, the hypothesis of an efficient money market is not in accordance with the widespread view that these markets are inefficient. Basu writes: 'A corollary of this proposition is that if the credit market is inefficient then the money-lender must be less than fully exploitative.'[36]

Empirical observations also invalidate the *monopoly-power* hypothesis. Basu shows in his theoretical model that: 'If one agent can ensure, under all circumstances, that the other will get no more than his fixed reservation utility, then it is in his interest to maximise output because that would maximise his own share.'[37] In the Philippines during the 1920s and 1930s, landlords in the rice sector were not interested in maximizing total production of their rice lands, and hardly took any steps to introduce better farming methods.

An alternative explanation is the *lender's risk-hypothesis*, proposed by the agricultural economist Anthony Bottomley. According to this hypothesis, when a rural lender gives credit, he or she runs the risk that the borrower will default and this increases the costs of lending. If we deduct the costs from the nominal interest rate, we get the effective interest rate, which is much lower.[38]

The lender's risk hypothesis finds some empirical support in research material from the Philippines. This explanation has already been suggested in the 1920s by the agricultural economists Evett Hester and Mabbun, who wrote that high interest rates were a protection against the risk of default.[39] In the mid-1950s Leopoldo de Guzman showed, on the basis of a large survey among farmers that the percentage of loans that were never repaid was 24 per cent.[40] The Philippine economist Benjamin Quiñones

[36] Kaushik Basu, 'Rural Credit Markets: The Structure of Interest Rates, Exploitation, and Efficiency', in Bardhan, *Economic Theory of Institutions*, pp. 147–65.

[37] Ibid., p.150.

[38] Anthony Bottomley, 'The Premium for Risk as a Determinant of Interest Rates in Underdeveloped Rural Areas', *Quarterly Journal of Economics*, 77 (1963), pp. 637–47.

[39] Hester et al., 'Some Economic and Social Aspects'.

[40] Leopoldo P. de Guzman, 'An Economic Analysis of the Methods of Farm Financing Used on 5144 Farms', *The Philippine Agriculturist*, 41, 8 (1958), pp. 460–78.

has tested the various hypotheses concerning interest rates using survey material from the late 1970s on informal loans to rice farmers. He rejects the monopoly-power hypotheses and instead hypothesizes that administrative cost, cost of fund, and risk premium are the major components of interest rates on informal loans. Among these components, *risk premium* is the most substantial. Lenders are shown to run a high risk that the borrower does not repay the loan, or does not repay in time. Quiñones is able to confirm these hypotheses on the basis of his survey material.[41]

A notable feature of landlord–tenant systems is that tenants constitute a heterogeneous group. From the point of view of the landlord there are old and trusted tenant families versus newcomers, loyal clients versus notorious troublemakers. The landlord does not maintain patron–client relations with all of his or her tenants, only a handful is trusted and favoured, and others are treated with more distance. Credit allocation is an important instrument of control. Landlords tend to be selective in providing loans, by patronizing some and excluding others.

However, this policy of discriminating between potential borrowers can create dissatisfaction and dissent among the tenants if it is done openly. Basu hypothesizes that if a lender wants to charge two borrowers different interest rates, he will have to couch it in some *universalizable* principle. This can be done when the people's need for credit varies over time. And when the lender cannot charge a certain tenant less on personal grounds, he can make the interest rate depend on the length of time for which the loan is taken. In doing this, he can indirectly impose a lower charge on the favoured tenant.[42]

Two general features of informal credit, therefore, are: (a) short-time loans entail higher interest rates than long-term loans; and (b) smaller loans entail higher interest rates than larger loans. Kaushik Basu has tried to prove these theorems on theoretical grounds. For the Philippines these correlations have been empirically demonstrated by De Guzman on the basis of an extensive survey of a large sample of farmers carried out in 1954–5. The

[41] Benjamin R. Quiñones, 'Explaining Variations in Interest Rate in Informal Rural Financial Markets in the Philippines' (Ph.D. thesis, University of the Philippines at Los Baños, 1982).

[42] Basu, 'Rural Credit Markets', p. 154.

material clearly shows inverse relationships between the period of the loan and the interest rate and the size of the loan and the interest rate: short-term loans below 20 pesos had an average interest rate of 55.4 per cent per annum; long-term loans above 500 pesos had an average interest rate of 14.4 per cent.[43]

The picture of traditional landlord largesse as part of patron–client relations is not correct. On average, landlords gave small amounts of loans, varying from small amounts at zero interest, and small amounts at high interest rates to larger amounts at lower interest rates. Landlords favoured some tenants and excluded others in this credit allocation. This picture emerges from surveys from the 1920s through the 1960s. Hester and Mabbun (1924) who summarized the results of eight surveys held in the years 1921 and 1922 among tenants, found that 52 per cent of the tenants were encumbered with loans, with an average of 52 pesos per tenant family, but varying from 12 to 100 pesos per tenant. Of these loans 84 per cent were from the landlord, the rest from other persons. Of the loans, 60 per cent were classified as consumptive and 40 per cent as productive.[44] During the 1930s indebtedness among tenants increased significantly and there was widespread unrest and dissent about usurious interest rates.[45]

Low Purchasing Power as an Indicator of Poverty in the Rice Region

This paper's main proposition is that in the Central Luzon plain landlords were not able or willing to perform their supposed role as patrons in such a way that they would provide sufficient credit to their tenants to help them bridge the long period of scarcity and income deficits. This means that the tenant population in the plain, constituting the majority of the population, had a very low level of purchasing power. This proposition can be tested with the help of data on merchandise sales in the pre-War period. In order to highlight the position of the population in the plain, we will compare these data for different crop regions.

[43] De Guzman, 'An Economic Analysis', pp. 471–3.

[44] Hester et al., 'Some Economic and Social Aspects'.

[45] *Fact-Finding Survey Report* (Manila: Department of Labor, 1936–7), pp. 217–35.

The indicator used is the merchandise sales per capita for several provinces for a number of years, viz., 1918, 1928, 1934, and 1936. The Bureau of Internal Revenue collected data on merchandise sales, because a sales tax was levied on sales by manufacturers and peddlers who had gross annual sales of at least 200 pesos. Although these data are not absolutely reliable, and although they include both sales of produce and of consumer items, they provide a rough indication of the degree of prosperity in an area. Dividing the provincial figure of merchandise sales for a certain year by the population figure for that year, the resulting figure of merchandise sales per capita is obtained.

We created three cropping regions, by selecting for each crop (coconuts, sugar, and rice) three provinces which had a very strong specialization in that crop. We decided to omit provinces with mixed cropping patterns, and to focus as much as possible on pure cases, in order to show the income effect of each specific cropping system. The coconut provinces are mainly located on the eastern side of the archipelago, where rainfall is more or less spread out over the year, or with a short (at most two months) dry period. Consequently the coconut regions have a high degree of mixed cropping, with corn, fruits, and vegetables growing between the coconut trees. Sugar cane is grown in areas with a longer dry period, as the crop needs an extended dry period. The three provinces selected were almost sugar-cane-monocrop areas before the War. For the rice region we have selected three provinces from the Central Luzon plain. In this rice-monocrop region with only one rice harvest, both mixed cropping and a second crop were absent.

The results of this exercise are shown in Table 8.1. The figures show that in 1918, per capita merchandise sales were much higher in the coconut provinces than in the sugar and rice areas. In 1928 the prices for coconut products were on the decline, and the income in the coconut provinces went down, which shows in the reduced level of per capita merchandise sales. During the economic crisis of the 1930s the income in all three cropping regions went down, as indicated by the declining levels of per capita merchandise sales.

The salient feature of this comparison is that the rice regions systematically had the lowest level of per capita merchandise sales, indicating very low levels of per capita purchasing power. This confirms the picture of extreme poverty in these regions, that emerges from other sources as well.

TABLE 8.1: Average per capita merchandise sales, by crop region and by province, for the years 1918, 1928, 1934, and 1936

(in pesos)

	1918	1928	1934	1936
Coconut region				
Tayabas	123	81	19	24
Samar	88	40	8	11
Misamis	90	49	15	20
Average	100	57	14	18
Sugar region				
Negros Occ.	23	41	32	37
Pampanga	26	21	12	11
Tarlac	34	30	16	17
Average	28	31	20	22
Paddy/rice region				
Nueva Ecija	23	27	11	13
Pangasinan	21	19	8	3
Bulacan	35	21	11	10
Average	26	22	10	9

Sources: For 1918: merchandise sales from *Statistical Bulletin of the Philippine Islands, 1920*, 3 (1921), pp. 208–9; population figures from the 1918 Philippine Census, quoted in *Statistical Bulletin of the Philippine Islands, 1929*, 12 (1930), Table 1. For 1928: merchandise sales from *Statistical Bulletin of the Philippine Islands, 1928*, 11 (1929), p. 165, Table 102; population figures from *Yearbook of Philippine Statistics, 1946* (Manila: Bureau of the Census and Statistics, 1947), Ch. 2, Table 10. For 1934: merchandise sales from *Philippine Statistical Review, 2, 1* (1935), p. 53; population figures from *Yearbook of Philippine Statistics, 1946*, pp. 11–14. For 1936: merchandise sales from *Philippine Statistical Review*, 4, 1–2 (1937), p. 58; population figures from *Yearbook of Philippine Statistics, 1946*, pp. 11–14. For each province, total merchandise sales have been divided by the population to produce per capita figures.

Conclusion

An extensive literature on production relationships in agriculture casts landlord–tenant relationships in the mold of patron–client ties and attributes to patrons in traditional society benevolent attitudes towards their clients. Patrons are supposed to help their clients in times of need and to extend credit during the lean season and crisis periods. This is also a general view of rural conditions in the Central Luzon plain in the Philippines, before the Pacific War. This paper argues that this view is not correct, as it overestimates the capability and the willingness of traditional rural patrons to provide assistance and credit.

The rice economy which developed in the Central Luzon plain since the 1910s, was a monocrop ecology in a semi-arid climate zone, allowing for one rice crop per year, with relatively low yields of paddy per hectare. The whole region was characterized by high tenancy (sharecropping) rates, and the landlord–tenant relationship became the dominant labour relationship until the early 1970s. Tenants were vulnerable to various kinds of income risk and they had to cope with a long period without income. They were dependent on landlords to provide them with loans to bridge this period.

In the literature on landlord–tenant relationships, one finds contradictory characterizations of these ties. During the 1920s and 1930s, authors emphasized the prevalence of usury and exploitation, but in anthropological studies of the 1970s these relationships have been depicted as rather benevolent patron–client relationships, with the landlord in the role of patron, providing insurance and support to the tenants in times of need, although they lost that function in later times. The question then is, to what extent have landlords been able to provide credit to their tenants.

This paper argues that landlords have never supplied much credit to their tenants and that they have not provided the insurance needed and expected. The traditional picture of benevolent patrons taking care of their clients, and supporting them in their needs, is not correct. Landlords were selective in their dealings with tenants, and provided credit without or with low interest rates to a few loyal clients, but charged high interest rates to others, or excluded them from the credit flow.

The main reason for this situation is that rice cultivation was not a very profitable business. Paddy yields per hectare have remained very low from the 1920s through the 1960s, with a national average of 1,000 kg of paddy nationally, and an exceptionally high level of 2,000 kg of paddy per hectare in the province of Nueva Ecija only. Irrigation facilities were virtually absent in the Central Luzon plain. Under these conditions landlord families did not have much capital available for financing their tenants. Landlord families had other use for the money earned from their landholdings, viz., investment in the education of their children and the purchase of real estate in Manila. A rural banking system which could absorb rural savings, did not come into being before the 1950s, and it was never very successful.

Connections

9

The Hosay Massacre of 1884: Class and Community among Indian Immigrant Labourers in Trinidad

Prabhu P. Mohapatra

In the afternoon of 30 October 1884, the tenth day of the month of Muharram, processions of Indian labourers made their way along the three main roads that passed through the cane fields and sugar estates, finally converging on the town of San Fernando in South Trinidad.[1] The processions marked the high point of the

* A version of this essay was presented at the Conference on 'South Asian Labour: Linkages Global and Local' held at the International Institute of Social History, Amsterdam, in October 1995. I am grateful to the conference's participants and especially Dirk Kolff for their comments. This essay in its present form owes much, in style and substance, to Catherine Le Grand's extensive and generous suggestions. My colleagues at the Research Centre 'Religion and Society' at the University of Amsterdam, Gerd Baumann, Patricia Spyer, Peter van Rooden, and Peter Pels, heard and read this paper with patience and encouraged me. I have benefited from the criticism of this paper by Dharma Kumar, Madhavan Palat, Ricardo Salvatore, and Suvritta Khatri. Archival research and fieldwork for this paper in Trinidad and London was made possible by research grants from the International Institute of Asian Studies, Leiden and the Wenner Gren Foundation of Anthropology, New York.

[1] The description of the Hosay festival and the shooting incident presented in the next few paragraphs are culled largely from *Correspondence respecting the Recent Coolie Disturbances in Trinidad at the Mohurrum Festival and with the Report thereon, by Sir H.W. Norman* (London, 1885) [hereafter *Norman Report*]. The best source for the Hosay Massacre to date is Kelvin Singh's documentary history of the incident with a long introductory essay and several extracts from contemporary newspapers and the *Norman Report*: *Blood Stained Tombs: The Muharram Massacre 1884* (London and Bangkok, 1988).

observance of Muharram, when the estates of the Naparima area brought out their *taziyas* or replicas of the tombs of Hussain and Hassan, the martyred grandsons of the Prophet. Carried on the shoulders of the devout or wheeled on carts, these *taziyas* were followed by crowds of labourers resident on the estates and residents of nearby villages. Accompanied by the resounding beats of the *tassa* drums, expert stick players displayed intricate skills of fencing avidly watched by their compatriots and other spectators. The processions were periodically interrupted with shouts and cries of 'Hosay Hosay' (the creolized version of the lamenting chant of 'Hai Hasan Hai Hussain'). This cry gave the festival its name; the replica of tombs (*taziyas*) were also called Hosay. The women in the processions threw rice on the *taziyas* and sang *mersiahs*, lamenting the deaths of Hussain and Hassan and mourning their martyrdom and the defeat of Hussain in the battlefield of Kerbala.

Much preparation had gone into the *taziyas* and making the processions a success. The estates formed the nuclei for the celebration of the festival, and labourers in each estate had pooled their resources to build the *taziyas*. On each estate on the first day of the month of Muharram, sacred earth from a designated spot had been dug and placed on a mound where a lamp was lit that would remain unextinguished till the end of the ten-day ceremony. Great artistic pride was taken in the building of the *taziyas* and their decorations. From the seventh night onwards, groups of labourers of each estate had gone out to the public roads with various Hosay memorabilia, mainly flags of different colours representing the martyrs and the estates. Fencing with fire sticks, mock stick play, and drum beating went on through the night. On these 'flag nights' it was customary for the flags of estates to touch each other, symbolically uniting the estates into a spiritual community. But the most spectacular display was reserved for the tenth and final day of the procession, when the *taziyas* or Hosays, magnificent multistoried cenotaphs of the martyrs, were brought out into the public road and displayed for the first time outside the estates. Each estate had been allotted a position in the grand procession that slowly made its way along the main road to San Fernando. This grand procession, when the *taziyas* (some of them as high as 30 or 40 feet) were displayed to public gaze, was the most important part of the Muharram celebration in the West

Indies. The procession that year, as in every year since 1855, when Hosay was first celebrated in Trinidad, headed towards the San Fernando wharf.[2] After marching through the town the gaily coloured Hosays were to be thrown into the sea, marking both the ritual end to the ten-day festival and symbolic renewal (since the spirits of Hassan and Hussain would return in the following year).

But the procession of 1884 was taking place in exceptional circumstances: the Government of Trinidad, in a proclamation published on 30 July 1884, and widely circulated among the estates, had banned processions on public roads (except by written permission of the magistrates) and more significantly prohibited their entry into the towns of San Fernando and Port of Spain. Defiance of the regulations merited a fine and imprisonment for six months. The Government was determined to enforce the ban. In September it rejected a petition from the labourers and headmen from 27 estates seeking a withdrawal of the proclamation and permission to enter the town with the immersion procession. Elaborate arrangements were made to enforce the regulation. The flagship HMS Dido had been summoned and anchored off the San Fernando harbour. Eighty armed police and a troop of soldiers from the St James barracks had been stationed in San Fernando alone. Three nights before the final procession, extensive scouting and patrolling had taken place around the estates by Justices of Peace, local planters, and the police. Police armed with 40 rounds of ammunition each, and backed by troops, were stationed at the entrance of the three main roads leading up to the town. Local notables and planters watched anxiously behind the armed contingent.

The processionists were doubtlessly aware of the arrangements made to stop them but seemed determined to carry on their way to San Fernando. Several planters and overseers and a few 'influential' Indian shopkeepers had attempted unsuccessfully to interrupt the procession and persuade the crowd to return to their respective estates. The first to reach San Fernando was the procession from the southern main road at the Les Efforts entrance to the town. A magistrate went towards the advancing crowd, ordered them to

[2] The first *taziya* ever built in Trinidad was in 1855 in the Philippines estate. Traditionally Philippines estate was accorded the pride of place in leading the Hosay procession into San Fernando. K.G. Grant, *My Missionary Memories* (Halifax, 1915), p. 20.

halt, and promptly read the Riot Act: an Act whose significance was completely lost to the intended audience who were shouting 'Hosay Hosay' and carried on with the mock stick fight. When the crowd was about 30 yards from the police line, the magistrate ordered the police to fire. The first shots rang out, the *taziyas* fell, and dead and wounded littered the ground. The rest of the crowd retreated in panic leaving their fallen *taziyas* and their wounded and dead comrades. The news of the shooting spread like wild fire and soon reached the other processions. Yet that seemed not to deter the processionists who moved towards the Mon Repos entrance of the town. It was later reported that on hearing the shots from the Les Efforts gate, some of the processionists refused to believe the news while others defiantly proclaimed: 'Let them [the police] shoot us too. . . . We will go to San Fernando.'[3] An hour later when the procession from the south–west reached the Mon Repos entrance it met the same bloody fate as its counterpart from the south. Here the crowd, though stunned, did not disperse for quite some time. When advised to leave, those in front replied, 'Shoot em all man' (meaning 'let them shoot us all'). The third smaller procession from the north–west direction seemed to have been dispersed without bloodshed.

Casualties were heavy: 120 dead or wounded (this figure does not include persons who received no treatment in the Government hospitals and were thus not recorded). On the day of the shooting 10 died; 6 others died within the next few days, and 6 more over the next few months—a total death toll of at least 22 persons. Furthermore at least 8 persons were maimed for life.[4] This is the heaviest death toll from a civil unrest in Trinidad's history, much higher than during the great strike of 1938 or the *Muslimin coup d'état* in 1990.

Indians had been brought into Trinidad as indentured labourers since 1845. By 1884, roughly 70,000 labourers, the majority of them from the Gangetic plains of India's Eastern United Provinces

[3] Testimony of James Drennnan before Coroner Wilson in *Norman Report*, p. 26.

[4] See note of the Protector of Immigrants, in D.W.D. Commins, *Note on Emigration to Trinidad* (Calcutta, 1891) [hereafter *Commins Note*], p. 42. It is interesting that in the official documents this is the only reference I have found as to the exact number of deaths and permanent injury which occurred during the Hosay shooting in 1884.

and Bihar, had arrived in Trinidad, constituting one-third of Trinidad's total population. In 1881 the bulk of the adult Indian population in Trinidad worked on its 109 sugar estates. A large number of them were indentured and bound to work on the plantations for a period of no less than five years for a fixed wage. While indentured, the workers were regulated by a series of immigration ordinances that penalized breach of contract by imprisonment and fines.[5] Further they were required to reside on the plantations and were punished if found outside the plantations without written permission from a manager or without a certificate exempting them from indenture. As against these restrictions placed on their free mobility the indentured workers were guaranteed a minimum fixed wage (25 cents) to be paid on completion of a task set by the manager. They were provided accommodation (barracks) and medical care on the plantation. A Government appointed Protector of Immigrants and his assistants were charged with their welfare. After a period of five years most Indian labourers still worked as free labourers on the plantations, though a growing number resided outside the plantations and worked as agricultural labourers. A few had acquired property as shopkeepers and bought Crown lands to set up independent farms.

Estimates of the total number who participated in the processions on 30 October 1884 varied. Most witnesses agreed that the number was in the range of 4–5 thousand. While the crowd was definitely smaller than usual it still represented a large proportion (one-third) of the total Indian population (both estate and non-estate) of the Naparima area.[6] Of the 93 injured whose names were recorded, 77 were Hindus, 15 Muslims, and 1 Christian; of the 18 dead (whose names we know) 13 were Hindus and

[5] No less then twenty separate offences were deemed to constitute breach of contract under the immigration ordinances, ranging from desertion to flouting sanitary requirements of the barracks. Most of the offences were related to work performance and related issues of indiscipline and disobedience.

[6] The Government's estimate of the number of participants in the San Fernando procession in 1881 and 1882 was 12,000. For estimates of the total number of participants in 1884, see the evidence of witnesses in the Coroner's enquiry into the shooting in *Norman Report*, pp. 14–18. In 1884, 15,000 Indians resided in Naparima Ward Union. Muslims constituted 16 per cent of the total Indian population in 1891. Calculated from Table XVIII, in Appendix, *Commins Note*, p. XXIX.

TABLE 9.1: Indian Population in Trinidad

Year	Estate		Non-Estate	Total
	Indentured Adults	Free Adults	Adults and Children	
1871	10,616	7,940	8,869	27,425
1881	11,418	10,062	27,340	4,882
1886	9,807	11,552	39,379	60,738
1891	10,782	12,702	42,734	66,228

Source: K.O. Laurence, *A Question of Labour: Indentured Immigration into Trinidad and British Guyana, 1875-1917* (London, 1994), Appendix II, p. 525.

5 Muslims. Of the persons injured and killed, 65 were indentured labourers and a similar number were free labourers.[7] These statistics shed light on the nature of participation in the Hosay of 1884. First, Hosay was clearly an estate based festival of the Indian labourers. Second, the overwhelming majority of participants in Hosay, like in the estate labour force, were Hindus. Finally, free and indentured labourers participated in rough proportion to their total population on the estates.

How do we understand this momentous event in the history of Indian labourers in Trinidad? First, how do we account for the unusual severity of colonial state repression? Second, what caused the Indian labourers to defy the colonial state and why did they choose the Hosay procession as an occasion to do so? Third, why did Hindus and Muslims together die to defend their right to celebrate a Muslim Shi'ite religious festival in Trinidad? It is important to note that in that same year communal conflict between Hindus and Muslims had become intense in several parts of India and increasingly the Muharram festival was an occasion for riots.[8] These questions can only be answered if we locate the significance of the Hosay festival and the procession among the Indian labourers in general and more specifically by careful elaboration of the context in which the festival of 1884 took place. I shall argue that both the intensity of colonial state repression and

[7] Statistics from *Norman Report,* Enclosure No. 7, in No. 10, pp. 86–95.

[8] In 1884 there were three incidents of rioting in India. In Agra a major Hindu-Muslim riot took place, two other incidents of rioting in Surat and Hyderabad happened between Sunnis and Shias. See S. Freitag, *Collective Action and Community: Public Arenas and the Emergence of Communalism in North India* (Berkeley, 1989), Chapter 4 for the Agra riots.

the defiance of the Indian labourers make sense only once we account for the ways in which the Hosay festival expressed the community and class identity of Indian labourers. While the Hosay festival served as a metaphor for the community of Indian labourers, its brutal suppression was a result of the deep-seated class antagonism on the plantations. Contrary to the dominant (official) explanation of the Hosay massacre I shall demonstrate through an analysis of the circumstances in which it took place that the procession of 1884 uniquely articulated the emergent community and class identity of the Indian labourers and that it was perceived as such by the protagonists, viz., the labourers, planters, and the colonial state. But how did the colonial state account for the Hosay massacre of 1884?

The Norman Report

We can begin by examining the official version of the event, the master text of which was the 'Report on Coolie Disturbances on Muharram in Trinidad' authored by Sir Henry Norman, the Governor of Jamaica, and presented to the House of Commons in March 1885. The British parliament asked Norman to conduct an enquiry into the event following questions raised in the legislative body. These questions originated in a letter sent to the Anti-Slavery and Aboriginal Protection Society in London and subsequently published in the *Times*. Written by J. Andre, a former member of the Bombay Civil Services who was resident in Trinidad at the time of the massacre, the letter had condemned the Trinidad Government for shooting down an unarmed mass of labourers in the course of their religious observance of Muharram. Andre had pointed out that, before the festival, there was acute discontent among the estate labourers due to the unilateral increase in task work and reduction of wages on the plantations. This he suggested was at the root of the 'disturbance'.[9] Henry Norman duly arrived on 1 January 1885 with the express object of inquiring into Andre's allegations. He completed his inquiry in seven days after collecting all 'relevant' papers and interviewing 34 persons. His account of the course of events and the causes leading up to the Hosay massacre became the official history of the event. His report was

[9] Letter of J. Andre, 7 November, in *Norman Report*, p. 74.

sufficiently authoritative to quell initial grumbling from the Colonial Office in London.[10]

Norman completely justified the colonial government action—claiming that it was both moderate and unavoidable. He argued that the Hosay procession was not religious in nature and dismissed Andre's allegation that the government interfered with the religious practices of the immigrants. Further he denied that the shooting of processionists had any connection with the sugar crisis, or grievances of the immigrants as a class about ill treatment by the planters or overwork on the estates. Yet his report was both cursory and one-sided in its conclusions. To begin with, he did not even bother to accurately enumerate the number of persons who had been killed in the shooting. According to him, only 12 persons were killed and some of the rest were only slightly wounded.[11] Yet the papers enclosed with his reports showed that 18 persons had already died by the time of his enquiry and four more were on the verge of death.[12] Norman glossed over the fact that the processionists had not attacked any of the numerous scouts patrols,

[10] The first reaction of the secretary of state of the colonies, Lord Derby to the shooting was that the police had been overzealous in enforcing the ban. Another official had commented that there was no evidence that there would have been danger in allowing the Indians to march through San Fernando and that the procession needed to be regulated rather than repressed by shooting more than a hundred people. See Governor of Trinidad's Despatch, 6 November, No. 287, in CO 384/149, Public Record Office [hereafter: PRO]. A Government of India official expressed disquiet over the large number of casualties, lack of preventive action on the part of the police and the absence of any overt attack on the police by the labourers. Minute of C.S. Bayley, 9 January 1885, in Revenue and Agriculture (Emigration), A Proceedings, No. 14–20, February 1885, NAI.

[11] *Norman Report*, p. 41. Later historians have often quoted the figure of 12 deaths provided in Henry Norman's report without checking even the papers enclosed in the report which show clearly that 18 persons were already dead by the time Norman wrote his report. Kelvin Singh cites a figure of 16 deaths in *Blood Stained Tombs*, p. 1. I have traced the death records of 19 persons from newspaper reports but it is clear that three others who were seriously injured had died soon after.

[12] See Letter of the Acting Surgeon General to the Governor of Trinidad, 5 January 1885: Enclosure No. 7 in *Norman Report*, p. 83, which clearly states that 18 fatalities had already occurred by that date. The list of injured and dead enclosed with this letter also shows that the condition of four more was critical and that they were not expected to survive.

Justices of Peace, or the police force that was mustered to oppose them at the entrance of San Fernando. Even though, by going on a procession on public roads, Indian labourers had broken the law, the maximum penalty for that was six months imprisonment, not summary execution. This was repeatedly pointed out to him in the depositions by some Indian labourers and also by J. Andre. Further, Norman did not seriously re-examine the government claim that allowing the procession in the town would have caused greater disturbance and loss of life than the shooting down of the processionists. In the process he did not take notice of the fact that while the government was empowered to regulate the procession and did not need to prohibit it, magistrates had been instructed to prohibit processions on public roads.[13]

The main cause of the confrontation, according to Norman, lay solely with the unreasonable defiance of authority by the Indian immigrants. The increase in absolute numbers of immigrants was matched by the growing insolence of the 'Coolies'. He wrote:

> After a residence of some time in Trinidad the 'Coolie' not only becomes a man of more independent spirit than he was when in India, but according to some reliable evidence, he often becomes somewhat overbearing. There is little doubt that the Indian immigrants looked upon the procession as a sort of means of demonstrating their power.

This unbridled exercise of power by the immigrants was further exacerbated, he argued, by lack of effective authority on the part of the colonial state in the past. Norman believed that 'Coolies have been induced rather to oppose authority, by being at times much indulged by an amount of consideration which could not permanently be extended to them.'[14]

[13] Sir George Campbell, a former Governor of Bengal and a liberal politician in England had pointed to this serious discrepancy in the Government's claim that every facility was provided to the immigrants to hold the procession except access to the cities of Port of Spain and San Fernando. Letter of Sir G. Campbell to Lord Derby, 10 March 1885, in CO 384/158, PRO. See also the Government circular to the stipendiary magistrates explicitly instructing them to disallow any procession, 5 August 1884, in *Norman Report*, p. 5. Rejection of some immigrants' application for taking out the procession on the public roads without entering San Fernando was pointed out in the evidence of the magistrate J.E. Johnstone in the coroner's enquiry, in ibid., p. 16.

[14] *Norman Report*, pp. 46 and 48.

The 'reliable' evidence that Norman presented was provided by officials and missionaries who bemoaned, 'Coolies have been becoming more independent and do not do salaam and so on as they used to do before.' Another said: 'In a childish sort of way the Coolies are overbearing; they required to be treated justly but firmly.'[15] The dominant explanation of the Hosay massacre then lapsed into the familiar colonial language of paternalism—Coolies as children and planters and government as benevolent but disciplining parents. The 'Coolies' who had been overindulged in the past needed to be taught a lesson. The evident crisis of the paternalist mode—that the wayward children had to be shot down *en masse* to bring them back into line—seemed to escape Sir Norman. He ended up reiterating that the immigrants needed to be 'firmly but kindly dealt with', if possible now itself by appointing a Protector with Indian experience.[16]

By assigning a perpetual childhood to the Indian labourers, Norman's explanation sought to restore the paternalist narrative. But it could do so only by denying agency to the Indian labourers and negating the possibilities of an alternative history of community formation and class conflict on the plantations.

Hosay: Religion and Community among Indian Labour

The first issue which Norman had to clarify was of course the ambiguous position of Hosay as a religious festival of the Indian labourers. Though a Muslim Shi'ite festival, Hosay was celebrated by both the Hindus and Muslims in Trinidad (as also in Guyana, Surinam, and Jamaica). Norman chose to resolve this ambiguity by denying any religiosity to the festival. He argued that Hosay could not be a religious festival as: 'although it is purely appertaining to the Mahomedans, is one in which most of the persons engaged in are Hindus, and the whole celebration in Trinidad has long since ceased to have a religious significance'.[17] Interestingly, the multi-religious character of Hosay had been little noticed and commented upon by the officials and planters until the decision to ban the procession was taken in March 1884. In July 1882, when the governor of Trinidad first sought permission from the Colonial

[15] Evidence of Arthur Child and Rev. Hendrie in ibid., pp. 65, 69.
[16] Ibid., p. 48.
[17] Ibid., p. 42.

Office to regulate the festival he did not make the participation of the Hindus in Hosay an issue. To most planters and officials, Hosay was plain and simple 'Coolie religion' and a day of amusement for the Coolies which was to be tolerated.[18] After the decision to ban the procession was taken in March 1884, and especially after the actual shooting in October, the Government, sensitive to the criticism of interfering with the religious practices of Indian labourers, deployed the argument about Hindu participation in the Muslim festival as a justification for its action. During the coroner's enquiry into the shooting, the government attorney sought to establish that the Hosay was not a religious festival. He did so on the basis that most of the participants in it were Hindus and that a section of the Muslims had in fact opposed its celebration. He then cited a petition received in 1881, signed by 107 Muslims who demanded that Hosay be banned as it was a form of idol worship and not prescribed by the Koran. The petition had been inspired by the Presbyterian missionary K.G. Grant.[19] Missionaries had been demanding the suppression of the open idolatry of the Hosay and in some ways worried about the attraction it held for the Creole population who seemed to join in the festival or procession enthusiastically.[20]

The real problem for the government and the planters lay not so much in the multi-religious character of the Hosay as in the nature

[18] See the letter of J. Scott Bushe to the Earl of Kimberley, 20 July 1882. Document No. 1 enclosed in ibid., p. 1. Widespread ignorance as to the religious aspects of Hosay is evidenced in the statement of the Manager of Philippine Estate, the first estate where Hosay was celebrated, in which he refers to the *taziyas* as 'Coolie gods' in ibid., p. 78.

[19] G. Garcia's submission in the verbatim report on the Coroner's Enquiry into the deaths during Hosay in *Port of Spain Gazette* [hereafter: *POSG*], 8 November 1884. See Evidence of J.C. McHugh, in *Norman Report*, p. 58, for the missionary involvement in the petition to ban Hosay.

[20] Creoles participated in the Hosay as spectators, and especially in the procession, as drummers and wheelers of carts, carrying the tabut. There is evidence that some Creole villagers also brought out their own *taziyas*. For such instances in British Guyana in 1873 and 1877, and Christian condemnation of such practices, see H.V. Bronkhurst, *The Colony of British Guiana and its Labouring Population* (London, 1883), pp. 362–4. In Trinidad's carnival, Creole bands imitated the Hosay procession and dressed as Indians with *taziyas*. See the *San Fernando Gazette* [hereafter *SFG*], 4 March 1882, and 10 February 1883.

of the Hosay procession which was viewed, by 1884, as the most threatening part of the festival. As Norman wrote later, the procession was one in which 'Coolies took rum and others smoked ganja or took it in sweetmeat and some would be unamenable to reason'—thus an event of irrational, drunken, and unmanageable revelry. Conflicts between various estates as to precedence in the procession had led to fights among the participants in 1865 and 1881, and were cited as reasons for promulgating the ordinance regulating the festival in 1882. But by 1884, when the regulations were enforced, it was not the internal conflicts between estates so much as the collective display of community power that appeared especially threatening to the planters and the government of the colony. Norman echoed this perception held among planters when he wrote: 'the procession had become the occasion of a sort of national demonstration of rather turbulent character . . . as a sort of means for demonstrating their [Coolie] power'.[21]

In March 1884, after the successful suppression of the carnival's midnight torchlight procession the government was being urged strongly by planters and their allies to ban the Hosay procession from the public roads and towns. In consultation with the leading missionaries, Morton and Hendrie, of the Canadian Presbyterian Mission, the Government now proceeded to distinguish the religious rites of the Hosay from the 'irreligious' procession. Thus the really religious parts of the festival, according to the government, were 'digging of sacred earth, and placing it in the sacred Tomb and its final burial', which were deemed the sole prerogative of the Muslims.[22] These activities could be performed within the confines of the estate. The public manifestation of Hosay where the Hindus and Creoles participated was now deemed irreligious and could be legitimately prohibited. When the ordinances regulating the Hosay celebration were published in July 1884, the non-immigrants, i.e. the Creole population, were banned. Licences for carrying out the religious rites could now be granted only to

[21] *Norman Report*, p. 46.

[22] The decision to ban the Hosay procession had been taken as early as 18 March 1884, in a meeting of the Executive Council in which the two missionaries were invited. The Immigration Department had been instructed to find out from the 'Muhammedan' headmen about the religious rites connected with the Hosay. Ibid., p. 3. The regulation of 30 July 1884, confined Hosay to the Muslims.

the 'Muhammedans', and processions were prohibited from public roads without a permit issued by a magistrate, and banned from entering the towns of San Fernando and Port of Spain.[23]

The denial of Hosay's religious character, especially of its processions, was necessary in order to delegitimize it and, thus, regulate and suppress it. The definition of religion adopted by the state distinguished the religious parts of Hosay from its secular parts, assigning the former only to the Muslims, and suppressing the latter. It stood opposed to the ideas the participants held about the festival. Their ideas were not necessarily all similar but the difference with the state conception of religion in 1884 was very marked indeed.

While Hosay in Trinidad shared many features that were prevalent in the Muharram in India, it had acquired special characteristics in the plantation setting of the colony. A first point to be noted is that in the West Indies, many Indian immigrants irrespective of religious affiliations participated in the Hosay. Thus, the Muharram celebration in Trinidad had little to do with its specific Shi'ite or Muslim origins and had been transformed into an ethnic festival expressive of the community identity of all Indian labourers. This did not mean that Hosay had been thoroughly 'secularized' and was devoid of religious significance for the participants. On the contrary, I shall argue that collective identity expressed through the performance of Hosay acquired strength and depth because of the religious beliefs of the participants. Hosay provided a complex of practices and beliefs that allowed for the expression of a shared sensibility derived from popular religious traditions prevalent in India. The idea of sacredness of the cenotaph, of acquiring merit through participation in the construction, parading, and worship of the *taziyas*, the reverence for the sacred banners and standards were common cultic features shared by low caste, artisanal Hindus and Muslims alike in many parts of India in the nineteenth century.[24]

[23] Full text of the Regulation in ibid., p. 4.

[24] Participation of the Hindus in Muharram in the nineteenth century is well documented. See P.D. Reeves (ed.), *Sleeman in Oudh: An Abridgment of W.H. Sleeman's Journey through the Kingdom of Oudh in 1849–50* (Cambridge, 1971), pp. 158–9. For the curious cult of Muharram among some Brahmins in north India, called the Hussaini Brahmins, see J. Wilson, *Indian Castes* (Bombay, 1877), Vol. II, pp. 29 and 134. For participation of

There is enough evidence to show that Hindus in Trinidad had a strong religious commitment to the Hosay. For instance they seemed to have believed that Hassan and Hussain were reincarnated every year during the Hosay and regarded them as benevolent spirits.[25] In Trinidad, one observer had noted: 'a tendency exists among the Hindus here to treat Hussain and Hassan as Deotas and thus add to their already incalculable number of gods, this fact is evident as small altars on which cock fowls are sacrificed to the two brothers are to be seen at several places in the island'.[26] Similar accounts of image worship of Hussain and Hassan were also noted in Guyana and Jamaica. It was common for the Hindu devotees to erect special *taziyas* as votive offerings for fulfilment of vows.[27]

It is thus not difficult to understand the force of sentiment behind the statement of Omaid, a Hindu labourer of Petit Morne, who told Norman: 'I am Hindu but I join the Hosay as it is the custom of all Coolies to do so in Trinidad.'[28] In this short statement which Norman chose to ignore in his report the labourer was articulating a notion of religion that was strongly inspired by what he perceived to be customary rather than orthodox and scriptural. Even the orthodox sections of Hindus as represented by the

---

Sunnis and Hindus in Muharram in Awadh, see Juan R. Cole, *Roots of North Indian Shi'ism in Iran and Iraq: Religion and State in Awadh, 1722–1859* (Berkeley, 1988), pp. 95–119, and for north India and Deccan, see Jaffar Sharif, *Islam in India or the Qanun-i-Islam*, trans. G.A. Herklots (Madras, 1863), pp. 159, 167. For Muharram's changing form over time in Bombay city, where Hindu participation declined towards the end of the nineteenth century, see J. Masselos, 'Change in Custom and Form of Muharram in Bombay', *South Asia*, new series, December 1982. For accounts of Hindu participation in Muharram in contemporary India, see D. Pinnault, *The Shiites:Ritual and Muslim Piety in a Muslim Community* (London, 1989), pp. 160–3, and A.R Saiyid, 'Ideal and Reality in the Observance of Muharram: A Behavioural Approach', in I. Ahmad (ed.), *Ritual and Religion among Muslims in India* (New Delhi, 1981).

[25] See John Morton's letter to *Trinidad Chronicle*, 11 April 1871.

[26] Letter of A. Weed in *SFG*, 20 January 1883.

[27] In 1923 Beckwith wrote a full anthropological account of Hosay in Jamaica mentioning several instances of votive offerings, and of vowing to provide a child to do service for the *taziya* procession. See M. Beckwith, *The Hussay Festival in Jamaica* (Poughkeepsie, 1923). John Morton refers to similar practices in Trinidad in *Trinidad Chronicle*, 11 April 1871.

[28] *Norman Report*, p. 63.

Babajees, or Brahmin priests, seemed to have regarded the practice of Hosay as perfectly compatible with their beliefs. A group of these Babajees were asked by the Governor in 1883 for their opinion on the banning of the Hosay procession through San Fernando. They unanimously reported that the Coolies would consider it a grave interference as they considered San Fernando to be a sacred place.[29] The same regard for the practical and customary aspect of Hosay was expressed in the petition which 32 labourers and headmen, 22 of whom were Hindus, wrote to the Governor praying for withdrawal of the proclamation banning the Hosay procession. They made no attempt to give any special reasons for participation of the Hindus in the Muharram. They wrote: 'your petitioners consider Hosein to be a special mark of your petitioners' religious belief, which they understand to be imperatively ordained for them to observe . . . that your petitioners consider to prohibit them from observing their religious rites when the moon calls your petitioners to do so would be detrimental to them and would consequently embitter their existence'.[30] Without denying differences among the labourers as to the motive for their joining the Hosay it is sufficient to note that around Hosay there had emerged a strong community identity of the Indian labourers irrespective of creed and caste in Trinidad. To the extent to which religion was a way of expressing that identity, Hosay to the Indian labourers was a religious festival.

But why and how did Hosay express the community identity of the Indian immigrants? Community identity can be best understood by examining its concrete manifestation in public and collective performances. Through collective performance, community was affirmed, powerfully inducing feelings of solidarity and a sense of belonging. A common sense of belonging is the result as well as the prerequisite of community performances.[31]

[29] Evidence of J.C. McHugh in ibid., p. 58.

[30] See the Petition in ibid., p. 8.

[31] Collective performance and community identity have been the subject of several excellent studies in South Asian historiography. Innovative use of Victor Turner's model of collective rituals as social process and of the dual concepts of structure and communitas is made in Arjun Appadurai, *Worship and Conflict Under Colonial Rule: A South Indian Case* (Cambridge, 1981) and also in Sandria B. Freitag's study of urban rituals of community in *Collective Action and Community*. See also several essays in Sandria B.

Experience of migration and the long sea voyage bound the Indian immigrants together and their closeness was enhanced further by the fact that most immigrants were recruited from the same linguistic and cultural region in India (nearly three-quarters of Indian immigrants came from the Bhojpur and contiguous Awadh region in the Gangetic United Provinces and Bihar). Further the plantation labour regime provided an overarching commonality of experience irrespective of inherited differences of creed and caste to the Indian immigrants. The primary identity of Indian immigrants in the plantation setting remained that of 'Coolie', nominally meaning an unskilled wage labourer but in fact a pejorative racial appellation for all Indians. Nothing marked out the Indian immigrant as the member of the lowest social group in Trinidad more than the spatial and temporal immobilization which was imposed by the five-year indenture. It was this attribute of immobilized labour implicit in the term 'Coolie' which was extended to the whole community of Indian immigrants and their descendants. Understandably, community aspirations of Indians were asserted in opposition to the 'Coolie' identity and the physical and cultural immobilization imposed by the indentured-labour regime.

The structure of Hosay and the procession provided an adequate frame for the expression of community aspirations of the Indian immigrants and their descendants. First of all, given the popularity of Muharram as an important public festival in northern India, most of the immigrants were familiar with the rituals and observances associated with it. The festival and the procession incorporated a spectrum of practices which allowed for participation by all the Indian immigrants irrespective of caste and religious affiliations. These ranged from the strictly religious observances of prayer, fasting, and keeping of vows and construction of the *taziyas* by the devoted to ostensibly secular ritual stick play, singing of *mersiahs* (in which women were most prominent), carrying banners and other memorabilias, *tassa* drumming, and spectatorship. Secondly, since the festivities

---

Freitag (ed.), *Culture and Power in Banaras: Community, Performance, and Environment, 1800–1980* (Berkeley, 1989). A different approach stressing conflicts between the upper and lower classes as central to construction of community and community performance was elaborated in Ranajit Guha, *Elementary Aspects of Peasant Insurgency* (New Delhi, 1983).

centered around the estates, the pooling of resources in the construction of the *taziyas* and participation in the procession as members of the estate reinforced the estate-based solidarity of all immigrant labourers. Finally, it was the procession in which various estates came together that allowed for the congregation of all immigrants from various estates, thus physically representing the whole community of Indians. The visual impact of the massed participants undoubtedly provided a powerful stimulus to community feeling as did the proud display of the magnificent structure of *taziyas* as unique cultural symbols of the community.

The processional aspect of Hosay was perhaps the most important reason for its popularity among the immigrants. The articulation of community identity in a processional form was especially important in the context of the spatial immobility of the community engendered by the indentured-labour system.[32] Through the Hosay procession, the community manipulated already existing spaces and places but gave them a new, albeit temporary, meaning.[33] The Hosay procession performed at least three functions which were crucial for the expression of community identity: an integrative, a transgressive, and a reiterative one.

[32] The importance of the processional representation of community identity in north Indian urban centres is explored in Freitag, *Collective Action and Community*, pp. 131–43. The special issue of *The Drama Review*, on 'Processional Performances' (29, 3 [1985]) has several essays on community representations and processions; see in particular the essay by Peter J. Chelkowski, 'Shia Muslim Processionals', pp. 19-30. Also relevant is Frank Korom and Peter J Chelkowski, 'Community Performance of Muharram Observances in Trinidad', *The Drama Review*, 38, 2 (1994), pp. 151–75, which analyses community participation in the Hosay Procession in contemporary Trinidad.

[33] I have been much influenced by Louis Maran's analysis of the spatial discourse articulated in processional forms. See his essay 'Notes on a Semiotic Approach to Parade, Cortege and Procession', in Alessandro Falassi (ed.), *Time out of Time: Essays on the Festival* (Albuquerque, 1987), pp. 212–20. The symbolism of space among Indian immigrants in Trinidad, especially in the context of the Hosay festival, has been excellently analysed in Ken Paramasad, 'Space as a Symbol: From Muharram to Hosay', in 'The Changing Socio-Historical Context of Cultural Symbols in the Indian Community in Trinidad with Comparative Reference to the Bhojpuri Speaking Region of India' (Ph.D. thesis, Jawaharlal Nehru University, New Delhi, 1993), Ch. 7. I am grateful to the author for allowing me to read his thesis and for sharing many of his ideas with me.

The route of the procession *integrated* normally segregated plantation communities and physically linked the bounded space of plantations with the city or town centre. Therewith the community was structured by the procession at the same time as it imprinted itself on the existing space. In its *transgressive* aspect, the procession narrated a counter-discourse to the normal spatial immobility imposed on the immigrants. By occupying the highway and marching through the centre of the towns, Indian immigrants laid claim to the public spaces which were ordinarily denied to them. While indentured immigrants were bound by law not to be outside the plantations without explicit permission of the managers, even non-indentured immigrants and their descendants were required by law to have on them certificates of exemption from indenture and were liable to be arrested as vagrants or deserters. Public spaces, highways, and towns were especially fraught places for the Indians. By occupying spaces and places in the procession, even temporarily, Indian labourers symbolically transcended both their 'Coolie' status and the implicit bounded space in which they were located. The Hosay procession then literally mobilized an immobile community.

However, the counter-discourse of space was not formulated in opposition to the established authority structure even though the procession did not draw its legitimacy from any explicit legal right to occupy spaces and places. Rather, the transgressive and liminal aspects were normalized through the *reiterative* function of the procession. By repeating over the years, fixed routes, destinations, and orders of estates in the procession, the community arrogated to itself an implicit right to occupy and march through public spaces. It was custom rather than any specific legal right which was invoked by the participants in the Hosay procession of 1884 to go to San Fernando. The heavy investment in customary spatial rights was also at the root of conflicts over orders of precedence in the procession. Custom also made space sacred as was asserted by the Babajees about San Fernando in 1883. By integrating, mobilizing, and reclaiming customary rights on public places and spaces, the Hosay festival and the procession powerfully articulated community aspirations and religious belief; the sacred and the profane were not separated either in the practices or in the minds of the participants. The reason why Hosay was to be regulated thus did not lie in its alleged irreligious nature. In order to understand why the Hosay in general, and the procession in particular, was regulated and finally suppressed one has to look at a different constellation of causes.

Hosay and the Crisis on the Plantations, 1882–1884

The Hosay massacre of 1884 took place during the severest crisis that the sugar industry of Trinidad had faced since the emancipation. The price of sugar which had been gradually drifting downwards since 1873 began to dip more precipitously from 1878–9 onward. Buffeted by the general depression in commodity prices and more directly by the dumping of bounty fed beet sugar on the British market, the average price of crystal sugar (cane) in the London market in 1880 stood at 50 per cent below the 1873 prices. The real crisis, however, became evident in 1884 when sugar prices suddenly plunged to half of the price of the previous year throwing the sugar industry into the deepest recession in its history.[34] Thereafter, prices remained low till the beginning of the First World War. The impact of this crisis was felt in all sectors of the Trinidadian society, overwhelmingly dependent as it was on sugar exports. But the sugar crisis had an immediate and acute impact at the point of production—in the cane fields and factories of the estates.

Planters had reacted to the emerging crisis in the early 1880s by increasing production and cutting wages and finally in 1884 by mass retrenchment of free labour. This strategy of intensification of production was felt by all sectors of the labouring classes but perhaps most intensely by the bonded indentured labourers who were compelled by law to work on the plantation at nominally fixed wages which, as we shall see later, could easily be much less than the statutory minimum. This then was the context in which the Hosay massacre took place and Henry Norman wrote his report.

But Norman had peremptorily dismissed any link between the sugar crisis, consequent wage reduction on plantations, and the Hosay massacre. He did so by blandly stating that 'It is a matter

[34] For a comprehensive account of the sugar crisis in the West Indies and British Guyana, see Walter Rodney, *A History of the Guyanese Working People* (Baltimore, 1981), pp. 19–30. Also R.W. Beachey, *The British West Indies Sugar Industry in the Late Nineteenth Century* (Oxford, 1957), pp. 110–18 and *passim*.

of fact that the Coolies are usually well fed, not overworked and are well treated in sickness.' Though the tasks had been increased since the fall in the price of sugar, complaints on this had fallen through on investigation, and in any case 'the Coolie who performs task work has to labour for fewer hours than those who work by time'. Further, Norman found the complaints on both sides to be 'much less numerous and less important than might have been expected'.[35] In spite of this summary treatment of an important issue, he did note that 'the Coolie is more prone to complain than he used to be and that he sometimes does so in an unruly manner and that generally he does not behave as well as he used to'. The specific form of 'Coolie' behaviour which was particularly reprehensible to him was that 'bodies of Coolies came to the Immigration office to present complaints in an overbearing way, carrying cutlasses and other agricultural implements'. By not punishing them, Norman believed that the government encouraged the notion among Coolies that they were powerful and could do as they pleased.[36] So even though their grievances were not legitimate, Norman did acknowledge both the existence of these grievances and, also, the specific form of action that the labourers had developed for their redressal.

In fact, even a cursory glance at the accounts of contemporary newspapers and of government reports prior to the Hosay of 1884 suggests a story quite different from what Norman set out in his report. From September 1882 onwards, the estates in Trinidad were rocked by a series of conflicts over wages and tasks between the planters and the indentured and free labourers. Such incidents numbering 25 involving large groups of labourers were reported in the contemporary newspapers in the two-year period between

[35] *Norman Report*, p. 47. It is significant that Norman only examined the planters' requests for endorsement of days lost on account of breach of contract. After 1875 such practices had become rare in Trinidad as the planters were not keen to follow bureaucratic procedures. Norman knew that the majority of the breaches of contract cases were never proceeded for endorsement, yet he cited the low rates of endorsement as an indication of the low level of conflict on the plantations. If he had examined the annual *Blue Books* he would easily have found statistics of criminal breach of contract cases and imprisonment statistics—a surprising omission given that Jamaica too had immigration ordinances for Indian labourers.

[36] Ibid., p. 48.

TABLE 9.2: Average Annual Committals for Breach of Contract

Year	Total Cases	Convicted
1874–5	2142 (20.2)	1117 (10.5)
1876–8	2959 (26.8)	1843 (16.7)
1879–81	2098 (27.2)	2033 (17.8)
1882–4	3378 (31.8)	2366 (22.3)
1885–7	3048 (31.1)	2270 (23.1)

Note: Figures in brackets represent the percentage of cases to indentured population.

Sources: *Blue Book* and *Annual Report of the Protector of Immigrants of Trinidad* for respective years.

September 1882 and October 1884—more than half of the total (recorded) between 1870 and 1901.[37] In September 1882, the first major conflict involving indentured labour broke out in the Cedar Hill estate. It was swiftly followed by similar disputes in six other estates. Disputes in six more estates broke out in 1883, climaxing in a massive wave of twelve major disturbances in 1884. These incidents of conflicts were marked by stoppages of work by the labourers, violence against the plantation officials, and collective marches by the labourers to the immigration offices in the towns. In many of these incidents armed police had been summoned by the planters. Stiff jail sentences for the 'ring leaders' followed.

The conflicts over tasks and wages were only overt manifestations of worsening labour relations on the plantations. Underlying them were the generalized tightening of screws on individual workers in the form of stricter regulation of tasks and increased work discipline. While we have very little direct information on how each worker responded, there is no doubt as to the increasing use by the planters of the official disciplining machinery in the form of imprisonment and prosecutions under the breach of contract provisions of the indenture ordinances. The annual figures of prosecutions demonstrate—*contra* Norman—a widespread and longer trend of individualized protest among the indentured labourers against the intensification of the labour process on the plantations.

[37] G. Tika Singh, 'Establishment of East Indians in Trinidad, 1870–1900' (Ph.D. thesis, University of the West Indies, St Augustine, 1985), p. 264. It is possible that several conflicts involving the smaller estates were not reported in the newspapers during 1882–4.

The average annual proportion of indentured labourers prosecuted under the ordinances increased continuously from 20 per cent in the early 1870s to its peak of almost 32 per cent during the 1882–4 period. The prosecutions were for a wide variety of charges, including desertion, absence from work, refusal to work, not finishing work, insubordination, abuse of overseers, and contravening hospital regulations. For those who were convicted under the ordinances, imprisonment ranging from seven days to three months was the most common punishment, followed by heavy fines.

I will focus on some instances of overt and collective actions of workers that erupted specifically during 1882–4 in order to explain how the crisis in sugar estates impacted the labour force, and to delineate the context in which the Hosay massacre of 1884 can be understood. While disputes over wages and tasks on the plantations were not unheard of in Trinidad before, there seems to have been a real increase in both the frequency and participation of labourers in such conflicts during 1882–4. It is during this period that the protest actions of the immigrant labourers acquired the dimensions of what can be termed strikes.

The strike cycle began with a massive disturbance in the Cedar Hill estate on 28 September 1882. The scale of the disturbance and its intensity took both the planting class and the Government by surprise. The apparent cause of the strike was considered a trivial matter by the Government. A Muslim labourer named Mowla Bux, who was on the verge of completing his indenture, was arrested on being found outside the estate without a pass. He was jailed for seven days and in the jail his head and beard were shaved. Mowla was apparently a religious leader, and was to lead the next Hosay festival in the estate. His humiliation was widely believed to have been engineered by an overseer in the estate who was particularly hated for having increased tasks and interfered with women on the plantation. On 28 September 1882 the forking gang in the estate, complaining of large tasks struck work; in the dispute with the overseer Lermont, they attacked him and two drivers[38]

[38] In the plantations, the immigrants were always represented by a headman or *sirdar* in disputes over wages and tasks, and in inter-immigrant conflicts. Appointed by the plantation management these headmen were known as drivers (a term which was carried over from the days of slavery). They were the main supervisors of work and heads of task gangs. The plantation overseer and manager controlled the immigrants through them.

with their implements, forcing them to flee. Immediately afterwards, the labourers marched *en masse* to the town with their implements, to complain to the Assistant Protector of Immigrants about large tasks, insufficient rations, and stoppage of pay. The mass deputation seems to have been the first of its kind in Trinidad. According to the Immigration Ordinances, indentured workers were allowed, with the permission of the manager, to go to the Protector of Immigrants to complain about task sizes, and the Protector was empowered to order reduction of tasks if they were larger than the tasks performed by free labourers. The Cedar Hill workers were, for the first time, collectively seeking the intervention of the Protector in a dispute over tasks. The whole band of workers then returned 'drunk with excitement' having been promised by the Assistant Protector that their grievances would be looked into. The next day, acting on a complaint by the overseer, a large batch of policemen along with the Assistant Protector appeared on the estate to arrest seven 'ringleaders' for rioting and assault. The mass of labourers freed the arrested men but a few hours later a reinforcement of armed police managed to take 36 men into custody. They were charged with rioting and assault.[39]

The Cedar Hill strike was quickly followed by strikes in nearby estates. On 9 October 1882, a batch of labourers in Fairfield went on strike, complaining of large tasks, and marched to the town carrying their implements to lay down their grievances before the magistrate and the local immigration agent. By the end of the month, strikes had spread to five other estates in the vicinity. In each case, the grievances related to over-tasking; and in a few cases, assault on the drivers and overseer followed by mass deputation to the Protector's office in the town implements in hand. The wave of 'strikes' surprised the government and planters alike, and wild rumors began to circulate.[40] What frightened the

[39] The account of this incident is to be found in Despatches of the Governor of Trinidad to the Secretary of State Colonies, 27 October 1882, and 8 December 1882, in CO 384/139, PRO and in *SFG*, 7 and 14 October 1882, and *POSG*, 16 December 1882.

[40] A patently absurd rumour, reported to the Government by one of the police informers, was that Indian labourers, mainly Muslims, were contemplating an uprising following the news of the Egyptian war. They were reported to have planned the killing of missionaries, the cutting of telegraph lines and the setting to fire of the main towns with pitch oil. Despatch of the Governor of Trinidad to the Secretary of State Colonies, 7 November, No. 260, CO 295/295, PRO.

planters was the rapidity with which one strike action followed another—so the planters concluded that a general uprising of the 'Coolies' was in the making. Some believed that the Hosay festival which was to take place on 22 November would be the occasion for the uprising. These frequent strikes were seen as previews to a general strike during crop season.[41] The Government was forced to appoint a commission of enquiry, and summon military and naval reinforcements, especially for the 1882 Hosay.

The commission of enquiry report was never made public primarily because it indicted the management in Cedar Hill and other estates for the disturbances. Though the commission discounted reports of a general Coolie uprising, since most actions on the part of labour were 'not owing to any general combined movement or to any general feeling of discontent among the immigrants population', it noted that 'some immigrants free or indentured thought it a good opportunity to agitate for an increase of wages'. Most disconcerting for the commissioners, however, was the method adopted by the workers to seek redress of their grievances. They observed that after every incidence of attack on a driver or overseer, the workers marched down to San Fernando in groups to complain of ill-treatment and large tasks: 'The mere fact of very large bodies of men marching down through the districts with their hoes and cutlasses has a most injurious and disturbing effect and is fraught with danger.'[42] The Hosay that year passed off peacefully. The war vassal HMS Flamingo was stationed off the San Fernando shore through 19–22 November, and the Governor remarked that 'her presence cannot have failed to have a salutary effect'.[43]

The rioting case against 28 Cedar Hill labourers, however, fell through in the Supreme Court due to a technical lapse on the part of the state counsels in the indictment. The labourers were set free.

[41] *SFG*, 28 October 1882, about the meeting of the planters and the apprehension of the uprising during Hosay. Also see *SFG*, 11 November 1882.

[42] This account is based on: 'Report of the Commissioners for Enquiry into the Cedar Hill Disturbances', Enclosure to Despatch from the Governor of Trinidad to Secretary of State Colonies, 8 December 1882, No. 287, in CO 384/139, PRO.

[43] Despatch of Governor to Secretary of State Colonies, 27 November 1882, CO 384/139, PRO.

The decision was roundly criticized by the local newspapers, planters, and the powerful planters' lobby in London, the West Indian Committee, which now mounted a sustained campaign for sterner action against worker indiscipline. The Colonial Office urged the Governor to mete out exemplary punishment in future instances of worker disturbances following the Cedar Hill incidents. In the case of the Woodford Dale strike, seven workers were given long prison sentences. As it happened, the technical leniency in the Cedar Hill case was immediately followed by harsh sentences being imposed on trivial charges made against labourers. Thus, on 16 December, the *San Fernando Gazette* reported the punishing of a group of indentured labourers from the Corinth estate with three months of imprisonment each, merely for using obscene language towards an overseer.[44] A few days later, a teenage labourer was charged with shirking work by the overseer, and no notice was taken by the magistrate that the boy suffered from a sore ankle. His mother and sister, who had come to court to attend the case, were noticed by the estate manager who promptly had them arrested for leaving the estate without permission, and the whole family was imprisoned for seven days.[45] These instances of stiff punishments were now increasingly seen as necessary to curb the tendency towards estate-wide strike actions.

The next year (1883), the strike cycle began on 28 July with the Petit Morne estate workers refusing to work on an extremely large task set for weeding. Demanding that the task of 4,500 sq. ft. be reduced to the customary 3,000 sq. ft., they marched to the town with their implements. When the task was moderated they refused to work till a particularly oppressive driver was removed, and they were allowed to elect their own driver.[46] Following closely on the heels of this strike, there occurred another strike in Usine St. Madeline, the large factory estate of the colonial Company, on the issue of large tasks. When workers of the estate went to the town to the Assistant Protector's office they were locked up for the night in the police barracks. The next day the Assistant Protector faced an extremely hostile labour force in the estate who forced him to get off his carriage and pushed it into the cane piece. In the Sevilla Park, Paradise, El Soccoro, Exchange, and Laurel Hill estates there

[44] *SFG*, 16 December 1882.
[45] *SFG*, 20 January 1883.
[46] *POSG*, 11 August 1883.

were strikes on similar causes and with similar actions by the labourers: mobbing of the overseers and managers followed by *en masse* march to the Protector's office in the town. The newspapers representing planting interests were now hysterical in their demand to teach the 'Coolies' a lesson. The *Port of Spain Gazette*, after reporting the prevalence of a spirit of mutiny and rebelliousness among the labourers in the Naparima district, urged the government: 'to show an unflinching front in uprooting the germs of rebellious spirits. . . . Coolies must be made to understand that they will be kept to their contract and that insubordination and violation of the law will be severely punished'.[47]

The crop season in 1884 began with a dramatic fall in the price of sugar in the London market, and in January and February three strikes were reported in Cedar Hill, Woodford Dale, and Esperanza. Quickly suppressed, these minor disturbances were merely harbingers of a large strike wave to peak in the following season. In February, though the government had successfully suppressed the Canneboullay midnight torchlight procession in the carnival in Port of Spain, there were clashes in San Fernando and Princes Town between the urban Creole residents and the Police. The latter opened fire in Princes Town causing two casualties.[48] The demand for suppression of Hosay now became louder in the press and among the planters. The *Port of Spain Gazette*, alarmed at the prospect of new 'Coolie outrages', now urged the government not to allow the Hosay procession:

> It is not a day too soon to provide against possible danger to public peace from the very fact that one-third of our population of the island is composed of men whose very thought and habit are antagonistic to our system of civilization. . . . [*If*] *we put into the hands of these men such a formidable weapon as the right to meet in thousands and march into the towns*, it may, sooner or later, be used to upset the very groundwork of society and produce disasters which will retard the progress of the colony by several generations.[49]

[47] *POSG*, 18 August 1883.

[48] The suppression of the torchlight processions was part of the colonial state's campaign to control the expressions of the urban lower-class protests in the carnival. For an account of the struggle over carnival and the transformations it underwent in the nineteenth century, see Susan Campbell, 'Carnival, Calypso and Class Struggle in Nineteenth Century Trinidad', *History Workshop Journal*, 26 (Autumn 1988), pp. 1–27.

[49] *POSG*, 1 March 1884.

The Government now seemed to heed to the collective urging of the planter class. In March, steps were taken to prepare for the suppression of the Hosay procession.

By July 1884, the tremendous fall in sugar prices had become apparent. Planters now went about retrenching their free labour gangs *en masse*, and drastically lowered the wages paid to the free labourers as they raised the task sizes of the indentured labourers simultaneously. In August 1884, the informal practice of cutting wages and raising tasks was formalized in a meeting of the estate owners in which they decided to collectively lower the wages of free labourers down to the minimum wage level of the indentured labourers, i.e. 25 cents per task.[50]

The workers responded immediately. A rash of strikes and work stoppages broke out all over Trinidad. Striking estate workers were now joined by non-resident free labourers from the villages. Thus, when the Exchange estate workers (mostly indentured labourers) marched to San Fernando with their implements, complaining of large tasks, they were joined there by the free labourers of Paradise Village who were protesting against the lowering of wages. The latter threatened to apply collectively for repatriation to India if the wage levels were not restored. The threat seemed to work as the Assistant Protector found both the level of wages too low and the size of tasks high in the estate and ordered a lowering of the task sizes.[51]

As the planter offensive became generalized, workers of various estates often reached the Protector's office at the same time, swelling the number of protestors. On 10 October 1884, there was a recurrence of violent protest on central Trinidad's El Soccoro estate. The labourers, complaining of large tasks and reduced wages, struck work. The overseer was beaten up and Mr Lawrie, the manager, put to flight; thereafter a large body of labourers with their agricultural implements, hoes, shovels, and cutlasses marched to the town. There they were joined by labourers from another estate who had also struck work and had come to the Protector's office to complain. The Police, summoned by the

[50] The planters could not legally pay lower rates than 25 cents as the rate of the indentured labourers pay was statutorily fixed. *POSG*, 16 August 1884.

[51] *POSG*, 9 August 1884.

Protector, tried to arrest the ring leaders, the usual tactic used to disperse the crowd, but the labourers freed the arrested men. Then, the armed police was called in and they arrested the leaders to take them to the police station, upon which the 'whole mob of Coolies' followed the arrested men, demanding that all of them be arrested along with the five men. After some time, they were induced to return. The Protector went to the estate the next day and found the tasks to have been immoderately large, and ordered them to be reduced.[52]

The planters severely criticized the Protector for allowing the Coolies to march insolently into the town to complain, and for rewarding them by having their tasks reduced. A prominent planter alleged in a letter to the Governor that such leniency has given rise to the belief among Coolies that the Government is afraid to interfere with them 'on account of their large and growing number'. Emboldened by the success of their marches, the workers were constantly addressing 'murderous threats to those in authority' in every dispute on the plantations to such an extent that few managers now care to go about their duty unarmed—a state of affairs unparalleled in Her Majesty's dominion. . . .[53] These intimidating marches now had to be stopped at any cost, thundered the planters' mouthpiece, the *Port of Spain Gazette*:

> Let every facility be afforded to them [the labourers] to lay their grievances before the proper authorities, but to do that they must not be allowed to march to the town and Police stations, with their hoes and cutlasses. It should be made clear to them that irrespective of the merit of the case this, in itself, constitutes a serious offence, which in all cases will be severely punished. It should be made a rule that in all such cases the ring leaders will be punished and no heed paid to their complaints until they shall have returned to work.[54]

The approaching Hosay to be held at the end of October now evoked deep anxieties among the planters. The planters' newspaper articulated their deepest fears: the fact that the number of Indians

[52] *POSG*, 10 October 1884.

[53] Letter from G.W. Fenwick to the Governor of Trinidad, 20 October 1884, enclosure to Despatch from Governor of Trinidad to Secretary of State Colonies, 24 March 1885, CO 384/155, PRO.

[54] *POSG*, 18 October 1884.

constituted fully one-third of the total population and, perhaps, more than half of the adult population. But more worrying was the fact that they, as a community, had nothing in common with the rest of the population:

> They are among us but not of us. They are united while we are divided. They are violent fanatics in religion: disciplined and well kept in hand by their priests who teach them to connect questions of caste and questions of religion with affairs of everyday life. . . . Life itself becomes a matter of little moment to them when put into the scale against anything affecting their religious fanaticism.[55]

The spectre of a militant plantation labour force unified by religion haunted the planters. The fear of the imminent Hosay and the class mobilization of the Indian labourers had fused in the minds of the plantocracy. The Government had, in the meanwhile, rejected the petition of the headmen of 27 estates asking for a withdrawal of the ban on the procession. Yet, planters were still not convinced of the Government's determination to stop the procession. On 11 October, three weeks before the Hosay procession, the *Port of Spain Gazette* expressed fears that once again the Government would succumb to the pressures of the Indian immigrants, allowing them to break the law and enter the towns with only a few persons arrested in the aftermath. The paper ominously pointed to the recent happenings in Surinam where seven Indian workers had been shot down during the disturbance in the Marienburg plantation.[56] Rumours of massing of arms by 'Coolies' became rife as planters became increasingly hysterical.[57]

The spate of strikes in October, and the increasingly militant combination displayed by workers laid the ground for the Hosay massacre. There were strikes on 18 October in the Union Hall and Laurel Hill estates, with a serious assault on the manager. As late as 28 October, two days before the Hosay procession was to be taken out, the labourers of the Petit Morne estate had marched to the Assistant Protector's office complaining of large tasks.[58]

[55] Ibid.
[56] *POSG*, 11 October 1884.
[57] *POSG*, 25 October 1884.
[58] Ibid., and evidence of Mr Pasea in *Norman Report*, p. 71.

All about Timing: The Temporal Dimension of the Strikes and the Hosay

The first thing that struck me about the series of conflicts that took place during 1882–4 is their timing. The incidents occurred most prominently, in some years exclusively, during the months between August and November. Of the 25 reported incidents of strikes and disputes over tasks and wages, 23 took place during these months—16 alone in the month of October. What is noticeable is that these months are very much in the heart of the so-called 'slack work season' in the plantations. Sugar cane cultivation in Trinidad, unlike British Guyana, had two clearly marked seasons. During the dry months, between January and June, work on the plantations was in full swing. This was the main season for sugar production and cane harvesting, when the work day in the factories and fields could often be 15 hours or longer everyday. In the slack season, from July until December, there was a marked decline in the intensity of work in the field. Factories were closed, the only work left was that of weeding, and in some cases, planting. It was the period when work was scarcer for free labourers.

Why were the strikes and disputes regarding wages and tasks almost exclusively in the slack season? Does the temporal bunching of strikes tell us anything about the strategies of the planters and the nature of workers' protest? Clearly, during crop time, the planters were unwilling to provoke conflicts with the workers because so much depended on the timely harvesting and milling of the sugar canes; it was the period when all hands were required for work since the ripened sugar cane had to be harvested within a very short time. This was when the planters were the most vulnerable to mass strikes: planters were often willing to hire free labourers at higher than normal wages. This was also the period when workers, both indentured and free, could increase their earnings by doing more tasks.[59]

On the other hand, during the rainy season, between July and December, the workers were most vulnerable—and the planters had the upper hand. The tasks of weeding, trashing and planting canes could be postponed without any threat to the immediate production schedules. Legally, the planters were obliged to provide

[59] *Commins Note*, pp. 9–12, for seasonality of earnings and work on the plantations in Trinidad.

work to the indentured gangs during this period while they could dispense with the free labourers. So the first steps towards economizing on any plantation would often be to shed their free labourers who were usually paid a higher wage than the indentured workers. But in periods of crisis even the wages of the indentured labourers could be reduced and their tasks extended. Planters were forbidden by law to have task rates below 25 cents for indentured labour. But they were free to expand task sizes as long as these remined equal for indentured and free labourers. So the planters reduced the wage rates for free labourers and increased the task sizes of the indentured labourers. This dual strategy was brought to bear most severely on the labourers during the slack season of 1884, but had been tried out earlier in the slack seasons of 1882 and 1883. Many of the tasks for the slack season were carried over to the crop season, especially weeding and trashing of cane, so the planters tried to set task sizes during the slack season that could then be cited as standard for the busy period. For these reasons, the slack season usually became a period of tussle between the planters and the workers over wage rate and task size.

The labourers defended what they considered as customary task sizes and wage rates. Customary task sizes and wages varied from estate to estate and from season to season. During a period of heavy rainfall, 'when the dirt sticks to the hoe', workers resented even the normal size tasks since the time needed to complete them would be much longer. They compared task sizes and the intensity of work by timing how long it took to finish a task or earn a certain amount of money. This is how most workers compared the tasks they were assigned in September 1884 with what they were accustomed to do in the Brothers and Williamsville estates.

Due to the institution of an enquiry commission in September 1884, we have detailed reports as to the effect of work intensification on the wage levels of both free and indentured workers on these two estates.[60] The estates had a recent change of management which promptly set about to raise tasks and reduce wages. The response of the workers was to go in a body to complain to the Assistant Protector of Immigrants in San Fernando and surround

[60] 'Report of the Commission to Enquire into Coolie Complaints on Brothers and Williamsville Estates', in enclosure to Despatch of Governor of Trinidad to Secretary of State Colonies, 24 March 1885, No. 75, in CO 384/155, PRO.

the house of the manager. Armed police was summoned by the manager to arrest arbitrarily chosen 'ring leaders'. The commission surmized that the tasks had been increased both in size and quality of work. Independent appraisers (a manager, an overseer, and drivers of other estates) found the standard weeding tasks stiff but fair in one case and definitely hard and larger in size in another. In front of the commission, the labourers, both free and indentured, complained bitterly about large tasks and drastically reduced earnings. The complainants ranged from an experienced worker of 22 years to a new immigrant of six months. The gist of their complaints was that they now had to spend two days to complete a task which they used to finish in one day. Weeding task sizes had been arbitrarily increased from the customary 3,000 sq. ft. to 3,600 and 4,200 sq. ft. Workers complained that in many cases they were asked to do two or three kinds of work while the size of their task was retained. Thus, along with weeding, each worker had to also do banking and boucanning (making rows for planting cane), which was customarily done by two persons. All the labourers interviewed by the commission compared their present tasks with what they were accustomed to earlier, in terms of time and earnings.[61] The wages of free labourers had been reduced from 30 cents a task to 25 cents. They were put to work along with the indentured workers at the very moment the tasks of the latter were increased. The Coolies' complaints were put graphically by Jeetu who said: 'I was sent here to work, not to get killed. I am not dead but my stomach is dying.'[62] The defence of customary task sizes was important to all sectors of the labour force but more so to the indentured gangs as they were bound to perform the tasks on pain of imprisonment—free labour at least had the option of walking out even if it meant loss of wages.

What does the bunching of strikes during 1882–4, and especially in the slack season, signify? Firstly, it is evident that the strikes and conflicts over wages were precipitated by increasing task sizes and falling wages. To that extent, the action of the labourers was largely defensive rather than an aggressive attempt to increase the existing wage levels. As the task and wage rates of the indentured

[61] Evidence of Bahadoor, Ramsingh, Jagartar and Khooda Bux in ibid.
[62] Evidence of Jeetu, ibid.

and free labourers became linked there was an objective basis for the united action of workers.

Secondly, it is now possible to understand the significance of Hosay in the context of increasing collective action by the workers on the plantations during 1882–4 and, more specifically, within the slack periods of production. We must keep in mind that the annual festival of Muharram was observed according to the lunar calendar which differed by a period of eleven days from the Christian calendar. As missionary John Morton explained:

The Muharram begins from the new moon of the Arabic month Muharram and lasts ten days. The Mohammedan year consists of 12 lunar months. These months are made to consist of 30 and 29 days alternately. Their new year day will therefore happen every 11 days earlier than the preceding year and this causes the Hosay to wander around our year.[63]

It is significant that during 1882–4, Muharram in its cyclical annual wandering, entered the busy strike season (the slack season for estates) for the first time in thirty years since it was first observed in 1855. In 1882, the Muharram fell on 22 November, in 1883 on 11 November, and in 1884 bang in the heart of the strike season on 30 October.

The temporal conjunction of the strike season (I am now using it as a shorthand for the frequent conflicts over tasks and wages that occurred between 1882 and 1884, and especially in the months between August and December) with the Hosay procession allowed for the transformation of estate level conflicts over wages and tasks into collective political action of the entire labour force. Yet, what was the process and structure of transformation by which class conflict on the plantations in this period was powerfully represented in the community performance of the Hosay procession of 1884? This can be best understood if we compare the ways in which class action and community identity was represented and communicated by the Indian immigrant workers in this period.

All about Processions: Strike and Hosay

An ubiquitous feature of strike actions by plantation workers during the 1882–4 period was the procession to the town, when workers marched in a body with their agricultural implements to

[63] Letter of J. Morton in *Trinidad Chronicle*, 11 April 1871.

lay down their grievances before the Protector of Immigrants. First reported in the Cedar Hill strike of 1882, the march to the town with agricultural implements was then associated with all subsequent strikes. There has been an old connection between work stoppages or strikes and processions in the history of the workers' movement worldwide.[64] What is of interest is the form of strike procession developed by the workers in the context of indentured-labour regimes on the plantations. These processions had specific features and communicated distinct meanings.[65]

In the first place, the presentation of the complaint in a 'body' rather than through a representative or an individual was a novel feature of these strikes as it shortcircuited the established structure of grievance redressal. In several instances, the drivers (supposedly the workers' representatives) were party to the disputes and object of workers' complaints. By going in a body, the workers asserted their right to collective rather than individual representation of their grievances. The collective presentation of their grievances was devised by the workers as a counter to the customary style of management in which ring leaders were picked up to be prosecuted in cases of industrial disputes under charges of incitement to stop work. No doubt, individuals representing the body were often the first to be arrested. Thus the *Guyana Daily Chronicle*, noting the emergence of the new strike form adopted widely in Trinidad and spreading to Guyana during the 1882–4 period, remarked: 'The Coolies are under the impression that when one or two of their number leave the estates to make known their grievances they are arrested as ring leaders, charged with vagrancy and eventually sent to the prison for the usual term of seven days, hence the reason for their turning up in a body.'[66] An instance of the effectiveness of

[64] Susan Davies points to the etymological links between strikes and processions, an early meaning of strike being 'to set out on foot', or 'to walk out'. For a fine analysis of the performative aspects of strike processions in Philadelphia in the nineteenth century, showing both the possibilities and limitations of their communicative potential, see her *Parades and Power: Street Theatre in Nineteenth Century Philadelphia* (Berkeley, 1988), Ch. 2, and her essay 'Strike Parades and the Politics of Representing Class in Antebellum Philadelphia', *The Drama Review*, 29, 3 (1985), pp. 107–16.

[65] Walter Rodney was the first historian to notice and write about the novel form of strike processions, developed by indentured plantation workers in the nineteenth century. See his *A History of the Guyanese Working People*, p. 153.

[66] *Guyana Daily Chronicle*, 8 August 1883.

such collective action in preventing arbitrary arrests of the leaders was evident in the El Soccoro strike of October 1884. The massed workers had demanded that they all be arrested along with the 'ring leaders', forcing the authorities to release the arrested men.

What was the significance of the processions of labourers to the town with agricultural implements, and what messages did they convey? Marching through the cane districts with their implements, the labourers of an estate sent out unmistakable signals to their counterparts on other estates. The demonstration effect of the march was evident in the quick succession with which neighbouring estates also adopted the method. By marching together the workers were safe from individual arrests by the policemen—since they obviously had not obtained permission to leave their estates. Carrying of implements immediately signified that they had struck while on work and could not be accused of absence from work or refusal to work which merited severe penalties. Thus the strike processions always carefully negotiated the thin line that separated the legal from the illicit, those actions which were permitted from those that were disallowed by the authorities. Thus the workers' processions and their protests in the plantations were marked by ambivalence, as they conveyed both defiance and deference towards those in authority. A typical instance of this was visible in the Brothers and Williamsville strike in September 1884, when workers after marching to the town returned to surround the house of the manager who immediately called in armed police to disperse the crowd. But when asked later by the commission of enquiry, many labourers replied 'Mr Dickie is our Mother and Father; where else are we to go but to his house.'[67] Given the nature of the authority structure on the plantations, the workers' recourse to paternalism appeared pragmatic and was often effective. When the workers marched to the town to complain to the Protector of Immigrants they tried to mobilize the paternalist rhetoric of protection of the state in their class grievances against the planters.

[67] Evidence of Ruggin Singh and Bahadoor in 'Report of the Commission to Enquire into Coolie Complaints on Brothers and Williamsville Estates'. For a thoughtful analysis of the ambivalence involved in workers' protest actions in the Indian context, see Dipesh Chakrabarti's classic account of jute workers' protest in Calcutta in *Rethinking Working Class History: Bengal 1890–1940* (New Delhi, 1989), Ch. 5.

Yet by carrying agricultural implements with them, the plantation workers at the same time infused a significant element of militancy into the strike procession. The prominent display of agricultural implements in these marches invoked deeply held fears among the planters of a mass uprising. As one Colonial Governor from Guyana wrote to the Colonial Office in 1880: 'We must remember that the agricultural implements placed in the hands of the Coolies constitute them at any moment as an armed force. . . .'[68] Though there was never any attempt on the part of the workers to do anything more than display these implements during the procession, planters read the potential for an armed uprising in them. With each such strike procession, the reaction of the planters, as I have shown earlier, became more hysterical. It was thus that acts of complaining or petitioning, in which the immigrants were primarily positioned as supplicants could be transformed into threatening gestures, the complaints becoming demands and the petitions becoming collective assertions of rights.

The strike processions of the workers during the 1882–4 period had multiple semiotic and semantic levels. Their frame of significance was the structure of power relations that flowed from the indentured-labour system. The strike procession acquired such significance because the workers had devised it in the context of a labour regime that not only disallowed, repressed, and made illicit withdrawal of their labour power in any form but also denied any representation of that action. By leaving work, and *marching in a body with their agricultural implements* to the Protector's office in the town, the workers combined both the withdrawal of their labour power (strike) and an appropriate representation of that act. Thus, the response of the workers to the planters' offensive during the 1882–4 period was marked by the development of a vocabulary and style of protest with specific goals and appropriate actions. The strike procession emerged as a creative and, in some cases, effective form of communication of their protest. The Hosay festival of 1884, temporally located in the strike season, thus became infused with semiotic and semantic charge derived from the protest marches of the workers.

Yet it was not through simple analogy that this crossover of meaning and style between the strike procession and the Hosay occurred. To start, let me note the evident difference between these

[68] Cited in Rodney, *A History of the Guyanese Working People*, p. 153.

two forms. The Hosay procession appears as the opposite of the daily conditions of indentured labour on the plantations. In the first place, it is remarkable how little of the labouring aspects of the participants' lives were represented in the procession. Beginning with the dress the participants wore, the gay beating of *tassa* drums, the ritual emblems of flags, banners, lances with the hand stuck on it, and finally the elaborate *taziya*, the replica tomb itself in its glittering tinsel and multihued magnificence form a sharp contrast to the drabness and daily grind of labour on the estates. Yet everything about the strike procession, including the dress the workers wore and the implements they carried, reminds one of their labouring conditions. If in the plantations the workers experienced ignominy in the category of 'Coolie labour', hemmed in by law and planter power, stripped of all other qualities, in the Hosay they experienced and represented themselves as a full-fledged moral and cultural community. To put it more starkly, if in the strike procession the workers seemed to carry their workplace symbolically with them, in the Hosay they seemed eager to leave it behind. And if the strike processions of workers emphasized and pointedly drew attention to their labouring conditions, the Hosay derived its meaning from its marked contrast with the same conditions.

Having noted this, I want to emphasize that opposition and contrast are still a relation and I would draw attention to this shared relational field in which both Hosay and the workers' processions were placed. As elaborated earlier, the temporal coincidence of Hosay with the strike season on plantations (during 1882–4) structured this field of relations. Both Hosay and the strike processions were, in a way, about representation of collectivities dramatically staged in public space. They both transgressed the bounded space in which the Indians were placed, i.e the plantations. Public space and citizens' rights were denied to the Indians, whether labourers or not. The symbolic occupation of public space was crucial to the representation of collectivity in both instances of class and community. The ideal public space in plantation societies in the West Indies remained the town—the seat of government, the site of civic rituals *par excellence*. It is not mere chance that both Hosay and strike processions aspired to be in the town. It was there that both class and community could become visible; literally become present to public gaze.

What undergirded these similarities of forms and vocabularies of collective representation between class action and community performance was that they were aimed at, and drew their legitimacy from, what the participants considered a defence of custom. In one case, the workers defended customary wages and tasks and, in the other, the customary right to proceed to the sea to immerse the *taziyas*. Finally, of course, public performance in both cases was marked by ambivalence of deference and defiance. In the Hosay there was no attempt to attack persons in authority yet the size of the mass itself, the deafening cry of 'Hai Hussain', 'Hai Hassan', and the ritual mock stick play could, given the context, infuse fear among planters in 1884. So that while one Coolie could say 'the government looks upon us as its children and they would not shoot us', the others might proclaim defiantly 'shoot one shoot all', meaning 'let them shoot us all'.

It is true, however, that the basic unit of collectives, in both cases of strike and Hosay processions, was the estate. Each estate brought out separate Hosays and often there was intense competition between the estates about orders of precedence in the procession ending sometimes in bitter fights. But on the other hand the Hosay procession, while being internally differentiated, performed a crucial function in integrating and bringing together labourers of all the estates. To the extent that each of these estates had similar sets of paraphernalia, and performed similar ritual actions, the Hosay procession presented them as a single community to the public gaze. The strike processions were usually composed of the workers of individual estates, though in October 1884 there was an incipient tendency for workers of different estates to appear in the town together. The possibility that these separate groups could merge into an indistinguishable whole was enhanced by their incorporation into the Hosay. In this sense at least, the Hosay procession embodied the ideal of the strike procession, i.e. a collective presentation of the whole class of labourers.

I shall point out here some aspects of the 1884 Hosay procession which were infused with the emergent class practices, and actualized the ideal strike procession. The Hosay procession of 1884 presented a novel feature. Most witnesses to the Norman commission emphasized the fact that though at the beginning each estate had their separate *taziyas* and smaller processions, as they reached the boundaries of San Fernando they had merged completely. One witness referred to 'the perfect sea of sticks' that advanced towards the town. Most witnesses said that men from all the estates had mingled to such an extent that it was not possible to distinguish different estates. An analysis of those who were killed or wounded in the shooting showed that they were from various estates (28 different estates in the two processions). Thus, at least during the final stretch leading up to the town boundary, the different estate formations had substantially merged, though the leading estates had the largest fatalities, like Petit Morne, Union Hall and Wellington.[69]

In a way the Hosay also actualized the embryonic strike processions of the estates. Only in very rare instances could the strike in one estate lead to sympathy strikes in other. But that is exactly how the Hosay of 1884 began.[70] The Esperance workers had, according to their manager been 'ready to give up the idea of leaving the estate, but as soon as they saw the Wellington and Picton Hoseas advancing along the public road they got excited and were carried away by their country men from these estates'. On the afternoon of 30 October the Philippine estate labourers apparently had been cowered and cajoled by their manager not to join the procession and the estate gates had been shut. In the meanwhile, an impatient crowd from the Wellington, Picton, and Esperance estates had formed outside and clamoured to be let in and take the Philippine *taziya*. 'If there are no men among the Philippine Coolies and if they were all women then we will take the Tazia', said one of them as they carried the *taziya* and the Philippine labourers followed them. The Retrench estate labourers, when warned by their managers that they would be shot if they joined the procession, said 'what Philippine Coolies do we will do' and followed the swelling mass on the road. This was repeated in very many estates where the hesitant workers were emboldened by the workers of other estates and followed them or were practically forced to do so. La Plaisance labourers followed the Bien Venue workers who themselves had followed the Taroub labourers. Petit Morne labourers apparently compelled the workers of Reform. It was thus that from estate to estate a tidal wave of processions was

[69] Calculated from the list of casualties, Enclosure No. 7, *Norman Report*, pp. 77–85.

[70] The account of this paragraph is from various statements of managers of estates submitted to the Norman commission. Ibid., pp. 81–5.

created that swept through the estates carrying all the workers with them.

In sum, the shared repertoire of style and content between the Hosay of 1884 and the series of strike processions preceding it could powerfully translate meanings developed in one set of actions to the other. The temporal conjunction of the strike season and the Hosay procession in 1884 was no doubt crucial for the conflation of class and community action in a single form. It was not only experienced as a unified moment by the labourers themselves but more importantly was communicated to and read as such by the state and the planters. This explains both the intensity and determination of the Indian labourers to oppose the ban on the procession, as well as the brutal suppression by the colonial state.

The Aftermath

Aided by the colonial state, the planters inflicted a massive defeat on the emergent working-class movement in Trinidad when they shot down 22 workers in the Hosay. They succeeded in imposing reduced wages on free labourers on a large scale and increased the tasks of the indentured labourers. In 1890, when Commins visited Trinidad, he could not but note the sharp decline in wages that had occurred between 1883 and 1890: for free labourers a fall of 25 to 50 per cent, and a definite increase of task size for indentured labourers.[71] Workers arrested for participation in the strikes before the Hosay were heavily punished with long prison sentences.[72] The shooting was followed by an ordinance in June 1885 that prohibited indentured labourers from complaining to the Protector in groups of more than five members at a time and banned the carrying of agricultural implements while going to complain, with severe penalties for transgression. In the immediate aftermath of the shooting, planters and their allies, among them missionaries and newspapers, uniformly noted the sharp decline in the scale of disputes in the plantations. John Morton, a leading Presbyterian missionary, had assured the Norman commission that: 'Since the riots the Coolies have much improved in demeanour; before they

[71] *Commins Note*, pp. 6–7 and 10.

[72] In the El Soccoro case five persons got prison sentences, ranging from two to four years. In the case of the Laurel Hill estate four 'ring leaders' were convicted for two years each. *POSG*, 20 December 1884.

had become very overbearing.' Most newspapers applauded the firm action taken by the government in upholding the 'majesty of Law', and pointed to the improved labour relations as a result of the shooting.[73]

But the results of these actions were not unequivocal. Workers were forced to adopt a more indirect style of protest, this time by leaving the plantations—there was a large and permanent exodus of free labourers from the estates which Commins later termed a 'secession from the estates'.[74] The exodus was apparently triggered by a strange rumour sweeping through the sugar districts: the Governor had proclaimed that the free labourers were not to accept wages below 25 cents for a task on pain of imprisonment for three months. The *Port of Spain Gazette*, which reported this rumour, suspected a renewed island-wide conspiracy by the Indian immigrants while *Public Opinion* appealed to the loyalty and good sense of labourers not to abandon the estates in their time of trouble.[75] The loss of some of the best and most experienced workers to the sugar industry was a gain to the cocoa industry which now experienced a sharp upturn in its fortune.

Conflict on the plantations did not cease altogether and neither did the tradition of collective action such as marching to the town, though after the enactment of the 1885 ordinance they did became less frequent.[76] Conflicts over tasks and wages remained largely confined to the estates and took the form of protests, like absenteeism, refusal to obey orders to finish and begin tasks, and occasionally violence against the plantation officials. This was reflected in continuing high rates at which indentured workers were prosecuted for breaches of contract provisions of the

[73] Evidence of John Morton in *Norman Report*, p. 69. See the reaction to the shooting in the selections from contemporary newspapers published in Singh, *Bloodstained Tombs*, Ch. 8.

[74] *Commins Note*, p. 7.

[75] *POSG*, 9 May 1885, and *Public Opinion*, 6 February 1885.

[76] A few days after the Hosay shooting, workers of a remote estate marched a long distance to the town to complain to the Protector. Six of them were arrested and immediately imprisoned on charges of incitement to stop work. *POSG*, 20 December 1884. After the enactment of the new ordinance in 1885 prohibiting mass processions, there were still a few instances of this form of protest—the most celebrated being in 1900 when 64 workers of Harmony estate were imprisoned for having marched to the town to complain of ill-treatment by the plantation manager. Laurence, *Question of Labour*, p. 267.

indenture ordinances. Towards the end of the indenture period, the use of prosecutions became very frequent and reached the heights of the 1880s with an annual rate of prosecution regularly exceeding 30 per cent of the indentured labourers. This high rate of prosecution was subject of several commissions of enquiry, and was one of the important arguments used by the Indian nationalists against the indenture system leading to its eventual abolition in 1917.[77]

Regarding the Hosay, strict enforcement of the 1884 regulations following the shooting drastically altered the character of the festival. It was now rigidly confined to the estates and no procession was ever taken out through the public roads of San Fernando and Port of Spain. Denied this vital expressive form, the festival died a slow death on the sugar estates in the south where there was a maximum concentration of the Indian population. As a vital festival of the Indians, Hosay survived only in a small pocket in the St. James-Peru suburb of Port of Spain; there it continues to be a major festival to date.[78] Prohibition of participation of non-immigrants (that is the Creole population) contributed to the increasing cultural separation between the Indians and the rest of the population of the island.[79] The sharp distinction between the religious and the non-religious part of the

[77] Trinidad's prosecution rate had reached 39 per cent by 1907–8 and declined slowly in the years afterwards. See the discussion on Trinidad's prosecution rate in *Report of the Committee on Emigration from India to the Crown Colonies and Protectorates*, 1910, House of Commons Parliamentary Papers, XXVIII, 1910 (Cd 5192–4), pp. 57–8, and *Report to the Government of India on the Conditions of Indian Immigrants in Four British Colonies and Surinam*, House of Commons Parliamentary Papers 1914–16, XVII (Cd 7744–5), pp. 21–8. See also Laurence, *Question of Labour*, Ch. 13 on the question of a high prosecution rate being an issue for the eventual abolition of the indenture system.

[78] See Singh, *Blood Stained Tombs*, p. 31, for an explanation of the survival of Hosay in this suburb of Port of Spain. For an account of the contemporary celebration of Hosay in Trinidad, see Korom and Chelkowski, 'Community Process and the Performance of Muharram Observances', and Frank Korom, 'Memory, Innovation and Emergent Ethnicities: The Creolization of an Indo-Trinidadian Performance', *Diaspora*, 3, 2 (1994), pp. 135–55.

[79] The issue of relations between the Creoles and Indians in the context of Hosay needs to be explored in detail. The crossover in style and participation between carnival and the Hosay would be a significant area for research in changing forms of popular culture of Trinidad. It is perhaps not without significance that in the immediate aftermath of the Hosay massacre the

festival made after the 1884 regulations, contributed to the decline of Hosay as a festival of the entire Indian community. It was now the prerogative of the Muslims only to apply for permission to celebrate the festival. In 1929, permission for the St James Hosay was denied as there were several Hindu applicants. It is interesting to read the petition sent by a group of Muslim youths seeking a re-examination of the order. They wrote:

> It appears sir that it has been represented to the Honourable Inspector General of Constabulary that this festival is to be carried on by the Hindus. We repudiate this fact sir, it is true that there are a few Hindus who have subscribed to build the *tazia* and the moons but sir you will readily understand that we young people now growing up are trying to break down all these distinctions and to remember that we are all East Indians.[80]

How different is this petition from the one sent to the Governor 45 years earlier, when no special pleading for participation of the Hindus in the Hosay was made! It is also significant that the petitioners refer to the emergence of distinctions that they wish now to erase by constructing an identity as 'East Indians'. In the aftermath of the 1884 Hosay, there was, therefore, a retreat into a more sharply defined religious community. The rise of Brahmanical Hinduism in Trinidad can be traced to this period when Hosay was in decline, with several consequences for the expression of low caste and unorthodox values in the community festivals. So one paradoxical effect of the suppression of the Hosay as a community festival was to increase community awareness, sharpening the boundaries between the Indians and the rest of the population and, also, among the Indian immigrants between the Hindus and the Muslims, the two major religious groups.

---

carnival of 1885 in San Fernando had a full-scale depiction of the shooting of the Indian labourers, enacted by the Creoles. Placed alongside another scene depicting the anti-tax movement among the Creoles, the tableau of the Hosay massacre in the carnival conveyed the popular resentment against the brutal treatment meted out to the Indians by the colonial state. This was in sharp contrast to the general support which the police action received from the elites of the island. *Public Opinion*, 24 February 1885.

[80] 'Petition From Muslim Youths', 22 July 1929; No. 152/1929 in General Letters to the Protector of Immigrants Office, Vol. 1929, Trinidad National Archives.

In this paper, I have tried to understand the multiple layers of meaning embedded in the Hosay massacre of 1884 by locating it in the history of class conflict and community formation among the Indian immigrant labourers. I have argued that the intensity of colonial state repression as well as the defiance of the Indian labourers can be explained by the way in which the Hosay of 1884 uniquely combined the class and community identities of the Indian labourers. By focusing on collective performances of class *and* community, I have tried to show the ways in which they mutually reinforced each other. If Hosay became a vehicle for the expression of class grievances, it did so by amplifying its expression of community aspirations. The experience of sharpening class conflict during the sugar crisis infused the community festival with oppositional workers' values. It was the fusion of class and community forms in the Hosay that most threatened the planters and the colonial state, and the shooting down of the 22 participants was meant to break the links between these two forms. Yet, as I have indicated, the success of the planters and the state may not have been so unequivocal.

10

Aurora and Ananta: Protagonists in an Epic Transition

Sudipto Mundle

Introduction

When Arvind Das first invited me to contribute to a festschrift for Jan Breman, his friend and professional colleague of many years, I readily agreed. Jan is an old friend. Contributing to a festschrift for him is a privilege. At the same time, I was faced with a dilemma. What could I write as an economist that would be appropriate for a festschrift in honour of a distinguished social anthropologist. Statistics and algebra are the tools of our trade. We economists analyse the behaviour of firms and markets, industries, sectors, and whole economies. The social anthropologists work with real life people—individuals and groups of individuals—as they interact in everyday life. I finally decided to revisit the transition from agrarian to industrial society, a theme that I have visited many times through my professional life, but approach it this time from what might be an anthropologist's point of entry, normally individual experiences of the transition.

There are many ways of stylizing facts and theorizing about the long-term dynamics of history. Marx and Weber, Toynbee and Braudel, Hicks, Landes and North are but a few of the better known examples of the many ways of organizing our images of the past. Two epic transitions which frequently reappear in these varieties of interpretations of the past are the rise of settled

* The views expressed in this paper are personal views of the author. These are not necessarly shared by the Asian Development Bank.

agriculture and the transition from agriculture to industry, i.e. the Agrarian Revolution and the Industrial Revolution. Historians, anthropologists, political scientists, and economists have all been interested in these two great turning points of human history, the passage from one to the other, and the links between them.

Development economists have been interested in the second turning point in particular, the transition from agrarian to industrial society, because the latter is also the traverse across the great divide between underdevelopment and development, the passage from mass poverty to mass prosperity. In a collection of papers on *Rural Transformation in Asia* which Jan and I published some ten years ago, the only academic project in which we have directly collaborated, we carried two papers on the subject.[1] Both were written by economists and dealt with economic aspects of the transition. Indeed, in the field of development economics there is a vast literature, led by the seminal work of Arthur Lewis and Harris–Todaro, which deals with this aspect.[2] Less has been written on the political and social aspects of this great transition. Important exceptions include the contributions of Breman and his colleagues in the Amsterdam group on workers and entrepreneurs engaged in this transition in western India.[3]

The latter half of the twentieth century saw this transition gather momentum in dozens of countries in Asia, Africa, and Latin America. Millions migrated from their rural farming communities to new modes of urban living in crowded and ever expanding cities. In its sheer scale this great global migration from the village to the city dwarfs any earlier migration episode in history, whether

[1] Jan Breman and Sudipto Mundle (eds), *Rural Transformation in Asia* (Delhi, 1991).

[2] W. Arthur Lewis, 'Economic Development with Unlimited Supplies of Labour', *Manchester School*, 22 (1954), pp. 139–91; John R. Harris and Michael P. Todaro, 'Migration, Unemployment and Development: A Two-Sector Model', *American Economic Review*, 60 (1970), pp. 126–42.

[3] Jan Breman, *Of Peasants, Migrants and Paupers: Rural Labour Circulation and Capitalist Production in West India* (Delhi, 1985); Mario Rutten (ed.), *Capitalist Entrepreneurs and Economic Diversification* (Rotterdam, 1991). For a recent analytical review see Sudipto Mundle, 'Agriculture–Industry Linkage: a Review and a Suggested Reconstruction', Keynote Paper at the Conference on Industrialization in a Reforming Economy: a Quantitative Assessment, Delhi, Delhi School of Economics, 20–2 December 2000.

it be the rural–urban migration of industrializing Europe, the great migration from Europe in the colonization of America and Australia, or the forced migration of labour among the European colonies in Asia, Africa, and Latin America that Breman and others have written about.[4]

Moreover, this new phase of rural–urban migration is still a process in the ascendant. As the economist Harry Oshima once put it, development is a transition from a situation where about two-thirds of the population is dependent on agriculture to one where two-thirds of the population is dependent on industry and services.[5] By that metric only a few countries in Asia, Africa, and Latin America have completed or nearly completed the transition. The rest are still on the way. The first few decades of the twenty-first century will see a peaking of this process.

In other words, the agriculture–industry transition of the latter half of the twentieth century, and its culmination in the early twenty-first century is a global human drama of epic proportions, unprecedented in human history. It is a process which will have transformed the lives of the large majority of six billion people who inhabit this world—mostly in China, India, and other developing countries of the Third World. Yet, we rarely perceive this as such an epic historical process. This is partly because in these transitional generations we ourselves are living through this process, and see nothing particularly extraordinary about our everyday lives. It is also because the transition is a long process stretched out over several decades. It is not a short dramatic event such as the horrors of war and the holocaust, or the conquest of space, the electronic revolution, and the biotechnology revolution which more easily capture the human imagination. It is really quite remarkable how little we know about the experiences of the hundreds of millions of people who are all protagonists in this epic human drama.

The story below is the story of two such protagonists. Arvind and I were exchanging e-mail messages about the theme and this

[4] Jan Breman, *Control of Land and Labour in Colonial Java* (Leiden, 1983).

[5] H.T. Oshima, 'Human Resources in the Agro-Industrial Transition, in International Economic Association', in S. Chakravarty (ed.), *The Balance Between Industry and Agriculture in Economic Development*. Vol. 3: *Manpower and Transfers* (London, 1989).

story when he departed for Amsterdam. I did not hear from him again. It is fortunate that some of his colleagues carried on with the project; and that the festschrift for his friend Jan has now been completed. This is how he would have wanted it.

The Encounter

Ananta Acharya met Aurora Fernandes at a dinner party in South Forbes Park, an elite residential quarter of Metro Manila, Philippines, much favoured by presidents, cabinet ministers, the leaders of business, diplomats, and the occasional expatriate managers of multinational enterprises. The president of a leading policy think tank in New Delhi, and one time Chief Economic Adviser in the Government of India, Ananta was in Manila to participate in a meeting for the establishment of an Asian economic monitoring arrangement to pre-empt a repeat of the 1997 financial crisis. He had stayed on for an extra day after the meeting to see his friend Ramesh Shetty. A close friend from their student days, Ramesh was now the Resident Representative of one of the international agencies in Manila.

Ananta was visiting Ramesh in his elegant South Forbes Park bungalow. The two friends were meeting after several years and they had much to catch up on. Aurora was there too, a bright and self-confident young girl of 22 years. With her hair tied back in a neat bun, wearing a crisp striped dress in white and pastel blue, she confidently moved about the living room offering canapes to go with the drinks before dinner. She had come to Ramesh's house some two years ago to work as a maid. Ananta was impressed with the young girl's self-confidence and her fluent English speech. It was quite unlike what he was used to back in India. He asked Aurora what her name was, and how she came to speak such fluent English.

As he listened to their conversation, Ramesh was struck by the irony of the event that was unfolding before him. Ananta had started life in a poor farming family, just as Aurora had. Both migrated from their villages to make a living in the urban world. However, their lives had moved along very different social paths. Here was Ananta, a well-known economist in India, leading his country's delegation to an international conference, and an honoured guest in Ramesh's house. And here was Aurora who had followed a more humble route. She too was in Ramesh's house, attending to his honoured guest. What accounted for their different fortunes he wondered? Perhaps Ananta too was struck by the irony of his chance meeting with Aurora. He questioned her closely on her origins, her past life, and how she came to be where she was.

Origins

Aurora was born and raised by her grandmother in the *barangay* of Bayomrang, a small village of 5,000 persons in the northwestern province of Pangasinan on the main island of Luzon in the Philippines. When she was a few months old her mother had to leave Aurora with Aurora's grandmother, and return to her husband's village in the same province to help him farm their small patch of land. They were too poor to employ anyone, and the patch of land was in any case too small for that. So Aurora was raised by her grandmother, her aunt, and other maternal relatives during her first few years. Her mother would visit her every week and buy her small necessities for school. But Aurora remembers that she could not even afford to buy a proper school bag.

After a few years the arrangement became unviable, so Aurora went to live with her parents. Her father's *barangay* was an even smaller village of some 400 families, mostly small farmers and fisherfolk. They lived in a small thatched bamboo hut with no electricity or piped water. Aurora is the eldest of eight brothers and sisters. Though small, the family plot is fertile and close to a river, enabling irrigation. They grow corn, rice, and vegetables, but it is barely enough to feed a family of ten and still provide a marketable surplus to meet their meagre monetary needs. As the family expanded, food became scarcer and Aurora had to increasingly take on the household chores as her mother directed all her time to helping her husband on the land, ro grow as much as they could. The shortage of food and money was a constant, nagging burden.

Despite this desperate struggle for survival the parents were determined to see all their children through school. Aurora mentioned that her father always said that even if he could give them nothing else he had to give them an education, because he did not want them to suffer the way he had suffered. It helped that the school was a public school and virtually free. Still there were costs of books and clothes for school, and the children had to be given something to eat during their day at school.

Aurora finished her elementary school at the age of 12 years, but then there was no more money to buy even her minimum requirements for high school. So during her vacation Aurora accompanied a relative to the nearby town of Bulacan where she got her first job as a fruit sellers' assistant. It paid her 500 pesos (about $10) per month. In two months she earned 1,000 pesos, of which she needed 500 for her high school. The rest she gave to her mother. She did the same every vacation and so paid her way through high school. As the eldest of eight siblings, Aurora says, she had to grow up quickly and learn the value of earning money at an early age. There was not much time for enjoying her childhood.

Ananta too came from a small farming family, but it was not nearly as deprived as Aurora's family. There were also other interesting differences in their origins, Ramesh noted, as he compared Aurora's life story with what he already knew of Ananta's life history. Ananta Acharya was born as the youngest of three sons in a Brahmin family in the village of Korongrapady in the South Kanara District of Karnataka province in India. The family owned some land. However, it is taboo for a Brahmin to plough the land. So Ananta's father earned his living as a professional cook in the town of Bellary 300 miles away, cooking for weddings and other social functions like the modern day caterers.

As a Brahmin, Ananta's father had four years of schooling in Sanskrit; however this was of little use in his cooking. He would visit home for a month every year during the inauspicious rainy season, when there was very little work for professional cooks. He would buy each of his three children a set of clothes during his visits, and leave Rs 200 with his wife as the household budget for the whole year. The amount never changed over the years though prices rose. If the father missed his annual visit, the children had to manage with their old clothes for one more year. Their mother was married at the age of ten years and had never been to school. However, she had a great fascination for education, and taught herself to read and write. She also learned some devotional singing since her father had been a well-known classical singer.

The family lived in a simple village house with no toilets and electricity. Though of modest means, the family was not in great penury like Aurora's family. Rice, pulses, and vegetables were all grown on the family farm. Tamarind fruits were sold to buy jaggery. The family also owned a few cows and Ananta's mother sold some milk to supplement their money income.

Ananta was very proud of his elder brother, the first high school graduate in the family, and adopted him as a role model. After completing elementary school in the village, Ananta attended a Christian high school in the nearby town of Udipi. Throughout this period Ananta was an impish young lad, full of pranks and thoroughly enjoying his childhood years, quite a contrast to Aurora who became an adult in early childhood. Ananta was no great scholar, he had told Ramesh, and nobody expected him to go far in life. However, he did not have to earn in his childhood to see himself through high school like Aurora. The one deprivation which he did share with Aurora in this early stage of life was the disadvantage of a rural origin. Both teachers and students at the high school in Udipi looked down on him as a country bumpkin, not smart and articulate like the other urban boys.

Divergent Paths

After finishing high school Aurora took an important decision which would set the course of her life for many years to come. She decided to abandon any plans for further studies, and travel to Manila to seek her fortunes. In the Philippines, for most rural–urban migrants in search of a better life all roads lead to Metro Manila, a gigantic urban conurbation spanning seven different cities, home to a third of the population of the Philippines, and the economic base for generating the bulk of the country's national income. It was the same for Aurora. She accompanied her cousin, who had earlier relocated to the city, and had promised to help Aurora find a job in Manila. Why had she chosen this path, Ramesh wondered. Why had she not paid her way through college with vacation jobs, the way she had worked her way through school? Perhaps the strain of studying and also earning to supplement the family income had proved too difficult to sustain. Perhaps it was the lure of the city. Perhaps a bit of both.

However, finding a job in Manila proved harder than what Aurora had expected. She first went to Cavite, one of the seven cities of Metro Manila where she could stay for a while with relatives. She looked for a job in a factory there. The factory wanted adults with Social Security accounts. You had to be of 18 years of age to become a member of the Social Security System.

Aurora was only 16 years old. She couldn't get the job. Disappointed, she returned to her village. An aunt was at the time searching for a helper in her beauty parlour-cum-refreshments shop in the nearby town of Camiling. She decided to hire Aurora. So Aurora was back in the urban world, even if not in the metropolis of Manila. She worked in her aunt's shop for two years. It was her first real exposure to the world of the urban adult. She enjoyed her work and met a lot of different people. Men courted her, and she even had a tentative relationship which finally went nowhere.

At the end of two years, Aurora found herself back in Manila in search of a job. She had no special skills, no education beyond high school, and no experience to qualify her for a job in factories or offices. She finally found a job as a maid in Ramesh's house, where she has continued to work. Maid's jobs do not rank very high in the professional ladder. Yet, in value terms it was more paying than many blue collar and even some white collar job, especially if you were lucky enough to land a job in an expatriate home at the upper end of the maids' job market. You earn about the same as department store assistants and clerks in small offices, but the board and lodging comes free with the job. On balance, Aurora could live reasonably comfortably, feed herself, buy a few clothes and accessories from time to time, and still send more money home to support the family than she would have in any of the other jobs. In her own way, Aurora had 'arrived'. She had found her little niche in the city, a place she could call home, and a job that now made her the main breadwinner of her family.

Ramesh felt quite pleased when he heard Aurora tell Ananta that the Shetty's were like a second family for her. He wanted to believe that she meant what she said. Perhaps she had reason to think so. Of late, most of Aurora's duties had been cut down to give her a chance to continue her studies. She had joined one of the computer training colleges in the city a year ago, and was doing quite well. The salary she earned allowed her to pay her college fees and still send some money home. She woke up early and did some of her chores before going to college. The rest she finished on her return. In the evening she studied and did her homework to prepare for the next day. It was a tough life, but at least she had now recovered her lost opportunity to complete college. She now had another chance to move upward into the ranks of the middle class.

Ananta's own path of 'arrival' in the urban world was not nearly as tortuous. He had finished school with a first class in his final exams, and easily got admission at the Mahatma Gandhi Memorial College. Paying for his college education was also not a real issue. His father had not been too keen to see Ananta through, however, this was mainly because his father thought that college education was a waste of time and money. After all, his own four years of Sanskrit education had not been of mush use. The shortage of money was not really a problem. The important thing for Ananta was for him to complete his studies. He had a tough routine. He had to wake up early and work in the farm before going to college. As a Brahmin, he could perform other tasks but not plough, which too he did on the sly. Then he and his brother would cycle to college in the town of Udipi. The eldest brother was now living away and was well set on the way to a Ph.D. He would visit home occasionally, give his mother the expenses for running the house, and then visit Ananta's college, where he would give his brothers a treat.

Ananta had initially hoped to study physics like his elder brother. However, the head of the physics department, who didn't seem to like Ananta very much, discouraged him. Ananta shifted to economics and, from then on, excelled in his performance. Nevertheless, his father did not want to support him further through a Master's degree. So Ananta went to live with his brother in Ahmedabad, and took his Master's degree there from the University of Gujarat. He also took up part-time jobs at this stage to help pay his way. It was at this time that he first met Ramesh Shetty, then a student at the Indian Institute of Management. He also met some excellent professors, who were impressed by his motivation and encouraged him to pursue a career as an economist.

After completing his Master's degree Ananta joined a research institute in Ahmedabad. Institutional politics then drove him out of there, and he followed his faction leader to the University of Saraswada. He also completed his Ph.D. there. However, the university was not among the best in the country for economics, and Ananta found it difficult to land an academic job with a Ph.D. from Saraswada University. Nevertheless, his contacts from his Ahmedabad days helped him a great deal, and he was able to secure an appointment with a research institution in Delhi this time. From then on, Ananta made rapid progress. Hard work, effective networking, and a large number of publications soon established him as a leading economist in his field. He also undertook numerous foreign assignments as a visiting fellow at universities and as a consultant to various international agencies. By the time he completed fifteen years at the institute, he had already risen to the top and taken over as the president and chief executive of the Institute.

Looking Ahead

Aurora had finished telling her tale to Ananta. He asked her what her aspirations were for the future? Interestingly, Aurora did not focus on her own career. She did say that she hoped to get a job as a computer programmer, first in a small company, and then move on to a major company. However, she mentioned this only as a means to an end. Her main aspirations were to somehow educate her siblings, so that they would not have to struggle the way she had struggled. This was also her father's main aspiration, Ramesh recalled, as he listened to her. Her other aspiration was to provide her parents with some of the simple comforts they had never had, such as a tin roof to replace the thatched roof of their hut. Eventually, she would like to marry and settle when she found a suitable man.

Once again Ramesh found himself comparing the simple aspirations of Aurora with those of Ananta, just as he had mentally compared their origins at the outset of Aurora's tale. He reflected on the very different future that lay ahead for Ananta. Both Ananta and Aurora had started life in a simple farmer's home in rural society. Both of them had eventually migrated to the city, but after following very different paths. Today Aurora was hoping to pull herself into a middle class life, see her siblings through school, and drag her parents out of poverty. Ananta, on the other hand, had already reached the top, a mandarin at the apex of a billion strong Indian society. His international assignments had enabled him to see his two children through good universities in the United States and they were both well settled abroad. His son was a computer engineer in Seattle, and his daughter an analyst with a Wall Street firm in New York. He himself was also quite well known internationally, increasingly called upon to join or chair various committees and conferences all over the world—a player in the exclusive world of a small global elite. For a boy who was born in a simple farmer's home with no electricity and no toilet, he had indeed travelled a long distance.

Conclusion

In the short story that has been recounted above I have altered some names, and places, and events to preserve the privacy of the two protagonists. Nevertheless, the story is a substantively accurate representation of the lives of two real individuals. At the level of their personal histories, the transformation which the two individuals have experienced in their personal lives is enormous. Yet, as a societal phenomenon it is not remarkable at all for the transitional generations of the late twentieth and early twenty-first centuries—the hundreds of millions of persons who have been migrating from rural to urban areas as one developing country after another completes the transition from an agrarian to an industrial society. Ananta's story may appear awesome, but there are thousands of Ananta's in the new elites of India, the Philippines, and other developing countries throughout the world. The current President of India had origins even more humble than those of Ananta. Nevertheless, this new elite of rural–urban migrants is indeed a small minority compared to the large majority of rural–urban migrants who have been less upwardly mobile like Aurora. A comparison of their divergent social migration paths raises a number of interesting questions.

It is useful in this context to recall E.H. Carr's famous causality example about Jones, the drunken driver of a car with defective brakes, who knocked down and killed Robinson at a blind corner that had poor visibility while the latter was crossing the road to buy cigarettes at the corner shop.[6] Carr used the example to illustrate an important distinction between real and accidental causes in history. Clearly if Robinson had not been on his way to buy cigarettes, he would not have been killed that night. In that sense, Robinson's heading for the cigarettes was one of the combination of events on that fateful evening that led to his death. However, it would be silly to infer from this that if people stopped buying cigarettes, it would reduce the number of deaths from traffic accidents (it would certainly reduce deaths from cancer, heart disease, and other health hazards of smoking but that is a

[6] E.H. Carr, *What is History?* (London, 1961).

different matter). Thus, Robinson's going to buy cigarettes cannot be *generalized* as one of the causes of traffic accidents. In that sense, it was a trivial or *accidental* cause, not a *real* cause of the traffic accident.

On the other hand, Jones' drunken driving, the defective breaks, and poorly lit blind alley can each be treated as generic or *real* causes of traffic accidents. Less drunken driving, less defective car breaks, and better lit streets could, each one in itself, reduce the incidence of traffic accidents.

Let us now return to the story of Aurora and Ananta and their divergent social paths of migration, and apply this test of causality. What can we say were the *real* causes of Ananta's greater upward mobility, relative to Aurora, in the course of his migration to the city? *Real* causes that are generic and would better enable us to predict the social paths of rural–urban migrants.

One set of causal factors I would like to set aside are the differences in individual capabilities. I shall set these aside not because they are unimportant, but because they are less interesting. Aurora is an intelligent and determined young lady. However, it would be an altogether different matter to assert that she is as intelligent, hard-working, and motivated as Ananta. I have no doubt that Ananta's high intellectual capability, diligence, and motivation were instrumental in his rapid rise to the top. So too was Ananta's admiration for the eldest brother, as was Ananta's desire to emulate him. Nevertheless, such inherent differences in individual capability are not very interesting as explanatory factors underlying variations in the degree of upward mobility among rural–urban migrants. They are not interesting from the perspective of public action because they are not variables which can be manipulated by such action to make the agriculture–industry transition a more 'friendly' development process. We, therefore, focus on factors other than such differences in individual capability.

Perhaps the most striking feature that stands out from this perspective is the key role of education, the intellectual capital of the migrant, in determining the social migration path or the degree of upward mobility. If we were to ask what was the single most important factor that diverted Aurora to a migration path different from that of Ananta's, the answer would have to be the lack of adequate education. Had Aurora continued her studies beyond high school, and graduated with a college degree, she would most probably have migrated to a middle-class urban life.

It should be emphasized that such upward mobility would have been a high probability, not a certainty. In the household where Aurora works in Manila, there is a cook with a bachelor's degree. In many homes in Manila, and even more so in Hong Kong, Taipei, Singapore, and other global cities, one is likely to encounter Filipina maids who are college graduates. More so outside the Philippines rather than inside, because the brightest and best educated usually migrate to higher paid jobs abroad. At a friend's home in Geneva, where I was a house guest, I once met a young Filipina lady who arrived in the morning to do the dusting, and vacuum the floor. I was told that she held a graduate degree. I asked the lady why she had travelled all the way to Geneva to work as a cleaning woman despite her high level of education. She explained that her cleaning woman's job enabled her to live comfortably herself, and still send more money home than the total salary she could have earned in a clerical or teaching job in Manila. Of course, the job of a household help in Manila is not the same as that of a cleaning woman in Geneva. Had Aurora gone to college, as Ananta had, she would most probably have moved on to an easier middle-class life, as Ananta had.

The importance of education in determining the path of social migration was not unknown to either Ananta's family or Aurora's family. Ananta's father had been reluctant about Ananta's higher education, and had refused to pay for it. From his vantage point as a professional cook, a high school education may have seemed quite enough. However, Ananta's mother more than made up for this lack of paternal enthusiasm, and all the three brothers had gone to college. Ananta and his role model elder brother had even gone on to earn their Ph.Ds. Perhaps this had something to do with the cultural milieu of a Brahmin family, and again perhaps not. Aurora's father is a poor Catholic farmer in the Philippines, and he too had repeatedly told his children that he was prepared to forego everything, so long as he could educate his children. It is also Aurora's main aspiration to earn for her siblings the educational opportunities she had missed; and she is extremely grateful to the Shettys that they have now given her the same opportunity.

The importance given to education by both Ananta and Aurora is of course not uncommon. It is a value that seems to cut across all classes and throughout the world. The upper classes drive their children to make sure that they get to the best universities, in order to maximize their upward mobility. The poor, for their part, accept enormous deprivation to ensure that their children get an education. These revealed preferences of civil society raise important questions about public policy, the emphasis that governments should give to the development of social infrastructure relative to physical infrastructure; and also the relative allocation of resources between primary education and secondary and higher education.

The second link in this chain of cause–effect linkages is the scarcity of economic resources. Aurora knew the importance of a college education for migrating to a white collar urban job, yet she had to give it up. The summer jobs had been enough to see her through school, but not enough to see her through college, and her parents just could not afford it. Ananta, on the other hand, had no such problems. His father was reluctant to see him through college, but mainly as a matter of choice and not for lack of resources. In the end, the rest of the family prevailed, and all three boys went to college. From a materialist perspective, we would be led to say therefore that it is not education *per se* that determines the social path of rural–urban migration, but the initial resource endowment of a family. It is the latter which determines its *access* to education and hence the social path of migration.

However, it is possible to further extend the chain of causal links. The resource endowment of the family must be reckoned relative to family size. Aurora belonged to a family of nine children. Had it been a family of only three children, like Ananta's, the family could have doubled its per capita income from the same farming plot. That would surely have enabled her to complete her college education, and given her a good chance to migrate to a middle-class urban life. But that was not to be. Was it purely chance that Aurora was born into a family with eleven mouths to feed, whereas Ananta was born into a family of only five? Or were there more systematic factors at work? Aurora's family belongs to a culture where contraception is not acceptable. In a different cultural milieu they might have practised contraception to have a smaller family, and reached a higher per capita income. Aurora could have had a college education and, potentially, a social path of rural–urban migration similar to that of Ananta.

If we can speculate on this counterfactual possibility, then we can also consider other counterfactual scenarios. Thus, Aurora's parents could have had their family of eleven, but also owned twice or thrice the amount of land her father actually owned. Their per capita income would then have been two or three times as high, and Aurora could have had her college education and a middle-class urban life. As a third possibility, culture, family size, and family land endowment could all be the same, but the government could be offering virtually free education even at the college level, as many countries still do. Once again Aurora could have had her college education and migrated to a middle-class urban life.

The main purpose of these counterfactual scenarios is to demonstrate that even in our simple two-case comparison of alternative social paths of rural–urban migration, there is no simple unilinear causal explanation of the alternative paths of migration. Applying Carr's test of real and accidental causes, each of the factors identified above could be extended from the particular to the general. A variation in any one of the elements identified in the two-case comparison, everything else remaining the same, would lead to a different outcome in general. It could raise or lower the probability of a migrant moving into alternative social paths of migration. Thus our simple story would lead us to hypothesize that cultural practises, economic resource endowments, and public policy jointly determine the variations in social paths of rural–urban migration.

I started out by telling a simple real life story about two individuals who met in a chance encounter in Manila. They both had similar origins in modest farm households, though admittedly with different resource endowments, and they ended up in very different social niches in the city. We could see these two life stories as purely random individual cases, with no larger historical significance. Alternatively, we could see the two life stories as representative of the hundreds of millions of rural–urban migrants in an epic global transition from agrarian to industrial society in the Third World, as I have suggested. Seen in this latter perspective, their contrasting stories lead to a hypothesis about the set of causal factors which determine the variations in the social paths of rural–urban migration. It would be interesting to ask whether this hypothesis can be sustained by scientific empirical analysis.

Implications

11

Refuting Labour History's Occidentalism

Marcel van der Linden

> *I use the term 'occidentalism' when the horizon of the social and cultural sciences extends no further than the frontiers of researchers' own type of society, and their interest in the rest of the world remains limited to the 'centre's' impact on the 'periphery'.*
>
> JAN BREMAN, 'Over oriëntalistiek en occidentalistiek', *De Gids*, 154 (1991), p. 504

Jan Breman has no explicit macro-theory. Although much of his work deals with exploitation and class contradictions, he is not a Marxist. Nor, though he often cites Max Weber approvingly, is he a pure Weberian. Breman does not like abstract discussions. He wants first of all to build up 'an empirical basis', since without a foundation of this kind theorizing often loses touch with its object. He has observed, for example, that 'reports which are based on factual research are often particularly critical of conceptualization.'[1] On the great debate over the dominant mode of production in Indian agriculture, he has noted critically that it 'broke down in extremely mechanistic schemas and abstract argumentation, which on closer inspection had a mystifying rather than an enlightening effect on everyday praxis'.[2]

* This article is translated by Peter Drucker.

[1] Jan Breman, *Wage Hunters and Gatherers: Search for Work in the Urban and Rural Economy of South Gujarat* (Delhi, 1994), p. 7.

[2] Ibid., p. 375.

A multifaceted, detailed reconstruction of causal mechanisms is more important to Breman than theoretical purity, as his conceptual framework shows. He uses a vocabulary in which Weberian, Marxist and other influences are intermingled. He speaks regularly of the 'proletariat', for example, but the terms refers for him to all those who do not possess means of production of their own, regardless of what relations of production they may be enmeshed in. Breman is thus referring to a 'negatively privileged ownership class', the same class to which Max Weber consigned unfree workers, the declassed (*proletarii* in the sense of European Antiquity), debt peons and 'the poor'.[3] This is thus a far broader concept than that of Marx, who reduced the proletariat to 'doubly free' wage workers.[4] Breman's conception of capitalism seems more reminiscent of Adam Smith's conception than that of Karl Marx, because it is defined above all in terms of trade-based divisions of labour and the effort to accumulate money.[5] Often Breman uses words with several different meanings, and only the context makes it possible to know what he means by them. The concept 'mode of production' for example, sometimes refers in his work to production processes and sometimes to an economic system.[6] Scholars who fail to appreciate Breman's layered deployment of concepts can easily fall into mistaken interpretations.[7]

[3] Max Weber, *Wirtschaft und Gesellschaft* (Tübingen, 1922), p. 178. Compare Jan Breman, *Of Peasants, Migrants and Paupers: Rural Labour Circulation and Capitalist Production in West India* (Delhi, 1985), pp. 66–74.

[4] '[T]his worker must be free in the double sense that as a free individual he can dispose of his labour-power as his own commodity, and that, on the other hand, he has no other commodity for sale . . . .' Karl Marx, *Capital*, Vol. 1, trans. Ben Fowkes (Harmondsworth, 1976), p. 272.

[5] Adam Smith, *The Wealth of Nations* (London, 1991), Book I.

[6] Breman speaks for example about 'a more aggregate mode of production' and about the plantation industry as 'a mode of capitalist production'. Jan Breman, *Taming the Coolie Beast: Plantation Society and the Colonial Order in South-east Asia* (Delhi, 1989), p. 23 and Ch. III.

[7] The most striking example of a mistaken interpretation (perhaps in part the result of insufficient knowledge of Weber's writings) can be found in Tom Brass, 'Immobilised Workers, Footloose Theory', *Journal of Peasant Studies*, 24 (1997), pp. 337–58. Brass argues in this article, among other things, that Breman misunderstands 'Marxist theory in general, and in particular those concepts (proletarianisation, deproletarianisation, repeasantisation) which are crucial to a Marxist analysis of agrarian change and the role in this of unfree labour' (p. 339). This remark could only be made by someone who fails to see that Breman, despite his Marxist-sounding terminology, is in fact an eclectic thinker with neo-Weberian leanings.

Thanks to his empiricism, Breman often prefers to speak about continuums instead of polarities. He mentions a 'continuum' leading from free to unfree labour; he observes that 'an economic continuum has been established between town and country'.[8] And since the richness of empirical data always takes pride of place for Breman, he can interpret the same empirical phenomenon (e.g. *halipratha*) in different ways over the years without seeing this as problematic.

Like Max Weber, Jan Breman seems to assume that 'the number and nature of causes that have determined any one specific event . . . are always infinite'.[9] But while Weber's standpoint is that we can create order in 'this chaos' only because our culturally determined opinions always make us attribute 'importance and meaning' to only 'part of individual reality',[10] all such epistemological relativism is alien to Breman. He is driven by the fact that we live in a world 'which is weighed down as never before by the realisation of a frightful lack of distributive justice'.[11] On the one hand he therefore orders reality on the basis of his own powerful moral and political commitment, but on the other hand he also tries to arrive at as complete a picture of causal configurations as possible. He sides with the labouring poor, but talks with managers, big landowners, and other authorities as well.

Marxists have maintained with good reason that the 'deeper' logic of development and its dynamic contradictions can never be unearthed with this kind of empirical approach. But Breman's method also has a demonstrable, compensating advantage. The truth is that many Marxists think that they already know the 'essence' of social developments. For this reason they think that it suffices simply to subsume new facts into an old theory. Breman's

[8] Jan Breman, Arvind Das and Ravi Agarwal, *Down and Out: Labouring Under Global Capitalism* (New Delhi and Amsterdam, 2000), p. 33.

[9] Max Weber, 'Die Objektivität sozialwissenschaftlicher und sozialpolitischer Erkenntnis' (1904), in *Gesammelte Aufsätze zur Wissenschaftslehre* (Tübingen, 1988), pp. 177–8.

[10] Ibid. See the critical analysis in Wolfgang Lefèvre, *Zum historischen Charakter und zur historischen Funktion der Methode bürgerlicher Soziologie* (Frankfurt am Main, 1971).

[11] Jan Breman, 'De strijd voor maatschappelijke gelijkheid in India', in Anne Gevers (ed.), *Uit de Zevende: Vijftig jaar politieke en sociaal-culturele wetenschappen aan de Universiteit van Amsterdam* (Amsterdam, 1998), p. 408.

brand of empiricism is much more open to unexpected or unknown phenomena. It is just this lack of preconceptions that makes Breman's scholarly writings so innovative. In this brief essay, I would like to illustrate this quality in one limited part of Breman's research.

Breman's academic writings are usually pigeonholed under rural sociology or development studies. But they also constitute a contribution to labour history, the history of the working classes in the broad sense of the word. Breman's contributions to this field can be divided into two parts. First, there are his explicit historical studies, such as his history of bonded labour in precolonial and colonial Gujarat, or his study of colonial labour policies in the Netherlands Indies and Belgian Congo.[12] Second, are his contributions, each of which was written separately as a contemporary analysis, but which in combination form a longitudinal series. This is true in particular for his many studies, from the 1960s to the present, of labour relations in Gujarat, which—read one after the other—afford terrific insights into middle-term regional development.[13]

Until now, historians have scarcely taken any notice of all these publications, which from their point of view fall too far outside the mainstream. Not only is Breman not an 'official' historian himself, but also—and this is probably more important—his approach diverges considerably from what until recently was the norm among labour historians. Historians of the working classes have not only occupied themselves for a long time almost exclusively with a small part of the world, that is the advanced capitalist countries and Eastern Europe/Russia, they have also conceived the object of their study in a very narrow and ultimately Eurocentric way. A number of remarkable preconceptions can be identified in the enormous stream of publications that have

[12] Jan Breman, *Patronage and Exploitation: Changing Agrarian Relations in South Gujarat, India* (Berkeley, CA, 1974); idem, 'The Village on Java and the Early Colonial State', *Journal of Peasant Studies*, 9 (1982), pp. 189–240; idem, *Taming the Coolie Beast*; 'Primitive Racism in a Colonial Setting', in idem (ed.), *Imperial Monkey Business: Racial Supremacy in Social Darwinist Theory and Colonial Practice* (Amsterdam, 1990), pp. 89–121.

[13] See above all the trilogy: Jan Breman, *Patronage and Exploitation*; *Of Peasants, Migrants and Paupers: Rural Labour Circulation and Capitalist Production in West India* (Delhi, 1985); *Footloose Labour: Working in India's Informal Economy* (Cambridge, 1996).

appeared since the discipline's first days in the 1860s. The typical worker to which the traditional labour historians devoted their attentions was a 'doubly free' individual (in the Marxian sense), usually male, employed in the transport sector (docks or railways), mines, industry, or large-scale agriculture. His (or sometimes her) family seemed to have above all a consumptive or reproductive function: wages were spent there and children were raised there. Protests were taken seriously mainly when they took the form of strikes by trade unions or left-wing political parties.

When, from the 1950s on, more contributions began appearing on the labour history of colonies or former colonies, they initially made the same Eurocentric assumptions. They too focused on mineworkers, dockers, plantation workers, etc., and neglected families and the work that took place there. They too mainly sought out strikes, trade unions, and political parties. Naturally, different historians' political leanings could be very different. J. Norman Parmer's thorough *Colonial Labor Policy and Administration* (1960) for instance, on the rubber plantation industry in Malaya during the last decades before the Second World War, looked at workers through the eyes of entrepreneurs and authorities. Jean Chesneaux's *Le mouvement ouvrier en Chine de 1919 à 1927* (1962) was written from an official Communist standpoint; while Guillermo Lora's *Historia del movimiento obrero boliviana* (1967–70) was a Trotskyist work.[14]

Later attempts often tried to develop a less Eurocentric approach. Path-breaking works include Charles van Onselen's *Chibaro* (London, 1976) on mine labour in Southern Rhodesia and Ranajit Das Gupta's *Labour and Working Class in Eastern India* (Calcutta, 1994) on plantation workers, miners, and textile workers in Assam, Bengal, and elsewhere. These new developments have been covered over the years by a series of collections of essays.[15]

[14] J. Norman Parmer, *Colonial Labor Policy and Administration. A History of Labor in the Rubber Plantation Industry in Malaya, c. 1910–41* (Locust Valley, NY, 1960); Jean Chesneaux, *Le mouvement ouvrier en Chine de 1919 à 1927* (Paris, 1962); Guillermo Lora, *Historia del movimiento obrero boliviana* (3 vols, La Paz, 1967–70).

[15] Richard Sandbrook and Robin Cohen (eds), *The Development of an African Working Class: Studies in Class Formation and Action* (London, 1975); Peter C.W. Gutkind, Robin Cohen and Jean Copans (eds), *African Labor History* (Beverly Hills, 1978); Robin Cohen, Peter C.W. Gutkind and

I am convinced that Breman's work can make an important contribution to the ongoing reorientation of labour history. And while it may sound paradoxical, I think that his *explicitly* historical writings—while very valuable in themselves—are less important in this respect than his sociological studies of south Gujarat since the early 1960s. For while the explicitly historical studies, particularly those about the Netherlands Indies, investigate fields that other authors have also written about, the results of Breman's Indian fieldwork are exceptionally innovative, path-breaking in the true sense of the word. Precisely the studies that were not intended as contributions to the historiography can draw labour historians' attention to biases that they need to overcome in order to understand the logic of developments in underdeveloped and newly industrializing capitalism. Below I give a capsule description of several 'lessons' that we labour historians can learn from Breman's Indian writings. These are not so much iron rules as methodological hints.

It all began when Breman decided in the early 1960s to study the 'vast agrarian proletariat of tribal origin' in south Gujarat.[16] That was a remarkable decision, for (as Breman himself noted): 'In those years rural studies tended to neglect agricultural labour.'[17] Those were the years in which scholarly interest in the subject began to germinate, as could be seen in the pioneering work of Daniel and Alice Thorner and Dharma Kumar.[18] Through these studies and his own fieldwork Breman quickly discovered that the social reality in south Gujarat was far more complex than the textbooks had led him to suppose. Landless agricultural labourers were not a product of colonialism, but had existed in great numbers as early as the beginning of the nineteenth century. Not only was the waged labour force in the countryside thus far older than was

---

Phyllis Brazier (eds), *Peasants and Proletarians: The Struggles of Third World Workers* (London, 1979); Barry Munslow and Henry Finch (eds), *Proletarianisation in the Third World* (London, 1984); Michel Agier, Jean Copans and Alain Morice (eds), *Classes ouvrières d'Afrique noire* (Paris, 1987); Shahid Amin and Marcel van der Linden (eds), *'Peripheral' Labour? Studies in the History of Partial Proletarianization* (Cambridge, 1996).

[16] Breman, *Beyond Patronage*, p. vi.

[17] Ibid.

[18] Daniel Thorner and Alice Thorner, *Land and Labour in India* (London, 1962); D.K. Kumar, *Land and Caste in South India: Agricultural Labour in the Madras Presidency during the Nineteenth Century* (Cambridge, 1965).

usually assumed, but there had always been a 'multiplicity' of relations of dependency and exploitation.[19] Up until the mid-twentieth century the landless rural population had to a great extent been part of a pluriform unfree labour system, in which people often remained bound by debt to a landlord for generations in a relationship of bondage and patronage.

These forms of attached labour began to be worn away in the late colonial period. The 'unfreedom' gradually disappeared, so that the landless could decide for themselves whom they would hire their labour power to, but at the same time they lost the 'basic subsistence security' that the patronage system had previously provided them with. 'The disappearance of the elements of patronage which had helped to conceal the earlier abundant supply of rural labour put an end to the state of unfreedom in which this class used to live, but not to the stark poverty that accompanied it.'[20] In recent decades Breman has spent most of his scholarly energy on analysing the fate of the agrarian lower strata that have been 'freed' through this process. Because these strata seemed to be geographically mobile in their search for work and were also moving to the cities, Breman soon broadened his field of research towards rural *and urban* underclasses. In the course of the last 40 years he has developed six insights that I would like to mention explicitly, because they can also be very useful in other times and places to people studying the development of labour relations.

First insight: focus on households, not individuals. While most class analyses (including Marxist ones) take individuals as their starting point, Breman soon discovered that it was better to use households as his units of analysis. In doing so he was, perhaps unconsciously, following Joseph Schumpeter's old suggestion: 'The family, not the physical person, is the true unit of class and class theory.'[21] By a quite different route from the Austrian economist, Breman had arrived at the conclusion that households of the lower strata are budget-pooling institutions, in which the incomes of several different people are aggregated:

[19] Breman, *Patronage and Exploitation*, p. 8.

[20] Breman, *Beyond Patronage*, p. 264.

[21] Joseph Schumpeter, 'Social Classes in an Ethnically Homogeneous Environment' (1927), in idem, *Imperialism and Social Classes* (Oxford, 1951), p. 148.

Only by looking at the household, in which many if not all of its members are involved or do want to be involved either partly or completely in the labour system, can we begin to understand the relative elasticity with which they are able to counter unemployment, severe fluctuations in income, and other similar vicissitudes. It also explains that mood of resignation, so striking to an outsider, with which they abandon the chance of a position, when the opportunity of a job is foregone for seemingly irrational reasons.[22]

Once one takes households, rather than individuals, as the starting point, then all sorts of all—too—simple dichotomies can be seen in perspective. For in one family, people with varied and shifting socio-economic positions can live together and support each other.[23]

Second insight: the working class is much larger than the labour elite. Breman's focus on broad layers of 'wage hunters and gatherers' in all their variety also led him to look differently at the 'pure' working class, employed mainly in the formal sector, than was usual among left-wing, critical scholars. Breman observed that the classic proletariat in the European and North American sense not only was not very numerous in underdeveloped capitalism, but that it moreover did not constitute the vanguard of class struggle. In itself this observation was of course far from new. Ever since the early 1960s a Third Worldist current had existed that asserted just the opposite, that the so-called 'real' working class was inclined towards conservatism. The best-known advocate of this position was Frantz Fanon. In his *The Wretched of the Earth* he wrote: 'In the colonial countries the working class has everything to lose. . . . It is these elements . . . who because of the privileged place which they hold in the colonial system constitute also the "bourgeois" fraction of the colonised people.'[24] Fanon counterposed to these

[22] Breman, *Wage Hunters*, pp. 60–1.

[23] This does not imply that the household-family is necessarily a picture of peace and harmony. On the contrary, members do not necessarily work for the common good of the household; they may be driven by selfish motives. Conflicts of interest are also possible, as well as oppression and resistance to oppression. See e.g. Judith Bruce, 'Homes Divided', *World Development*, 17 (1989), pp. 979–91; Diane L. Wolf, 'Daughters, Decisions and Domination: An Empirical and Conceptual Critique of Household Strategies', *Development and Change*, 21 (1990), pp. 43–74.

[24] Frantz Fanon, *The Wretched of the Earth*, Preface by Jean-Paul Sartre. trans. Constance Farrington (Harmondsworth, 1967), p. 86.

workers the peasants and lumpenproletariat, 'that horde of starving men, uprooted from their tribe and from their clan', to which 'the pimps, the hooligans, the unemployed and the petty criminals' belonged. Fanon saw the lumpenproletariat as the real vanguard: 'This *lumpen-proletariat* is like a horde of rats; you may kick them and throw stones at them, but despite your efforts they'll go on gnawing at the roots of the tree.'[25]

Jan Breman follows Fanon, in the sense that he too has little confidence in the minority of workers who are 'employed on the basis of regular employment and standardised working conditions and are thus able to lead a relatively secure existence'. But he warns against overestimating the homogeneity of this '*labour elite*',[26] given among other things 'the differences between salaried employees of major enterprises and government institutions on the one hand, and skilled blue collar workers on the other'.[27] Various 'ranks and categories' exist within the labour elite—a fact that becomes apparent in various circumstances, including in 'the numerous trade unions which, instead of defending class interests, seem to be more concerned with sectoral interest on the basis of status differences. A common front is only seen as regards the defence of these protected forms of labour.'[28] At the same time, Breman never placed his hopes in the lumpenproletariat, because his class analysis was much subtler than that of Fanon's.[29]

Third insight: the labouring poor consist of several sub-classes. Unlike Fanon, Breman does not think that there is only *one* alternative to this labour aristocracy. Under the top layer of privileged workers Breman distinguishes three more 'classes' within the 'working population'.[30] First there is the 'petty bourgeoisie', which

[25] Ibid., p. 103.
[26] Breman, *Wage Hunters*, p. 29.
[27] Ibid., p. 35.
[28] Ibid.
[29] Breman presumably agrees with Peter Worsley's rejection of Fanon's 'assertion that the employed are always "privileged", since the mass of unskilled labourers in the towns are hardly living high on the hog, and since the employed poor, too, are "sub-proletarian" in living standards and pursue "informal" income-opportunities (so that [there] is no clear border-line between "proletariat" and "sub-proletariat")'. Peter Worsley, 'Fanon and the "Lumpenproletariat"', *Socialist Register 1972*, p. 225.
[30] For what follows see Breman, *Wage Hunters*, pp. 30–32.

includes 'owners of small-scale enterprises, certain categories of one-man firms such as self-employed craftsmen, retail traders, shopkeepers, and those who earn their daily bread by economic brokerage, such as moneylenders, labour recruiters, contractors of piece-work or house industry, rent collectors, etc.' This is the group that corresponds more or less to what Sol Tax once called the 'penny capitalists'.[31] Second, there is the 'sub-proletariat', the largest segment of the working population, which includes 'ambulent craftsmen who each morning tender their labour and (paltry) tools in the urban marketplace, the houseworkers, street-vendors, and a long list of others, including the inevitable shoeshine'. This segment also includes 'the casual and unskilled labourers' and the workers 'employed by small-scale workshops and [the] labour reserve of large enterprises'. The third group, finally, is the lumpenproletariat, which Breman defines as 'the urban residue with criminal tendencies', the group of declassed people, 'who have broken all ties with their original environment, who have nowhere to live, and who have no proper or regular contact with others in their immediate surroundings'. Having fallen into a state of pauperization, 'they form a beaten and apathetic muster of lone men, women with children, children without parents, the maimed and the aged. Prepared for anything that will earn them a penny, the majority roam the streets begging, collecting old paper and bottles, and scavenging through the cities garbage for anything edible or usable'. Any 'rigid and static classification' must be rejected.[32]

Fourth insight: complicate the informal sector. The transitions between the different segments of the labouring poor are fluid, vague, and shifting. A substantial proportion of the labouring poor is counted as part of the 'informal sector', but Breman has serious doubts about this concept.[33] Many writers think of the informal sector as a relatively homogeneous group of urban self-employed people, while the reality is much more complicated than that. First of all, the informal sector is socially much more

[31] Sol Tax, *Penny Capitalism: A Guatemalan Indian Economy* (Washington, D.C., 1953).

[32] Breman, *Wage Hunters*, p. 33.

[33] See Breman's essay 'Dualistic Labour System? A Critique of the "Informal Sector" Concept', in Breman, *Wage Hunters*, pp. 3–45.

differentiated than is often supposed. Besides self-employment there is, for example, casual labour as well. In reality, the informal sector includes most of the aforementioned three sectors 'under' the labour elite. And it is exceptionally difficult, if not impossible, to split the informal sector analytically into different elements: 'The specific structure of the informal sector—dominated by exchangeability and discontinuity and knowing only a very slim margin between employment and unemployment—makes categorization according to the standard concepts and problems defined in terms of the formal sector a rather dubious affair.'[34]

Fifth insight: complicate the urban–rural dichotomy. An additional wrinkle is that the informal sector is no way an exclusively urban phenomenon. When the formal–informal distinction is restricted to urban labour, the concept 'loses some of its practical and policy relevance'.[35] The enormous geographical mobility of the labour force means that 'town and country cannot be regarded as separate economic sectors'.[36] More generally, there are too many stereotypes in the literature, as if all migration occurs from the country to the city or as if non-agrarian activities exist only in cities. This kind of sharp counterposition between rural and urban areas does not correspond to reality. In many respects it makes more sense to see a gradual transition, a 'continuum'. First, many extractive and industrial activities take place in rural areas. Plantations are a major example of this. Second, there is considerable geographical mobility *within* rural areas in the form of a seasonal movement of labour.[37] Third, the move from country to town is often temporary: 'Large groups of seasonal migrants wander wretchedly to and fro between town and country, recruited or rejected as need arises.'[38] And fourth, there is also movement from city to countryside: 'In the harvest season in particular, farmers from distant neighbourhoods will travel by tractor to such markets in [daily labour] markets in Valsad and Bardoli, for instance, to hire gangs of workers to harvest their crops.'[39]

[34] Breman, *Wage Hunters*, p. 61.

[35] Breman, *Footloose Labour*, p. 3; Breman refers to N.V. Jaganathan, *Informal Markets in Developing Countries* (New York and Oxford, 1987).

[36] Breman, *Wage Hunters*, p. 50.

[37] For example, ibid., pp. 182–8.

[38] Ibid., p. 9.

[39] Breman, *Footloose Labour*, p. 47.

Sixth insight: complicate migration processes. It is often assumed that people are either sedentary, and thus work where they live, or that they migrate over great distances. Breman shows however that there are all sorts of intermediary forms. Even in south Gujarat 'the predominant pattern of labour mobility is not migration but circulation'.[40] Breman distinguishes among several variants. In the first place of course is daily commuting, by workers in the formal as well as informal sector 'with a fixed workplace to which they travel daily', and by casual labourers who in 'the course of a few weeks or even days . . . will visit numerous locations, situated near or further away from the village, to perform the same or even different work each time: as helper in the building trade, loader-unloader on a lorry, navvy or road worker, or as agricultural day labourer'.[41] In the second place is seasonal work, which 'started in the first half of the twentieth century'.[42] As early as the 1920s Halpatis who worked as *halis* (bonded servants) took part in seasonal migration. 'By giving them permission to do so, the landed gentry avoided being held responsible for their livelihood in the slack season.'[43] These migratory processes cannot all be simply reduced to push- and pull-factors. Migration, above all circular migration, does not take place primarily because of a labour shortage in one spot and a labour surplus in another. On the contrary, sometimes workers go from A to B to work when at the same moment there are workers from B doing the same work in A. What is most important in such cases is the power of the employer: not only can workers 'from the outside world' be more easily let go at the employer's convenience, outsiders are also far easier to control:

> Labourers coming from elsewhere are often not familiar with the local customs and language; in the most literal of senses, they do not know their way around within the milieu in which they find themselves, and are defenceless in face of the power exercised over them at the work site, which was usually also the place where they took up residence.[44]

[40] Ibid., p. 33.
[41] Ibid., p. 35.
[42] Ibid., p. 44.
[43] Ibid. Breman refers to G.C. Mukhtyar, *Life and Labour in a South Gujarat Village* (Calcutta, 1930).
[44] Breman, *Labour Migration*, pp. 18–19.

This powerlessness is often strengthened because the employer makes sure that his labour force is made up of people with varied ethnic and geographical origins.

With these six insights, Breman has provided building blocks for a truly global, non-Eurocentric labour history. His approach demonstrates that we should re-examine all the schemas we were educated in on their merits. Why for example do we still take the formal sector as our starting point and consider the informal sector as a deviation from this norm? Shouldn't we turn the questions around? If the majority of the wage-earning labour force is involved in informal labour relations, isn't the conclusion obvious that 'more than the persistence of the informal sector economy, the emergence of the formal sector employment needs explanation'?[45] In short, Breman's writings constitute a great intellectual challenge. Since Breman himself has always stayed quite close to his empirical data, further interpretation of his research findings leaves more theoretically-minded people with a considerable amount of work ahead of them.

[45] Breman, *Footloose Labour*, p. 5. A similar point is made in Immanuel Wallerstein, *Historical Capitalism* (London and New York, 1983).

12

Bibliography of Jan Breman's Writings

Mario Rutten

Following his first publication on the population growth and demographic structure of Java in 1963, Jan Breman has built up a very impressive publication record of high international standing. The bibliography presented here contains only a selection of his writings. In order to make my task a feasible one, I limited the bibliography to an overview of Jan Breman's major academic publications: monographs, edited volumes, essays, articles in journals, and chapters in edited volumes. In total, this already adds up to 150 publications.

Besides the publications compiled in this bibliography, Jan Breman wrote many working papers as well as reports invited by national agencies (NAR or National Council for Development Co-operation) and international organizations (ESCAP, ILO, Asian Development Bank), and published numerous articles in newspapers and weekly magazines in the Netherlands (e.g. *De Volkskrant*, *NRC Handelsblad*, *Vrij Nederland*, *De Groene*, and *Onze Wereld*), in Europe (e.g. *Le Monde Diplomatique*), and in Asia (e.g. *Biblio* and *Illustrated Weekly*). He has received various awards for his publications. Moreover, many of his books and articles have been translated into Asian languages, such as Gujarati, Hindi, and Bengali, Bahasa Indonesia, and Chinese. The translations referred to in this bibliography are only a small sample.

From the beginning of his academic career, Jan Breman has pursued a consistent but wide range of thematic and geographical research interests. This is reflected in his publications. Most of them deal with labour relations in India and in Indonesia, both historical and contemporary, both urban and rural, and with issues related to development co-operation. Jan Breman's publications play an important role in the national and international debates on these themes among researchers and policy-makers. His writings are often cited and his arguments regularly discussed.

In compiling this bibliography of Jan Breman's work I received help from many people. I would like to thank especially Jildiz Heddes for collecting and processing most of the information, and Ilse Breman-Burke for her offer to help me in going through Jan Breman's bookshelves while he was away in Asia.

Viewing Jan Breman's tremendous academic productivity, this bibliography is only an approximation of his writings over the years. I am convinced that even if I were to have asked him to check the information, it would still have been an incomplete bibliography. Moreover, a bibliography of Jan Breman's work can never be more than a work-in-progress, already outdated at the time of publication. Even now, while writing this introduction, Jan Breman is about to publish two new monographs: one on rural labour in Indonesia (with G. Wiradi, *Good Times and Bad Times in Rural Java: Socio-economic Dynamics in Two Villages towards the End of the Twentieth Century*); the other on urban textile workers in India (*Changing Profile of the Indian Working Class: A Case Study of Industrial Labour in Ahmedabad*). I am convinced these two books will be followed by many other new publications in the future.

Monographs, Edited Volumes, and Essays

1963 *Java: Bevolkingsgroei en demografische structuur* (Amsterdam: Koninklijk Nederlandsch Aardrijkskundig Genootschap). 50 pp.

1969 With C. Boef and C. Gutter (eds), *Mooi rood is niet lelijk* (Rotterdam: Universitaire Pers Rotterdam). 172 pp.

1970 'Meester en knecht: een onderzoek naar de veranderingen in de betrekkingen tussen landheren en landarbeiders in Zuid-Gujarat, India' (Ph.D. thesis, Afdeling Zuid- en Zuidoost Azie, Antropologisch-Sociologisch Centrum, Universiteit van Amsterdam). 273 pp.

1971 *Djawa: Pertumbuhan penduduk dan struktur demografis* (Jakarta: Indonesian Demographic Institute). [Terdjemahan Karangan-Karangan Belanda No. 4.] 112 pp.

1973 With A. Peper, *Intentieplan Sociaal Beleid: Suriname: een voortgangsnota* (Paramaribo: Stichting Planbureau Suriname). 102 pp.

1974 *Patronage and Exploitation: Changing Agrarian Relations in South Gujarat, India* (Berkeley: University of California Press). 287 pp. [Indian edn: Delhi: Manohar, 1979.]

1976 With R. van Waesberge, *Suriname: een stukje Derde Wereld* (The Hague: NOVIB). 72 pp.

Een dualistisch arbeidsbestel?: een kritische beschouwing van het begrip 'De Informele Sector' (Rotterdam: Van Gennep). [Inaugural Address, Erasmus Universiteit Rotterdam.] 53 pp.

1979 *Kertas kerja pada lokakarya sejerah sosial-ekonomi pedesaan* (Jakarta: Kelompok Studi Asia, Institut Pertinian Bogor, Lembaga Penelitian Sosiologi Pedesaan). 50 pp.

1980 *The Village on Java and the Early Colonial State* (Rotterdam: Erasmus Universiteit). [Comparative Asian Studies Programme Series No. 1.] 54 pp.

The 'Informal Sector' in Research: Theory and Practice (Rotterdam: Erasmus Universiteit). [Comparative Asian Studies Programme Series No. 3.] 94 pp.

1983 *Control of Land and Labour in Colonial Java: A Case Study of Agrarian Crisis and Reform in the Region of Cirebon during the First Decades of the 20th Century* (Dordrecht: Foris Publications). [Verhandelingen van het Koninklijk Instituut voor Taal-, Land- en Volkenkunde No. 101.] 158 pp.

1985 *Of Peasants, Migrants and Paupers: Rural Labour Circulation and Capitalist Production in West India* (Delhi/Oxford: Oxford University Press/Clarendon Press). 472 pp.

1986 *Penguasaan tanah dan tenaga kerja: Jawa di masa kolonial* (Jakarta: Lembaga Penelitian, Pendidikan dan Penerangan Ekonomi dan Sosial). 230 pp.

1987 *Koelies, planters en koloniale politiek: het arbeidsregime op de grootlandbouwondernemingen aan Sumatra's Oostkust in het begin van de twintigste eeuw* (Dordrecht: Foris). [Verhandelingen van het Koninklijk Instituut voor Taal-, Land- en Volkenkunde No. 123.] 417 pp. [3rd revd edn: (Leiden, KITLV Uitgeverij, 1992). 551 pp.]

With J. Berting and P.B. Lehning (eds), *Mensen, macht en maatschappij: een bundel sociaal-wetenschappelijke opstellen* (Meppel: Boom). 212 pp.

With C.J.M. Schuyt (eds), *De bedreigde universiteit: oordelen en voorstellen* (Leiden: Martinus Nijhoff). 111 pp.

Het dorp in Azië als koloniale schijngestalte (Amsterdam: Universiteit van Amsterdam). [Inaugural Address, Centre for Asian Studies Amsterdam.] 64 pp.

1988 *The Shattered Image: Construction and Deconstruction of the Village in Colonial Asia* (Dordrecht: Foris Publications). [Comparative Asian Studies No. 2.] 49 pp.

The Renaissance of Social Darwinism (The Hague: Institute of Social Studies). [Dies Natalis Lecture.] 29 pp.

1989 *Taming the Coolie Beast: Plantation Society and the Colonial Order in South-east Asia* (Delhi: Oxford University Press). 321 pp.

1990 (ed.), *Imperial Monkey Business: Racial Supremacy in Social Darwinist Theory and Colonial Practice* (Amsterdam: VU University Press). [CASA Monographs No. 3.] 152 pp.

Labour Migration and Rural Transformation in Colonial Asia (Amsterdam: Free University Press). [Comparative Asian Studies No. 5.] 82 pp.

Humanisme en ontwikkelingssamenwerking: een herwaardering van goede intenties (Rijswijk: Nijgh en Van Ditmar Universitair). 81 pp.

1991 With S. Mundle (eds), *Rural Transformation in Asia* (Delhi: Oxford University Press). 532 pp.

1992 *Coolie Labour in Indonesia* [in Chinese] (Xiamen: Lujiang Publishing House). 335 pp.

Op zoek naar een menswaardig bestaan: de dynamiek van armoede en welstand op het platteland van West-India aan het einde der twintigste eeuw (Amsterdam: Koninklijke Akademie van Wetenschappen/Noord Hollandsche). [Mededelingen van de Afdeling Letterkunde, Nieuwe Reeks No. 55–5.] 92 pp.

1993 *Beyond Patronage and Exploitation: Changing Agrarian Relations in South Gujarat* (Delhi: Oxford University Press). 399 pp.

With T. Duquesnoy and R. Aerts (eds), *Een ereschuld: essays uit 'De Gids' over ons koloniaal verleden* (Amsterdam: Meulenhoff). 318 pp.

1994 *Wage Hunters and Gatherers: Search for Work in the Urban and Rural Economy of South Gujarat* (Delhi: Oxford University Press). 422 pp.

1996 *Footloose Labour: Working in India's Informal Economy* (Cambridge: Cambridge University Press). [Contemporary South Asia No. 2.] 278 pp.

Labour Nomads in South Gujarat (Surat: Centre for Social Studies). [I.P. Desai Memorial Lecture No. 8.] 37 pp.

1997 *Menjinakkan sang kuli: politik kolonial, tuan kebun, dan kuli di Sumatra Timur pada awal abad ke-20* (Jakarta: Pustaka Utama Grafiti). 346 pp.

Silencing the Voice of Agricultural Labourers in South Gujarat (Cambridge: Cambridge University Press). [Kingsley Martin Lecture.]

With P. Kloos and A. Saith (eds), *The Village in Asia Revisited* (Delhi: Oxford University Press). 450 pp.

1999 With J.P. Parry and K. Kapadia (eds), *The Worlds of Indian Industrial Labour* (New Delhi: Sage Publications). [Contributions to Indian Sociology, Occasional Studies No 9.] 442 pp.

2000 *The Impact of the Asian Economic Crisis on Work and Welfare in Village Java* (The Hague: Institute of Social Studies). [Dies Natalis Lecture.] 65 pp.

With A. Das and R. Agarwal, *Down and Out: Labouring under Global Capitalism* (New Delhi/Amsterdam: Oxford University Press/Amsterdam University Press). 156 pp.

2001 *Op weg naar een slechter bestaan: verwijdering van industriële arbeid uit de formele sector van de economie* (Amsterdam: Vossiuspers UvA). [Valedictory Address, University of Amsterdam.] 103 pp.

A Turn for the Worse: The Closure of the Ahmedabad Textile Mills and the Retrenchment of the Workforce (Amsterdam, Centre for Asian Studies Amsterdam). [Wertheim Lecture 12.] iv + 30 pp.

Articles in Journals and Chapters in Edited Volumes

1963 'Java: bevolkingsgroei en demografische structuur', *Tijdschrift van het Koninklijk Nederlandsch Aardrijkskundig Genootschap*, 80, 3, pp. 252–308.

1965 With C. Baks, E.W. Hommes, I. Ronner and K.W. van der Veen, 'De betrouwbaarheid van informatie in een kastesamenleving in Gujarat, India', *Sociologische Gids*, 12, 3, pp. 167–74.

1966 'Uitgestelde bevrediging, ondernemersgedrag en economische groei', *Mens en Maatschappij*, 41, 1, pp. 1–20.

With C. Baks and A.T.J. Nooij. 'Slavery as a System of Production in a Tribal Society', *Bijdragen tot de Taal-, Land- en Volkenkunde*, 122, 1, pp. 90–109.

1967 With E.W. Hommes. 'Sociologie en ontwikkelingsbeleid in niet-Westerse samenlevingen', *Sociologische Gids*, 14, 3, pp. 158–74.

1969 'Veranderingen in de betrekkingen tussen landheren en landarbeiders in Zuid- Gujarat, India', *Sociologische Gids*, 16, 6, pp. 395–402.

'Deferred Gratification, Entrepreneurial Behavior and Economic Growth', *Sociologia Neerlandica*, 5, 1, pp. 15–34.

1971 'Over oude en nieuwe afhankelijkheidsrelaties: de maatschappelijke context van patronage en makelaardij', in *Buiten de grenzen: sociologische opstellen aangeboden aan Prof. Dr. W.F. Wertheim* (Meppel: Boom), pp. 31–46.

'Sociaal wetenschappelijk onderzoek en interuniversitaire samenwerking', *Sociologische Gids*, 18, 1, pp. 60–1.

1974 'De oliecrisis en de Derde Wereld: ontwikkeling en onderontwikkeling: het proces van differentiatie in de Derde Wereld', *Internationale Spectator*, 28, 3, pp. 143–5.

'Mobilization of Landless Labourers: Halpatis of South Gujarat', *Economic and Political Weekly*, 9, 12, pp. 489–96.

1975 'Beleid en maatschappij in Suriname: de systematiek van "hosselen en pinaren"', *Beleid en Maatschappij*, 9, pp. 214–25.

With E.W. Dew and J. Brandsma, 'Suriname na de onafhankelijkheid', *Beleid en Maatschappij*, 9, pp. 2–44.

1976 'Modernisering en emancipatie in de koloniale en post-koloniale samenleving', in H.J.M. Claessen, J. Kaayk and R.J.A. Lambregts (eds), *Dekolonisatie en vrijheid: een sociaal-wetenschappelijke discussie over emancipatieprocessen in de Derde Wereld* (Assen: Van Gorcum), pp. 109–19.

'Pauperization of a Tribal Caste', in S. Devadas Pillai (ed.), *Aspects of Changing India* (Bombay: Popular Prakashan), pp. 255–61.

'A Dualistic Labour System?: A Critique of the 'Informal Sector' Concept', *Economic and Political Weekly*, 11, 48–49–50, pp. 1870–6; 1905–08; 1939–43.

1977 'Het nieuwe regime in Azië: de overgang van de weke naar de harde staat', *Internationale Spectator*, 31, 3, pp. 137–51.

'Labour Relations in the "Formal" and "Informal" Sectors: Report of a Case Study in South Gujarat, India [2 parts]', *Journal of Peasant Studies*, 4, 3–4, pp. 171–205; 337–59.

1978 'Seasonal Migration and Co-Operative Capitalism: The Crushing of Cane and of Labour by the Sugar Factories of Bardoli, South Gujarat [2 parts]', *Journal of Peasant Studies*, 6, 1–2, pp. 41–70; 168–209.

'Modernisering', in L. Rademaker (ed.), *Sociologische Encyclopedie: Deel 2* (Utrecht/Antwerpen: Het Spectrum), pp. 457–60.

'Ontwikkelingslanden', in L. Rademaker (ed.), *Sociologische Encyclopedie: Deel 2* (Utrecht/Antwerpen: Het Spectrum), pp. 480–4.

'Het dorp of Java en de vroeg-koloniale staat', *Symposium*, 1, pp. 187–215.

1979 'Ruraal beleid in India: voor de meesten het minst en voor de minsten het meest', *Internationale Spectator*, 33, 12, pp. 726–33.

With E.W. Hommes, 'Social Change in South Gujarat: An Introduction', in S. Devadas Pillai and C. Baks (eds), *Winners and Losers: Styles of Development and Change in an Indian Region* (Bombay: Popular Prakashan), pp. 3–17.

'The Market for Non-Agrarian Labour: The Formal versus Informal Sector', in S. Devadas Pillai and C. Baks (eds), *Winners and Losers: Styles of Development and Change in an Indian Region* (Bombay: Popular Prakashan), pp. 122–66.

'Mobilization of Landless Labourers: Halpatis of South Gujarat', in A.N. Das and V. Nilakant (eds), *Agrarian Relations in India* (New Delhi: Manohar), pp. 145–68.

1981 'Onderzoek voor en van het Nederlandse ontwikkelingsbeleid', *Internationale Spectator*, 35, 3, pp. 150–7.

1982 'Extension of Scale in Fieldwork: From Village to Region in Southern Gujarat', in O.v.d. Muijzenberg, P. Streefland and W. Wolters (eds), *Focus on the Region in Asia* (Rotterdam: Erasmus Universiteit Rotterdam) [Comparative Asian Studies Programme Series], pp. 83–92.

'The Village on Java and the Early-Colonial State', *Journal of Peasant Studies*, 9, 4, pp. 189–240.

1983 'De bodem van het stedelijk bestel in Azië: riksjalopers in Calcutta', *Internationale Spectator*, 37, 3, pp. 121–30.

'Het Nederlandse ontwikkelingsbeleid: de daden achter de woorden', *Beleid en Maatschappij*, 10, 7–8, pp. 195–201.

'The Bottom of the Urban Order in Asia: Impressions of Calcutta', *Development and Change*, 14, 2, pp. 153–83.

1984 'Het smalle spoor van het Nederlandse ontwikkelingsbeleid: herijking van bilateraal beleid', *Internationale Spectator*, 38, 6, pp. 309–15.

'Seasonal Migration and Co-Operative Capitalism: The Crushing of Cane and of Labour by the Sugar Factories of Bardoli, South Gujarat', in H.P. Binswanger and M.R. Rosenzweig (eds), *Contractual Arrangements, Employment and Wages in Rural Labour Markets in Asia* (New Haven: Yale University Press), pp. 131–42.

1985 '"I am the Government Labour Officer. . .": State Protection for Rural Proletariat of South Gujarat', *Economic and Political Weekly*, 20, 24, pp. 1043–55.

'Between Accumulation and Immiseration: The Partiality of Fieldwork in Rural India', *Journal of Peasant Studies*, 13, 1, pp. 5–36.

1986 'Over hobbies en lobbies: de uitbesteding van de Nederlandse ontwikkelingshulp', *Internationale Spectator*, 40, 6, pp. 353–63.

'Feiten graag, geen ficties', *Internationale Spectator*, 40, 9, pp. 545–46.

1987 'Whose Side are You On? The Fieldworker in the Arena of Class Conflict', *Netherlands Review of Development Studies*, 1, 1, pp. 67–83.

1988 'Groei zonder verdeling: de ontplooiing van het kapitalisme op het platteland van West-India', *Internationale Spectator*, 42, 9, pp. 554–62.

'Het beest aan banden? De koloniale geest aan het begin van de twintigste eeuw', *Bijdragen tot de Taal-, Land- en Volkenkunde*, 144, 1, pp. 19–43.

1989 'Extension of Scale in Fieldwork: From Village to Region in Southern Gujarat', in P. Bardhan (ed.), *Conversations Between Economists and Anthropologists: Methodological Issues in Measuring Economic Change in Rural India* (Oxford and New York: Delhi University Press), pp. 127–36.

'The Disintegration of the Hali System', in H. Alavi and J. Harriss (eds), *South Asia: Sociology of 'Developing Societies'* (London: Macmillan Education Ltd.), pp. 149–59.

1990 'Veldwerk en transformatieprocessen op lange termijn', in B. Fontaine, P. Kloos and J. Schrijvers (eds), *De crisis voorbij: persoonlijke visies op vernieuwing in de antropologie* (Leiden: DSWO Press) [Sociaal Antropologische Studies], pp. 57–67.

'Een staat van terreur: Kongo rond de eeuwwisseling', *Amsterdams Sociologisch Tijdschrift*, 16, 4, pp. 3–27.

'Agrarian Change and Class Conflict in Gujarat, India', in G. McNicoll and M. Cain (eds), *Rural Development and Population: Institutions and Policy* (New York: New York Population Council), pp. 301–23.

'Introduction: Race, a Class Apart', in J. Breman (ed.), *Imperial Monkey Business: Racial Supremacy in Social Darwinist Theory and Colonial Practice* (Amsterdam: VU University Press) [CASA Monographs No. 3], pp. 1–6.

'Primitive Racism in a Colonial Setting', in J. Breman (ed.), *Imperial Monkey Business: Racial Supremacy in Social Darwinist Theory and Colonial Practice* (Amsterdam: VU University Press) [CASA Monographs No. 3], pp. 89–122.

'The Civilization of Racism: Colonial and Post-Colonial Development Policies', in J. Breman (ed.), *Imperial Monkey Business: Racial Supremacy in Social Darwinist Theory and Colonial Practice* (Amsterdam: VU University Press) [CASA Monographs No. 3], pp. 123–52.

'From Cane Fields to Court Rooms: Legal Action for and against Rural Labour in Gujarat, India', in G. Shah (ed.), *Capitalist Development: Critical Essays: Felicitation Volume in Honour of Prof. A.R. Desai* (Bombay: Popular Prakashan), pp. 270–88.

'Even Dogs are Better Off: The Ongoing Battle Between Capital and Labour in the Cane Fields of Gujarat', *Journal of Peasant Studies*, 17, 4, pp. 546–608.

1991 'Over orientalistiek en occidentalistiek', *De Gids*, 154, 5–6, pp. 501–04.

'Civilisatie en racisme: een staat van terreur: Kongo rond de eeuwwisseling', *De Gids*, 154, 5–6, pp. 448–93.
'Kolonialisme, racisme en cultuurpolitiek', *De Gids*, 154, 5–6, pp. 339–42.
With S. Mundle. 'Introduction: The Perspective', in J. Breman and S. Mundle (eds), *Rural Transformation in Asia* (Delhi: Oxford University Press), pp. 9–25.
'A Note on the Colonial State', in J. Breman and S. Mundle (eds), *Rural Transformation in Asia* (Delhi: Oxford University Press), pp. 127–44.

1992 'De rekening vereffend: hoe het enkele hoofdpersonen in de Koeliekwestie aan de Oostkust van Sumatra verder is gegaan', in P. Boomgaard, H. Poeze and G. Termorshuizen (eds), *Aangeraakt door Insulinde: De boeken van drieëntwintig lezers* (Leiden: KITLV Uitgeverij), pp. 39–46.
'Een advocaat van kwade zaken', *De Gids*, 155, 6, pp. 476–92.
'Mobilization of Landless Labourers: The Halpatis of South Gujarat', in D. Gupta (ed.), *Social Stratification* (Delhi: Oxford University Press) [Readings in Sociology and Social and Cultural Anthropology], pp. 399–418.
'The Hali System in South Gujarat', in G. Prakash (ed.), *The World of the Rural Labourer in Colonial India* (Delhi: Oxford University Press), pp. 248–81.
With V. Daniel. 'The Making of a Coolie: Conclusion', *Journal of Peasant Studies*, 19, 3–4, pp. 268–95.
'Controversial Views on Writing History', *Itinerario*, 16, pp. 39–60.
'Kerja dan kehidupan buruh tani di pesisir Jawa', *Prisma*, 21, 3, pp. 3–32.

1993 'Ten Geleide', in J. Breman, R. Aerts and T. Duquesnoy (eds), *Een Ereschuld: essays uit 'De Gids' over ons koloniaal verleden* (Amsterdam: Meulenhoff), pp. 7–21.
'Het neerlandse cultuurpatroon door vreemde ogen', in J.C.H. Blom, J.T. Leerssen and P. de Rooy (eds), *De onmacht van het grote: cultuur in Europa* (Amsterdam: Amsterdam University Press), pp. 95–102.
'Op weg naar het ghetto: de transformatie van een moslim-sloppenwijk in Ahmedabad, India', *De Gids*, 156, 6, pp. 456–71.
'Publieke druk tot wettelijke bescherming van landarbeid in India', in *Liber Amicorum voor Prof. Mr. A.A.G. Peters* (Gouda: Quint), pp. 249–62.
'The Anti-Muslim Pogrom in Surat', *Economic and Political Weekly*, 28, 16, pp. 737–41.

1994 'Het verlopend tij van de ontwikkelingspolitiek: de kritische grens van Jan Pronk', *Socialisme en Democratie*, 51, 11, pp. 490–7.

'The Remaining Poor People: Restating the Social Question in a Global Perspective: A Response to Sandshom', in L. Boer and J. Rooimans (eds), *The World Bank and Poverty Reduction: Contributions to a Seminar, The Hague, November 17, 1993* (The Hague: Ministry of Foreign Affairs/Development Co-operation Information Department), pp. 15–19.

'Rural Impressions on the Urban Communal Carnage', *Internationales Asienforum*, 25, 3–4, pp. 335–43.

1995 'Een laat-kapitalistisch manifest: de catechismus van de Wereldbank', *Socialisme en Democratie*, 52, 10, pp. 447–59.

'De verzorgingsstaat is van de wereld', in *Van de wieg tot het graf? De toekomst van de verzorgingsstaat* (Amsterdam: De Volkskrant), pp. 33–35.

'Labour Relations in the "Formal" and "Unformal" Sectors: The South Gujarat Experience', in P.M. Mathew (ed.), *Informal Sector in India: Critical Perspectives* (New Delhi: Khama Publishers), pp. 171–89.

'Labor Get Lost: A Late Capitalist Manifesto', *Economic and Political Weekly*, 30, 37, pp. 2294–3000.

'The Creation of a Labour Surplus in Surat District, Gujarat, India', in S. Corbridge (ed.), *Development Studies: A Reader* (London: Edward Arnold), pp. 216–34.

With G.S. Bhalla and K. Chopra. 'Sur l'Asie', *Tiers Monde: Croissance, développement, progrès*, 36, 144, pp. 948–52.

'Work and Life of the Rural Proletariat in Java's Coastal Plain', *Modern Asian Studies*, 29, 1, pp. 1–44.

'De problematiek in de gammawetenschappen: commentaar op C.J.M. Schuyt', *Mededelingen der Koninklijke Nederlandse Akademie van Wetenschappen*, 58, 1, pp. 27–8.

1996 'Globalisering of het dreigende einde van ontwikkelingssamenwerking', *Socialisme en Democratie*, 53, 6, pp. 332–40.

'The Village on Java', in M.C. Hoadley and C. Gunnarsson (eds), *The Village Concept in the Transformation of Rural South-east Asia: Studies from Indonesia, Malaysia and Thailand* (Richmond: Curzon Press) [Nordic Institute of Asian Studies No. 20], pp. 3–28.

With B. White, 'Coercion and Quality in Indonesian Family Planning: A Response to Anke Niehof', *Bijdragen tot de Taal-, Land- en Volkenkunde*, 152, 1, pp. 144–7.

'Bali's Killing Fields Thirty Years Ago', *Economic and Political Weekly*, 31, 16–17, pp. 997–9.

'Indonesia: Beginning of End of "New Order"?', *Economic and Political Weekly*, 31, 32, pp. 2135–7.

With M. van den Berg and B. van Oijk, 'Pen op papier', *Socialisme en Democratie*, 53, 7–8, p. 459.

1997 'Armoedebestrijding in het kader van globalisering', in K. Lieten and F. van der Velden (eds), *Grenzen aan de hulp: beleid en effecten van ontwikkelingssamenwerking* (Amsterdam: Het Spinhuis), pp. 17–37.

'Labour Nomads in South Gujarat: Wage Hunters and Gatherers', in G. Shah (ed.), *Social Transformation in India* (Jaipur and New Delhi: Rawat Publications), pp. 532–80.

'The Village in Focus', in J. Breman, P. Kloos and A. Saith (eds), *The Village in Asia Revisited* (Delhi: Oxford University Press), pp. 15–75.

'Compassion and Calculation: The Business of Private Foreign Aid', *Development and Change*, 28, 4, pp. 791–2.

'Hong Kong, Big Brother is Eagerly Waiting for You', *Economic and Political Weekly*, 32, 17, pp. 867–9.

'On the Move: The Migrant Labour Market', *The India Magazine of Her People and Culture*, 17, 9, pp. 50–6.

'Labour Get Lost: A Late-Capitalist Manifesto: A Stylised Summary and a Critique', *1999: Zeitschrift für Sozialgeschichte des 20. und 21. Jahrhunderts*, 12, 1, pp. 83–104.

1998 'De strijd voor maatschappelijke gelijkheid in India', in A. Gevers (ed.), *Uit de Zevende Hemel: Vijftig jaar Politieke en Sociaal-Culturele Wetenschappen aan de Universiteit van Amsterdam* (Amsterdam: Het Spinhuis), pp. 395–409.

'W.F. Wertheim, de Sociologie van het Niet aan de Universiteit van Amsterdam', in J. Goudsblom, P. de Rooij and J. Wieten (eds), *In de Zevende: De eerste lichting hoogleraren aan de Politiek-sociale Faculteit in Amsterdam* (Amsterdam: Het Spinhuis), pp. 169–81.

'Azië, het blijft een mirakel', *Socialisme en Democratie*, 55, 2, pp. 51–7.

'The Rural Informal Sector Reconsidered', in R. Radhakrisha and A.N. Sharma (eds), *Empowering Rural Labour in India: Market, State and Mobilization* (New Delhi: Institute for Human Development), pp. 103–12.

'The End of Globalization?', *Economic and Political Weekly*, 33, 7, pp. 333–6.

'Arbeitsnomaden in der kapitalistischen Ökonomie von West-Indien: proletarisches Dasein auf dem Land am Ende des 20. Jahrhunderts', in V. Bader, et al. (eds), *Die Wiederentdeckung der Klassen* (Berlin and Hamburg: Argument-Verlag), pp. 193–211.

1999 'Van ontwikkelingssamenwerking naar internationale armenzorg', *Socialisme en Democratie*, 56, 9, pp. 375–87.

'The Study of Industrial Labour in Post-Colonial India: The Formal Sector: A Introductory Review', in J. Breman, J.P. Parry and K. Kapadia (eds), *The Worlds of Indian Industrial Labour* (New Delhi: Sage Publications) [Contributions to Indian Sociology, Occasional Studies No. 9], pp. 1–41.

'The Study of Industrial Labour in Post-Colonial India: The Informal Sector: A Concluding Review', in J. Breman, J.P. Parry and K. Kapadia (eds), *The Worlds of Indian Industrial Labour* (New Delhi: Sage Publications) [Contributions to Indian Sociology, Occasional Studies No. 9], pp. 407–31.

'Industrial Labour in Post-Colonial India (1): Industrializing the Economy and Formalizing Labour', *International Review of Social History*, 44, 2, pp. 249–300.

'Indonesia: Politics of Poverty and a Leaking Safety Net', *Economic and Political Weekly*, 34, 20, pp. 1177–8.

'Silencing the Voice of Agricultural Labourers in South Gujarat', *Modern Asian Studies*, 33, 1, pp. 1–22.

'Indonesia: More of the Same', *Economic and Political Weekly*, 34, 3–4, pp. 68–9.

'Industrial Labour in Post-Colonial India (2): Employment in the Informal Sector Economy', *International Review of Social History*, 44, 3, pp. 451–83.

'Ghettoization and Communal Politics: The Dynamics of Inclusion and Exclusion in the Hindutva Landscape', in R. Guha and J.P. Parry (eds), *Institutions and Inequalities: Essays in Honour of André Beteille* (Delhi: Oxford University Press), pp. 259–83.

'The Informal Sector of India's Economy: The State of the Art and the Art of the State', in F. Oshikawa (ed.), *South Asia under the Economic Reforms* (Osaka: The Japan Center for Area Studies) [Series 6], pp. 185–211.

2000 'Labour and Landlessness in South and South-east Asia', in D. Bryceson, C. Kay and J. Mooij (eds), *Disappearing Peasantries* (London: Intermediate Technology Publications), pp. 231–47.

2001 'The Impact of the Asian Economic Crisis on Work and Welfare in Village Java', *Journal of Agrarian Change*, 1, 2, pp. 242–82.

'Ontwikkelingsbeleid en goed bestuur', *Socialisme en Democratie*, 58, 6, pp. 276–81.

Contributors

CHRIS BAKS (1931), studied geography at the University of Amsterdam, where he obtained his Ph.D. in 1969 with a dissertation on the social implications of the abolition of land tenure in three south Gujarat villages (supervisor: Prof. Wim Wertheim). In 1964 he joined the anthropology department of Leiden University, and in 1974 he became Reader in anthropology at Utrecht University. He now lives in France.

ARVIND NARAYAN DAS (1948–2000) was a prominent social scientist and journalist. A former Senior Editor of the *Times of India*, he started publishing *Biblio: A Review of Books* in 1996. He wrote or edited eleven books, including *Does Bihar Show the Way?* (Calcutta, 1979); *Agrarian Unrest and Socio-Economic Change in Bihar, 1900–1980* (New Delhi, 1983); *India Invented: A Nation in the Making* (New Delhi, 1992; revd edn 1994); *Changel: The Biography of a Village* (Harmondsworth, 1996); and *Down and Out: Labouring under Global Capitalism* (New Delhi, 2000), with Jan Breman and Ravi Agarwal.

K.P. KANNAN (1949) is Fellow and Indian Planning Commission Chair Professor of Development Economics, Centre for Development Studies, Ulloor, Trivandrum, Kerala, India. His publications include *Of Rural Proletarian Struggles: Mobilization and Organization of Rural Workers in South West India* (Delhi, 1988) and, as co-author, *Health and Development in Rural Kerala* (Trivandrum, 1990). He is currently working on collective care arrangements for informal sector workers, child labour, and the political economy of the power sector. Jan Breman supervised his Ph.D. thesis at the Institute of Social Studies, The Hague.

MARCEL VAN DER LINDEN (1952) is Research Director of the International Institute of Social History in Amsterdam; Professor of Social Movement History at the University of Amsterdam; Editor of the *International Review of Social History* (Cambridge); Chair of the Dutch–Scandinavian research programme 'Changing

Labour Relations in Asia' (the Executive Committee of which includes Jan Breman), and Co-Director of the Amsterdam School of Social Science Research (co-founded by Jan Breman). He published widely on labour history and the history of ideas. His most recent book is *Transnational Labour History: Explorations* (Aldershot, 2003).

PRABHU P. MOHAPATRA (1961) is the Secretary of the Association of Indian Labour Historians, a staff member of the V.V. Giri National Labour Institute in Noida, and a Corresponding Editor of the *International Review of Social History*. He has contributed essays to *Studies in History* and to *The Journal of Peasant Studies*.

SUDIPTO MUNDLE (1949) is currently Head, Operations and Policy Coordination, Programs Department West, Asian Development Bank, Manila, Philippines. Earlier he was Reserve Bank Chair Professor at the National Institute of Public Finance and Policy, New Delhi, a Senior Fellow at the Centre for Development Studies, Trivandrum, and Economic Adviser in the Ministry of Finance, New Delhi. He is the author of numerous publications including *Surplus Flows and Growth Imbalances: The Intersectoral Flow of Real Resources in India, 1951–1971* (Delhi, 1981). He edited *Public Finance: Policy Issues for India* (Delhi, 1997), and co-edited with Jan Breman, *Rural Transformaton in Asia* (Delhi, 1992).

MARIO RUTTEN (1958) is Jan Breman's successor as Professor of Comparative Sociology at the University of Amsterdam. Jan Breman supervised his doctoral thesis which was published as *Farms and Factories: Social Profile of Large Farmers and Rural Industrialists in West India* (Delhi, 1995). Other publications include *Asian Capitalists in the European Mirror* (Amsterdam, 1994); *Small Business Entrepreneurs in Asia and Europe*, edited with Carol Upadhya (New Delhi, 1997); and *Rural Capitalists in Asia: A Comparative Analysis on India, Indonesia and Malaysia* (Richmond, 2002).

RATNA SAPTARI (1955) coordinates the Changing Labour Relations in Asia (CLARA) research programme at the International Institute of Social History in Amsterdam. Her publications include *Rural Women to the Factories: Continuity and Change in East Java's Kretek Cigarette Industry* (Amsterdam, 1995); and *Changing Labour Relations in South-east Asia*, edited with Becky Elmhirst (Richmond, UK, forthcoming).

WILLEM VAN SCHENDEL (1947) is Professor of Modern Asian History at the University of Amsterdam and Senior Research Fellow at the International Institute of Social History in Amsterdam. His publications include *Peasant Mobility: The Odds of Life in Rural Bangladesh* (Assen, 1981); *Three Deltas: Accumulation and Poverty in Rural Burma, Bengal and South India* (New Delhi, 1991); and *Reviving a Rural Industry: Silk Producers and Officials in India and Bangladesh, 1880s to 1980s* (Dhaka, 1995).

SEDIONO M.P. TJONDRONEGORO (1928) is Professor of Sociology at the Agricultural Institute, Bogor, Indonesia. His many publications include *Dua abad penguasaan tanah* (Jakarta, 1984; with Gunawan Wiradi), *Social Organization and Planned Development in Rural Java* (Singapore, 1984), and *Sosiologi agraria: kumpulan tulisan terpilih* (Bandung, 1999; with M.T. Felix Sitorus and Gunawan Wiradi).

PETER VAN DER VEER (1953) is Professor of Religious Anthropology at the University of Amsterdam, Co-Director of the Institute for the Study of Islam in the Modern World (ISIM) in Leiden; and Chair of the International Institute of Asian Studies, Leiden. His publications include *Gods on Earth: The Management of Religious Experience and Identity in a North Indian Peigrimage Center* (London, 1988); *Religious Nationalism: Hindus and Muslims in India* (Berkeley, 1994); and *Imperial Encounters: Religion and Modernity in India and Britain* (Princeton, 2001).

WILLEM WOLTERS (1940) is Professor of Economic Anthropology at Nijmegen University, since 1985. He has previously worked at the South-East Asia Department, Amsterdam University, and from 1974 till 1985 at the Department of Comparative Sociology, Erasmus University Rotterdam. In this last capacity he was a member of Jan Breman's staff. He has done fieldwork in the Philippines and in Indonesia, and is presently working on the economic history of South-East Asia. His publications include *Politics, Patronage and Class Conflict in Central Luzon* (The Hague and Quezon City, 1983), and *Conceptualizing Development*, with Otto van den Muijzenberg (Dordrecht, 1988).

